"Deaver's characters stood as close to ground zero as men can and live" —*The St Louis Post Dispatch.*

Philip Deaver's stories were written in "poetry that recalls Saul Bellow's greatest character, Henderson" (i.e., *Henderson the Rain King*) —*Kirkus Reviews.*

When Phil Deaver spoke, "people listened because his words glowed with respect, admiration, and wisdom. His passion for writing and the writing process was palpable. He was a writer's writer" —Diana Raab, PhD, author of *Healing with Words, Regina's Closet,* and other works.

Philip Deaver was "a fiction writer to his very core. Fiction was everything to him, a religion" —Richard Goodman, author of *The Bicycle Diaries: One New Yorker's Journey Through 9-11* and other works.

Philip Deaver's "piercingly direct stories" were "full of recognizable emotion concerning our interactions with the people who comprise our worlds, public and private—the relationships we've forged while climbing the frail scaffolding of human interaction that we can only hope will support us" —Ann Beattie, author of *Chilly Scenes of Winter* and many other novels and stories.

Also by Jeshel Forrester

Houseboating in the Ozarks (a novel)

The Connoisseur of Love (a novel)

The Beautiful Daughters of Men (poetry)

More Deaths than One (a novel)

Blaw Hunter, Blaw Thy Horn (a memoir)

Uluru (music album)

Alma Rose (music album)

Kamara (music album)

Jeshel (music album)

Dust on the Bible (music album)

The Old Churchyard (music album)

ONE DOG BARKED, THE OTHER HOWLED

A Meditation on Several Lives of a Minor American Writer

JESHEL FORRESTER

Hardie Grant

BOOKS

Published in 2023 by Hardie Grant Books an imprint of Hardie Grant Publishing

Hardie Grant Books (Melbourne)
Ground Floor, Building 1, 658 Church Street
Richmond VIC 3121, Australia

Hardie Grant Books (London)
5th and 6th Floors, 52–54 Southwark Street
London SE1 1UN, United Kingdom

www.hardiegrant.com.au

Hardie Grant acknowledges the Traditional Owners of the Country on which we work, the Wurundjeri People of the Kulin Nation and the Gadigal People of the Eora Nation, and recognises their continuing connection to the land, waters and culture. We pay our respects to their Elders past and present.

A catalogue record of this book is available from the National Library of Australia.

 A catalogue record for this book is available from the National Library of Australia

One Dog Barked, The Other Howled
ISBN 9781761450525

Publication commissioned by Courtney Nicholls
Publication managed by Hannah Louey
Cover design by George Saad
Cover concept by TDJ Shirley
Typesetting by Cannon Typesetting
Printed in Australia by Griffin Press, an Accredited ISO AS/NZS 14001 Environmental Management System printer.

 The paper this book is printed on is certified against the Forest Stewardship Council® Standards. Griffin Press – a member of the Opus Group holds chain of custody certification SCS-COC-001185 FSC® promotes environmentally responsible, socially beneficial and economically viable management of the world's forests

For TDJS (mahi tika ana)

Contents

"It must all be considered as though spoken by a character in a novel."

Roland Barthes

Preface

THIS IS THE story of a man who left instructions that the word "WRITER"—in capital letters—should be carved into the centre of his tombstone.

I live in New Zealand now. I've lived far away from America for more than half my life. As far away as I could get.

One small consequence is that my computer defaults to spelling and punctuating the New Zealand way. If I use an incompatible American spelling, my computer scolds me and tells me to change. I don't spell or punctuate the way I used to do.

When I finished an early draft of this book, I toyed with the idea of going back and changing everything to American English, for consistency. But I decided it's best to leave it as it is. So this book is written New Zealand style, except where the original was in American English. My spellings and punctuation, like my mangled accent when I open my mouth, are small reminders of the distance I've come, or gone.

So if you see an s where you think a z should be, or a u where it's not needed, or an re where you'd like to see an er, or too many consonants for the past tense, or periods missing after Dr or Jr or the St in St Louis, take a deep breath and suck it up.

In 2018, as Philip Deaver lay dying, I finished recording my third music album in as many years. I dedicated the CD to "Philip Deaver, il miglior fabbro" (the better craftsman), hoping he might yet have enough acuity to appreciate the sounds and lyrics. Those same words of dedication were used by Thomas Stearns Eliot, the English poet who hailed from St Lous, Missouri, when he honoured his buddy Ezra Pound with an inscription to *The Waste Land*. Eliot stole the words from Dante, without attribution—but no matter.

One of the songs on my 2018 album puts Rudyard Kipling's poem *Danny Deever* to music, in recognition of the nickname Phil was given shortly after his birth. It wasn't the first time I'd tried to pay tribute to Phil in music. On my 2016 album, one of the songs was *Black Top Road*, which included a rejigging of Phil's own lines from his poem *Diary of a Dead People Pleaser*: "Two dogs under a yellow moon / trot past your flat headstone, / one to howl and one to bark."

Both the poem and the 2016 lyrics were reflections on Phil's late father, a small-town physician. The song's chorus repeats the following lines: "Doctor, Doctor, speak but the word, / Come back and heal my soul / Take me in your folded hands / And never let me go." The archaic phrase "speak but the word" was borrowed from the New Testament (Matthew 8:8): a Roman centurion says he isn't worthy to have Jesus of Nazareth enter his home. "Speak but the word," he says to Jesus, "and my servant shall be healed."

Phil said *Black Top Road* was his favourite song. He didn't live long enough to hear *Danny Deever*.

Because Phil was the better craftsman, I've used his own words wherever possible instead of trying to interpret or paraphrase his ways of expressing himself. This book is about him, not me. I'm just a wayward sidekick on these parallel journeys, Tonto to his Lone Ranger, Boswell to his Johnson.

For some readers, indented quotations are annoying, as they can disrupt the smooth flow of lines of thought. But all things considered, it's best to let Phil speak for himself by quoting him. And a pleasant surprise in revisiting our correspondence has been to discover how eloquent he was, even when he didn't anticipate his words would be published. So, for better or worse, this book is quote heavy.

Because this life is Phil's, not mine, my own words and adventures are relevant only when they provide some context for what Phil was saying or doing. I don't need to say more about my half of the world. When I appear, as I must, it's only because Phil wouldn't make complete sense without me. As more than one mutual friend observed, we were "joined at the hip." Another colleague, who spoke at Phil's memorial service in Winter Park, Florida, said later: "I had deep affection for him. I guess it is impossible for me to think of him without linking you two together."

Phil often spoke of truth. "Truth" was the name of his very last story, in his last book, *Forty Martyrs*. He'd come to accept that "brutal truths needed to be told brutally," and he was alive to the paradox that certain levels of frankness, or even silence, could be "in effect, lies." He understood that truth itself has limitations, that (with all due respect to John Keats) it was not always beauty: "There was such a thing as too much" of it.

The most memorable character he left behind was the antihero named Skidmore. He had a mean streak, a "genius for meanness," but as Phil wrote in his story "Infield," his meanness "was rarely in outright lies, more often in brutally administering the truth." Phil may have been channelling William Blake: "A truth that's told with bad intent / Beats all the lies you can invent."

In 2014, before his ability to express himself in words began to fade, he wrote an online essay, "309 E. Scott: or Why Write Fiction?" He said he'd tried to write nonfiction, including a piece about his hometown of Tuscola, Illinois—"309 E. Scott" was the address of his childhood home. But he "couldn't control the line on [his] impulse for fiction." He wondered why he couldn't "tell a true story for once?"

Then, he demonstrated his conundrum by writing about a real-life return to his childhood home, with made-up names for the latest owners and other fabrications. The line between fact and fiction was blurred.

His conclusion? "Reality doesn't actually contain stories." He believed that "fiction and truth are complementary, not opposites":

> Our brains make stories from random activities and events. And so the simple act of picking and choosing what to tell in order to make a sequence of events to form a story is to fictionalize what really happened, to straighten out a very crooked line.

He cited Alice Munro, a growing influence in his later years, for the proposition that a story can be "autobiographical in feeling, though not, sometimes, entirely so in fact." He agreed: "There's such a thing as being too fond of what really happened … by being so terribly accurate we can miss the emotional core, the heart of why we're bothering to write the story at all."

Phil was a natural-born fabulist. Or if not natural-born, a beginner as early as the sixth grade and a fabulist-in-full by his 18th birthday. As eulogised by the writer Richard Goodman, Phil was "a fiction writer to his very core. Fiction was everything to him, a religion." And as Phil himself once put it, "Since I was a young kid, I've gone into fiction easily and with great pleasure. I can suspend my disbelief like nobody's business."

This memoir adheres to Phil's dicta about truth and fiction. I know things that no one else, living or dead, can know. And I want to tell those things with an aim that is true to the "emotional core." Phil Deaver had many other lives as well as the ones I knew, and like all of us he was subject to Oscar Wilde's apothegm that "he who lives more lives than one / more deaths than one must die." But Phil's other stories can be told by others, if they are so inclined.

If Phil was a natural-born fabulist, he was also a natural-born institutionalist, a word that might be generally defined as adherence to, or respect for, established forms and norms. An institutionalist is not necessarily a conservative person, in politics or style. But the ties that bind are never fully severed.

For example, Goodman's eulogy confirmed that "Phil was raised Catholic, and I don't think he ever left his faith, despite what he might have claimed":

> It was deeply there. He had a sense of Catholic guilt about him. He told me that after his father died a group of Catholic elders from his town took him on a silent retreat. It meant a great deal to him. It's not a coincidence that his first book was titled *Silent Retreats*.

And it's not a coincidence that his book of poetry was titled *How Men Pray* and came with a cover that evoked a Christian altar. His final book was *Forty Martyrs*, named for the small Catholic parish in his hometown, which unified everything for him, all the things he could never fully leave behind.

Another of Goodman's observations was that Phil was "rooted in the Midwest" even after he moved from Illinois to Indiana, then to Kentucky, then to Virginia, then to Florida. For Goodman, Phil's Midwestern roots were evident whenever he spoke, with his boyish enthusiasm, about something that interested him—and he found almost everything and everyone interesting. "He had a distinct way of talking, a Midwestern drawl with a slow cadence often leading to a bright punctuation of emphasis."

Phil's institutionalism was based on his Midwestern values. He maintained a lifelong respect for and deference to the role models, sporting heroes, and organisational structures of his youth, even when he knew they were diminished by human frailty. He valued society's recognitions and awards. Favourable feedback from reviewers, colleagues, or friends meant a great deal to him—not because he was immodest, but because he was genuinely surprised and gratified whenever his achievements were acknowledged—and usually such recognitions were long overdue.

Approval in big ways or small validated his sense of self, which was always vulnerable. He treasured his Flannery O'Connor Award and his O. Henry Prize—both of which came in 1988—for the remaining 30 years of his life. He couldn't quite believe he'd been selected. When Garrison Keillor of *The Writer's Almanac* saw fit to read some of Phil's poetry on national radio, he was gobsmacked.

He loved reading from his works to appreciative audiences in Florida bookshops, in the halls of academe, or back home in Illinois cafés or libraries. His tenured position at Rollins College was a dream come true and he wished it could have lasted forever. He beamed with quiet pride when his students said how greatly he'd influenced them, or when old friends told him his stories brought tears of joy or sadness to their eyes. If a John Updike or an Ann Beattie sent an encouraging word his way, he was on cloud nine. He would have cherished the spoken and written remembrances at the two memorial services that followed his death.

Phil and I had a great deal in common, including our politics, our Midwestern backgrounds, our youthful Catholicism, the years of our births, the intersection of our personal histories, our obsession with sports, and our love of literature. But where Phil was a self-confessed "people pleaser," as he described himself on many occasions, I was a natural-born contrarian, if not a full-blown iconoclast. If a mission statement had been stamped on my forehead during my teenage years, it might have been taken from Marlon Brando's Johnny in *The Wild One*—when he was asked what he was rebelling against, his answer was, "Whaddya got?"

Johnny didn't know why nothing could ever be quite right—and neither did I.

Or, as Phil once put it in a thinly disguised caricature in *Silent Retreats*:

> Skidmore was a razzle-dazzle guy. He could unanswer more questions in a week than most men in a lifetime. It had become a pattern in his life. Give him a relationship and a couple of months on his own resources, and Skidmore could bring more ruination than whole defoliation programs, whole societal collapses, whole holy wars.

Fair enough. But to put our differences yet another way, Phil was a good boy. In his later years, he even took to signing off on some of his emails, with a measure of irony, as "Good Danny." I wasn't good. I was bad.

Goodman wrote that Phil was "haunted" by winning the 1988 Flannery O'Connor Award for his book *Silent Retreats*, which was the first major turning point in his life as a writer. According to Goodman, he was "weighed down by the burden of promise that honor bestowed on him and not producing another book."

That observation carried some truth, but it wasn't quite fair. Phil's outstanding book of poetry, *How Men Pray*, was published in 2005. Many of his short stories appeared in literary journals after *Silent Retreats* was published. And as Goodman acknowledged, Phil's novel-in-stories, *Forty Martyrs*, was published to positive reviews in 2016, around the time he was diagnosed with the illness that would destroy his ability to express himself, then claim his life.

More importantly, if the length of Phil's resumé didn't quite match his expectations, that was in large part due to his generosity of spirit. Goodman again: "Phil was a great friend, loyal and caring":

> He did everything he could … to aid writers he admired or who he felt were deserving …. This to me is what separates many writers from others. Those who, like Phil, use whatever influence and funds they have, not to mention encouragement, to help emerging writers flourish and those who claim they will help, and don't. When Phil pledged his help, he kept that pledge.

He was even known to suffer fools gladly.

When the poet Allen Ginsberg died in 1997, his obituary in *The New York Times* described him as one of America's "minor poets," and some of Ginsberg's admirers were understandably miffed. But being celebrated as a minor poet was no mean achievement and it was not a sign of failure. Ginsberg was prolific, and sometimes he hit the mark. When he was good, he was very, very good.

Phil Deaver was, in a sense, the opposite of Ginsberg. He was not a public figure, and his list of works was not long, but his written words were invariably of a high standard. From modest beginnings and with "sweat equity" (as he called it), he too achieved the status of a minor American writer. The description is not pejorative. And coupled with it is the recognition by all who knew him that, as a human being of intelligence, compassion, and wit, there was nothing minor about him. If Phil was troubled by the volume of his output, I wish those of us who were actually familiar with his body of work could have assured him, on his way out the door, that he had achieved an enviable standard in almost everything he wrote—published or unpublished.

Quantity is overrated. As Phil's colleague, the Florida poet Russell Kesler, once wrote, "Volume usually means poor quality for me." Phil wasn't a volume guy, he was a quality guy, as a person and as a writer. He made up in quality for any perceived shortfall in quantity.

When John Updike died, leaving behind his substantial but uneven body of work, those of his fans with normal sensibilities, like Phil, were saddened. Not me, but then I was never a fan, and I don't have normal sensibilities. As the English critic James Wood observed, Updike was more style than substance. And in her *New York Times* farewell, Michiko Kakutani put another nail in Updike's coffin by stating the obvious: he was verbose, and he published way too much for his own good. For Updike, as for most people in most walks of life, a whole lot less would have been a whole lot more. Still, he managed to make a living from writing, as few people do.

The American playwright Paul Rudnick posited that "writing is ninety percent procrastination: reading magazines, eating cereal out of the box, watching infomercials." A writer can be hard at work when gazing out a window. If his or her procrastination is active, not passive, it comes with careful observation and attention to detail, which were defining characteristics of Phil's prose and poetry. He took his time, and he got it right—the way he wanted it.

Speed and volume can detract from a work product. Bob Dylan, Nobel Prize winner, probably wrote more WTF songs than anyone in history, along the way to creating an unparalleled canon of lyricism. And the guy who holds the record for missing the most game-winning shots in NBA history is ... Michael Jordan, because he attempted more game-winners than anyone else.

The defining event of Phil Deaver's youth was the death of his father in a car crash in 1964, when Phil (then known as Danny) was 17 years old. Ever after, in his correspondence, his fiction, his poetry, his readings, he alluded to that senseless tragedy, as if he could never quite believe it had happened and never quite figure out what to do with his feelings about it. One thing was clear: he could never leave behind the small hometown of his youth, Tuscola, Illinois, no matter how far away he drifted. Tuscola was his Hotel California: he could check out any time he wanted, but he could never leave. He wrote about Tuscola forever.

I couldn't quite understand his lasting obsession with Tuscola and central Illinois until the penny dropped, much later, at a Bruce Springsteen concert. The Boss was introducing "My Hometown," his song that goes, "Main Street's whitewashed windows and vacant stores / Seems like there ain't nobody wants to come down here no more / They're closing down the textile mill across the railroad tracks / Foreman says these jobs are going boys and they ain't coming back / To your hometown." The song is "about getting out / Packing up our bags maybe heading south," just as Phil had done.

In his introduction, Springsteen told us why the lyrics hit home for him:

> I had this habit for a long time. I used to get in my car and drive back through my old neighborhood in the town I grew up in. I'd always drive past the old houses that I used to live in, sometimes late at night. I got so I would do it regularly—two, three, four times a week for years. I eventually got to wondering, 'What the hell am I doing?'
>
> So, I went to see the psychiatrist. I said, 'Doc, for years I've been getting in my car and driving past my old houses late at night. What am I doing?'
>
> He said, 'I want *you* to tell me what you think you're doing.'
>
> I go, 'That's what I'm paying you for.'
>
> He said, 'Well, something bad happened and you're going back thinking you can make it right again. Something went wrong and you keep going back to see if you can fix it or somehow make it right.'
>
> I sat there, and I said, 'That's what I'm doing.'
>
> He said, 'Well, you can't.'

I laughed, the rest of the crowd laughed, and The Boss burst into song.

Phil often spoke about "dwelling in the past" and "arrested development." By arrested development, he meant being stuck at an emotional level because of some trauma suffered during childhood or adolescence. He believed arrested development was linked to disturbances in the parent–child relationship. He said I had it, and he had it, and most of our high school teachers and troglodyte coaches had it. It wasn't a good thing.

Phil may have been right about arrested development, but revisiting Tuscola was not my idea of fun. When I left town in the autumn of 1964, I wanted nothing more to do with the place. When I got the chance, I got ten thousand miles away from central Illinois and blocked Tuscola out of my brain, except as an occasional curiosity. If this was arrested development, I wasn't one to resist arrest.

Phil was the opposite. Everything he did was filtered, one way or another, through his memories of Tuscola, Illinois—and he was burdened, or gifted, with a photographic memory. He kept going back home, in his writing and in his life, to the town's streets and parks and buildings and people, because something bad—very bad—had happened to him at the moment he was preparing to leave home for the first time at the age of 17. He kept going back because he imagined, even though he knew better, that he could make it right again. If he went back to his youth often enough, maybe the story would have a different ending. Maybe his dad wouldn't be killed in that awful car wreck. Maybe it was all just a terrible dream and he'd finally wake up.

When Phil and I were kids, the gatekeepers to literature anointed F. Scott Fitzgerald and Ernest Hemingway as the giants of American fiction. Phil always had a soft spot for Fitzgerald, with his prodigious talent and good heart, but he (Phil) developed a love–hate relationship with the work of Hemingway. He liked some of Hemingway's early stories and admired *A Moveable Feast*, but he regarded most of his longer fiction as stunted in expression and emotion. Still, he'd often quote Hemingway, and one of his favourite lines came from Hemingway's 1936 story, *The Short Happy Life of Francis Macomber*: "We owe God a death."

Hemingway put those words in the mouth of his big game hunter Robert Wilson, whose full remark was, "By my troth, I care not; a man can die but once; we owe God a death and let it go which way it will, he that dies this year is quit for the next. Damn fine, eh?"

Like T S Eliot, Hemingway failed to attribute his words to their source—in this case, Shakespeare's *Henry IV, Part II*—and he botched the quote to boot. But again, no matter. His point, and Shakespeare's, was that to be born is to be indebted. One's death—Phil's death, his dad's death, your death, my death—settles the account.

When any person's account is finally settled and the debt is finally quit, potential claimants step forward with deluded or legitimate assertions of entitlement. Some want the decedent's spoils; others want the soul; others want only to take part in the farewell.

If the deceased person achieved a measure of fame or notoriety, erstwhile friends and lovers may jockey for their places in the legacy. If there are children, the best of them may want, more than anything, understanding and forgiveness. Mentors and benefactors, real or imagined, may expect some modest acknowledgement, spoken or unspoken.

Everyone with a seat at or near the table is likely to claim, with varying degrees of integrity, to have known the deceased in some special way. There will be anecdotes. There will be tall tales. There will be whispered secrets, *sotto voce*, for good or ill.

When Phil died, I was no longer welcome at the table, for good reason, and I made no claims upon him. All I had were a half-century of letters and 60 years of memories.

Finally, a disclosure of interest, of sorts. In the early 2000s, I was diagnosed with Asperger Disorder (AD), named for the Austrian paediatrician and Nazi collaborator Hans Asperger (1906–1980), who specialised in children's mental disorders. For those of you who aren't very familiar with AD, in the 1990s it was recognised throughout the world as an accepted diagnosis, distinct from autism. However, as of 2013, AD is no longer a separate diagnosis; rather, it's considered a mild form of autism, at the lower end of the autism spectrum. Still, in some quarters, the Asperger label persists, in reference to "high functioning" types of autism.

The symptoms of AD start early in life. They include discomfort in maintaining eye contact; delays in pragmatic skills, such as an inability to read body language, facial expressions, and other social cues that are obvious to most people; exhibiting limited emotions; communicating about one's self to excess; social awkwardness; a tendency to focus intently on a single subject matter, such as sports statistics or politics; repeating certain words and phrases when discussing favourite topics; and a fondness for routines. Solipsism may not be a synonym for autism or AD, but it's a characteristic.

For me, the list of odd behaviours may be expanded to evading invitations to social gatherings and avoiding formal occasions where certain behaviours may be regarded as appropriate—graduation ceremonies, funerals, weddings, team lunches, award presentations, staff meetings. I hide at parties. I shy away from grownup conversations. Especially about relationships.

I never rise for any country's national anthem, and I'd have trouble doing so if I tried. Somehow the patriotism gene escaped me. And I never bow my head in meditation or prayer when asked to do so by a reverent leader. I stare straight ahead, eyes fixed and wide, arms hanging free. I was born with the Catholic chromosome, but missed out on the piety gene.

AD is five times more common in boys than in girls. Famous people with the syndrome have included Andy Warhol, Dan Ackroyd, Darryl Hannah, Robin Williams, Sir Anthony Hopkins, Courtney Love, Bill Gates—and probably Abraham Lincoln.

Phil never knew about this diagnosis. Nor did the people who were acquainted with both of us, from our early years together in Tuscola to Phil's final incarnation in Winter Park, Florida. The signs aren't always obvious. People with AD tend to develop little tricks to get by, even before their odd behaviour finds a psychological label.

If I stick to my tricks, I'm okay. But if I get fooled into trying to act normal, it's at my own peril and the peril of everyone within my wingspan.

So I'm impaired. Who isn't? I have deficits. Who doesn't? With the benefit of hindsight, AD might help explain some of the things that happened. It might even explain why, or how, this book came to be written.

Like anyone who may aspire to be known as a "writer," Philip Deaver was a seeker of some form of truth. But as it was for D H Lawrence, so it was for Phil: "Lies are not a question of false fact / but of false feeling." And as the truths and lies of his yesterdays became the lies and truths of his tomorrows, the first question he asked himself, each day, echoed the words of Lawrence: "How great a liar am I?" The answer: a damned good one.

What follows is a love song.

PART ONE

CHAPTER 1

Till Like a Wheel of Turning Steel

"Nemo dat quod non habet." ("No one can give what they do not have.")

Legal maxim

ON 16 MARCH 1967, the Appellate Court for the Fourth District of Illinois handed down its opinion in the case of *Deaver v Hickox*. The court's decision turned on a narrow point of law—whether the trial judge in the Circuit Court of Champaign County had erred by admitting, over objection, an opinion by a state highway patrolman about the speed of two vehicles prior to a collision.

Following the initial trial in January 1966, the jury had awarded $165,000 in damages to Althea Samples Deaver, a nurse from nearby Tuscola, Illinois, for the death of her husband Philip F Deaver Sr, 44, a physician and surgeon. That was a lot of money in those days. The jury also awarded her $2,400 in damages for the death of her father, Lester Samples, 70, who died in the same accident. Lester was a newspaper man who taught history at Kearney State Teacher's College in Nebraska. He was small in stature and crippled from birth.

The crash happened at five o'clock on a Wednesday afternoon, the first day of July, 1964. One of the cars, a Buick Skylark, was driven by Dr Deaver. Mr Samples was seated in the Skylark to his right. He'd been staying with the Deavers in Tuscola since February, 1964, following the death of his wife—Althea Deaver's mother. Mrs Samples had suffered a sudden stroke in January 1964 at the Oklahoma City airport, after visiting the Deavers in Tuscola during the previous month.

Dr Deaver and Lester Samples were returning to Tuscola after shopping in Champaign. It was a rare day off for Dr Deaver, and he'd gone to Rogards, an art store in Champaign, to buy some supplies. He was a talented amateur painter and drawer.

For reasons that will never be clear, Dr Deaver chose to exit Champaign on the First Street Road instead of State Highway 45, which ran parallel to the west on the other side of the railroad tracks. Ahead of him on the outskirts of Champaign was a rural blacktop with a blind crossroad obscured by a field of summer corn standing six feet high. There were no traffic signs on those kinds of roads.

Ronald Hickox, a lad of 17 years from the rural township of Bogota (pronounced "Bo-gotta"), in downstate Jasper County, approached the crossroad from the west, driving a Ford Falcon. The intersection was not far from the Tolono farmhouse belonging to Hickox's relatives, the Reed family. Hickox was living with them for the summer and working near Champaign. At the time of the crash, he was driving home from work.

There was no evidence that either of the drivers had been drinking. And it was undisputed that Hickox tried to stop. He left at least 39 feet of skid marks before impact. How fast he was going wasn't clear. Estimates were as high as 65 miles per hour, and Hickox was still going at least 35 miles per hour at the moment of impact.

Hickox's Falcon crashed into Deaver's Skylark in the middle of the intersection, shoving it into the tall grass growing alongside the corner of the road. The Skylark came to rest upside down. Hickox's car skidded into the southeast corner, remaining upright, facing northwest. Both the Skylark's right door and the Falcon's front end were caved in by a foot and a half.

Dr Deaver and Lester Samples suffered head and chest injuries and died at the scene. They were wearing their safety belts, but it made no difference. Somehow, Hickox ended up beneath his Ford Falcon. He was told later that people who came to the scene had to jack up the car to remove him from underneath. He had multiple injuries over his body. He was taken by ambulance to Champaign's Burnham Hospital, where he was reported to be in fair condition. He lived to be the defendant in *Deaver v Hickox*, sued for the two wrongful deaths by Mrs Deaver, the doctor's widow and the administrator of her father's estate.

A year after the jury's verdict, the Appellate Court ruled that the trial court had wrongly admitted the patrolman's evidence as to speed, because he wasn't qualified as an accident reconstruction expert. The verdict in favour of Althea Deaver was vacated, and the case was sent back for a new trial.

The second time around, with new experts for the parties, the jury gave a verdict for Ronald Hickox. The trial judge, outraged, set aside the jury's verdict and ordered yet another new trial. But Hickox and his lawyers appealed before a third trial could start. And again, in 1970, the Appellate Court judges decided against Althea, concluding unanimously that the trial judge had abused his discretion by refusing to accept the jury's verdict. The judgment in favour of Hickox was reinstated.

What a nightmare for Althea. First, a dead mother in January, then a dead husband and a dead father in July, followed by four years of failed litigation. Althea's two children, Danny and Maureen, were still living at home at the time of the crash. Danny had just finished high school, and Maureen was entering her junior year.

But who really knew who caused the deaths? The only surviving witness was young Ronald Hickox, and (on the advice of his lawyers) he wasn't saying anything. For all anyone knew, he couldn't even remember the accident.

One thing was clear—Althea should have had a different lawyer. Jim Lemna, a Deaver family friend, didn't charge her a fee, but he should have hired a lot better expert for the original trial. The state patrolman had investigated many accidents, but he'd never previously testified as an accident reconstruction expert and he admitted, right there in the courtroom, that he was "speculating" about the speed of the cars. "Speculate" is not a word for an expert to use. It was, in fact, fatal to Althea's case. The other side produced a real expert from Purdue University, a specialist in braking ratios. In offering his opinions, he didn't speculate. What was the Appellate Court to do?

As the saying goes, free legal representation is worth what you pay for it. In addition to hiring an unqualified expert, Lemna advised Althea to turn down an $80,000 settlement offer from Ronald Hickox's insurance company, State Farm. That was a lot more than zero. But Lemna's advice to Althea was to refuse the offer and roll the dice.

Like most of these car crash cases, this one was really brought against the defendant's insurance company. Hickox was only insured by State Farm in the amount of $20,000. State Farm paid for his lawyers and covered the appeals, and it's not clear that Althea could have collected $167,400 even if the trial court's original verdict had been upheld.

At least Dr Deaver's life was insured. Althea managed to live modestly with the help of those insurance proceeds till she died, 28 years later.

The litigation left young Danny Deaver with a lifelong scepticism about the legal profession. He felt that lawyers didn't apply "normal logic" or "normal sense," but used a type of reasoning that was "so complicated it can come down on the diametrically opposite side of the truth."

Later, the *Deaver* case was sometimes cited as a legal precedent on the dangers of using an unqualified expert witness. It made its way into university law reviews and classrooms in Illinois and other jurisdictions, where its logic, normal or otherwise, was examined and discussed by law professors and law students.

The contents of the Buick Skylark were returned to the Deaver family in due course. Dr Deaver's medical bag was found in the car's back seat, along with the art supplies he'd purchased from Rogards earlier in the day: pastels, charcoals, and drawing paper.

Fifty-four years later—and three months after Danny Deaver's death—I tracked down Ronald Hickox via the Internet. I found a "Charlotte Hickox" with connections to Flora, Illinois, and phoned her from New Zealand. It turned out she was the wife of Ronald's younger brother Alan. She handed the phone over to Alan and I explained why I was trying to reach Ronald. Alan said he'd contact Ronald and see if it was okay. I gave him my email address.

On 2 August 2018, Ronald Hickox emailed his telephone number to me, inviting me to phone him. I did so immediately.

I explained that I'd grown up with Danny, that he'd been my best friend during our childhood years together in Tuscola, Illinois. Each of us—Danny Deaver, Ronald Hickox, and me—was 17 years old on the day of the car wreck that killed Danny's dad and grandfather. Ronald told me he was now 72 years old. He lived in Arkansas. He had seven brothers and two sisters. He was the oldest of the ten siblings.

He asked me to call him Ron. He said he'd been married for 49 years and had three sons, now aged from 42 to 48. He was especially proud of a granddaughter who was 18 years old and had just graduated from high school. He said he loved his family; his life had been good; he had worked in "electronics"; he said he had a good wife. He married her eight months after the end of the second Deaver trial. By then, he'd been in the Air Force for a while. After the last court appeal in his favour, the Air Force sent him to Puerto Rico to work on bomb navigation systems and electronics for the B-52 aircraft. His wife went with him. He said he never told her about the Deaver crash.

Then, he told me a story. He said it tied things together for him. One afternoon in 2006 (42 years after the death of Dr Deaver), he was changing a flat tyre on the grass at the side of a road when a car, driven by a 19-year-old boy who wasn't paying attention, ran over him. Ron was left with no pulse and he wasn't breathing. His lungs had collapsed. An ambulance was called, and he was resuscitated and taken to a nearby hospital. His injuries were too complicated for a small hospital. He was flown by helicopter to a bigger hospital, where surgeons cut him open "from top to bottom." After that, he spent three months in the hospital and made a full recovery.

When he came home, his brothers and sisters called on him to test his memory by asking questions about his childhood. They were happy to find that his mental faculties were sound.

Among the things he remembered was that when he was four to five years old, he was put to work on their father's farm. They lived outside Bogota, Illinois, a rural community of around 3,000 people. They had 500 chickens. From the age of five, Ron drove a tractor in the field. He was so small he had to press both feet on the clutch to make it go down. But he "got to play some too." As a 10-year-old, he helped his dad bring in the crops. It meant he was often taken out of school. When he reached high school, his grades suffered because he missed so many classes. He said he "was never an A student," but he managed to receive passing grades.

When he was a young boy, his dad often "horsewhipped" him. He said his dad was "good, but hard." Ron remembered that on one occasion he received 13 lashes. Because he was the oldest of the 10 Hickox children, his dad made all the other kids come out to the barn

8

to watch the whipping so they'd learn a lesson. Ron said he didn't hold this against his dad, who was the "hardest working man" he ever knew.

Then, Ron told me about the Deaver crash. In the summer of 1964, he was working at a job "detassling corn" near the small town of Bement, not far from Champaign. It was his first paid job. After work on the first day of July—a Wednesday—he was "hurrying" back to the house where he was staying, which belonged to the Reed family. He was in a rush because some cousins from California were visiting down south in Bogota, and he wanted to get back to the Reeds' house, change his clothes, and drive to Bogota to see them.

He acknowledged to me that he was driving too fast as he entered the Champaign cornfield. But he believed that both drivers—he and Dr Deaver—were at fault. There were no stop signs on the blacktop roads in the cornfields and neither driver was "driving like we should have been." He said a 17-year-old boy "doesn't have good judgment"—but at the same time, Dr Deaver didn't attempt to slow down before entering the crossroad. There were no skid marks behind Dr Deaver's Buick.

Ron remembered being lifted into a car and taken to a nearby hospital, and that the car seemed to speed up and slow down along the way. When he finally regained his senses, his father was there with him in the hospital. The first thing Ron asked his father was, "How are the people from the other car?" His father said, "They didn't make it."

Ron stayed in the hospital for three days. He had no broken bones—just bruises all over his body.

He said that the 1964 crash "always haunted" him, but "there was nothing afterwards" he could do about it. He couldn't change it. He couldn't bring them back. He said he never tried to put the crash out of his mind—he would always remember it, although he "wasn't really good" at processing bad memories. He said he didn't know how to express what he felt, that he couldn't find the words. "I wish it hadn't happened," he said.

He remembered the trial that followed, when Althea Deaver brought her lawsuit against him in Champaign. During the trial, he didn't say a word to Althea because his lawyers told him not to. But his father, who attended the trial, told Althea how terrible Ron felt about what had happened.

After the trial, his Air Force officers told him he was depressed, and that he had something he needed to work out. But he never received any counselling. He said his dad helped him overcome his depression.

He said he never learned much about Dr Deaver. It was "hard to do research" in those days before the Internet.

I told him that Danny—Philip Deaver—had become a writer and a poet, and that his written work could be found on the Internet. I said that a lot of what Phil wrote was about the crash and the loss of his father. Ron said he "liked poetry" and he would "look him up." I also told him he could find summaries of the trial online. He said he'd look those up too.

He said the accidents in 1964 and 2006 made him realise something: "When it's final, it's final." He said Danny Deaver had never tried to contact him.

CHAPTER 2

Whose Name Is Writ in Water

ON I JULY 1964, at the time of the crash and long before Althea's legal troubles played out, I was practising my moves on an outdoor basketball court in Tuscola's Ervin Park. I did this every chance I got, all through high school. Ervin Park was my home away from home, for basketball, baseball, swimming, tennis.

The news of the accident travelled fast. Dr Deaver was one of the most prominent people in Tuscola, a town of just 4,000 people. An hour or so after the crash, my dad called out my name from behind the wire fence of Ervin Park's swimming pool, which he managed for the town. I put down my basketball and ran across the grass, smiling but nervous. I always did what he told me to do. He looked grim. I wondered what I'd done wrong this time.

"Doc Deaver is dead," he said. He waited for my reaction. There wasn't one.

"He got killed in a car crash," he said. There was no mention of Lester Samples.

"You should go see Danny," he said.

I rode home on my bicycle. My mother was waiting there in the dining room, standing with my baby sister in her arms. My other two sisters and my three-year-old brother sat around the dining room table. They'd heard the news.

"You've got to go see Danny," my mother said. "He's your best friend. You've got to be with him."

I was unable to say anything. My legs gave out and I fell to the floor and churned in a circle on my back, pushing myself along our ragged carpet with the heels of my Converse basketball shoes. My eyes were closed and dry.

The next thing I remember, I was sitting with Danny Deaver on the front lawn outside his house. As the sun went down, he and I moved to the front seat of my Rambler station wagon, which was parked at the curb. We closed the windows. We were alone.

"We always talked about it," he said, "what it would feel like if one of our fathers died."

We were 17. Like Ronald Hickox. Losing a parent was the worst thing either of us could imagine. It was, in fact, unimaginable, fictional, something that happened to other people, to characters in stories.

"And now it's happened to me," he said.

I said nothing. There was nothing to say.

And then he said: "I'm still wondering how it feels."

He'd learned of the deaths from his younger sister Maureen when he returned home after a hot and humid day baling hay.

Days passed. Althea was sedated. My dad, always there when someone died, called on her. He tried to talk with her. He tried to pray with her.

A group of Tuscola high school kids, friends of Danny's and Maureen's, gathered in the living room of the Deaver home, saying silly things, telling Althea there should be a memorial, a monument, as if a piece of rock would make any difference, as if a stone could bring back the dead or give meaning to a life on earth.

"He was a great man," said Wish Dunne, the pharmacist's daughter. No one disagreed.

Two days after the crash, on the afternoon of my 18th birthday, a private funeral for Mr Samples was held at Tuscola's Waddington Funeral Home. His body was sent back to Nebraska for burial.

The following evening, the Fourth of July, a visitation for Dr Deaver began at 6pm at Waddington's, under the watchful eye of the funeral director Tack Green. He'd ordered that the casket be closed. At eight o'clock, we said the rosary. Then, I walked from the funeral home to Ervin Park to join my family at the Independence Day fireworks. Together we oohed and aahed with the rest of the crowd as the dark sky gave way to shards of light. Then we went home. The next morning, a Sunday, Dr Deaver's funeral service was held at the Forty Martyrs Catholic Church, with Father Casey presiding.

For at least the next seven years, Danny had dreams that his father was still alive. Much later, in 1988—about the time his first book, *Silent Retreats*, was being published—he wrote to me: "The closed casket and the fact that I was off to college and couldn't stay home and face the death, as Mom and Maureen did for a couple of years before Maureen left home, allowed me to psychologically keep him alive."

Another "closed casket" appeared in the opening paragraph of his story, "The Valence of Common Ions," as narrated by his character "Daniel." A 28-year-old woman, a nurse, had been "killed in a collision at an intersection." It was a pointless and shocking death. A photograph of the dead woman in her nursing uniform stood next to her closed casket:

> But to take that picture and extract reality from it, and place that reality in the dark gray metallic casket. Hard to do for a stranger, let alone loved ones … . Embalmed. Ready for the grave. Goodbye.

CHAPTER 3

Yet Brokenly Live On

A WEEK AFTER DR DEAVER's funeral, the second half of the
summer of 1964 picked up where it had left off. I practised
my moves on the basketball court and my dad ran the swimming
pool. The Deavers were given space to grieve together, by themselves,
and to sort out their affairs.

But by the end of July, Danny and I were making plans. We
would take a trip out west, to Nebraska and Colorado, in my family's
Rambler station wagon. It would be our last big adventure together
before starting college in September. Danny was bound for St Joseph's
College in Rensselaer, Indiana, a Catholic college founded in 1889 by
the Missionaries of the Precious Blood. I was going to Eastern Illinois
University in nearby Charleston, a state institution with a proud
tradition of mediocrity.

In years to come, I couldn't imagine how Althea Deaver could have
allowed her only son to travel by car from Illinois to Denver and back,
five weeks after her husband and father had been killed in a wreck.
A quarter of a century later, at around the time of *Silent Retreats*,
Phil wrote to me to explain:

My mom was on the edge of cracking the summer of the accident. The doctors didn't think she could take care of me anyway, and certainly at the time she wasn't strong enough to say no if we pushed to make the trip, which we did. I managed to be gone with you in August, then head out to college in September. She was helpless to stop us from going on the trip.

All summer, before the crash, we'd been challenging one and all to doubles tennis matches at Ervin Park. Any pair of locals who would take us on. And there were some good players in town, most of them grown men. We billed ourselves as "The World's Greatest Tennis Team," which was weird because we weren't any good. But we had a lot of energy, and we specialised in mind-games. We wore white sailor caps, white T-shirts, cut-off jeans, and tennis shoes with no socks. Sometimes we served underhanded or between our legs. We liked to position ourselves at unlikely places on the court, all but inviting our opponents to hit the ball to the sweet spot we'd left wide open. And somehow we beat everyone in town except for two middle-aged guys, Rudy Kalmar and his partner, who'd been to university on a tennis scholarship.

So when we loaded the Rambler in August, we threw in our tennis racquets and our sailor caps. We also took a couple of scruffy baseballs and two big Japanese leather mitts so we could play catch along the side of the highway whenever we felt like it.

From Tuscola to Nebraska, we were able to tune in to the St Louis Cardinals' games on the car radio, which had a lot better reception than our crackly transistor radios at home. The best broadcasting team in baseball history, Harry Caray and Jack Buck, kept us entertained for hours on the road.

Our first stop was Quincy, near the banks of the Mississippi River, the town I'd lived in before Tuscola. My dad's basketball team had won a state championship for Quincy College and made an unlikely run in the national tournament.

I hadn't been back to Quincy since the family left but I still remembered my way around. I showed Danny where we used to live, where I went to grade school, where I'd ridden my bike with baseball cards clothes-pegged into the spokes to make it sound like a motorcycle. I showed him the college chapel with its concave ceiling where the enormous face of Jesus stared down and scared the hell out of me. I retraced my steps to the larger St Francis Solanus Catholic Church where I'd embarrassed myself by wearing my Davy Crockett hat up to the communion rail, and to the school stairs where bad boy Joey Sohn gave the middle finger sign to a nun.

We drove over to the home of the Rapp family, but my old friend Johnny Rapp had already left for college. Like Danny's dad, his father was a doctor. The stack of boards behind the Rapp garage was still there, where I'd stepped on a nail that passed clean through my right foot. Danny and I talked in the back yard with Johnny's mother, who recognised me even though I was a foot taller and a whole lot skinnier.

We crossed Quincy's Bayview Bridge into Missouri and headed south for a St Louis Cardinals baseball game at the old Busch Stadium (Sportsman's Park, which was to be demolished two years later). We'd been to dozens of games with our dads. We were there in 1957 for a Sunday afternoon game, hoping to see Stan the Man Musial get his 3,000th hit. Danny kept raving on about Musial's weird batting stance at the plate. Stan didn't get it done that day, but he did it later in the week with a double into the Wrigley Field ivy.

We were there on April 14, 1961, when Wally Post, the Cincinnati Reds outfielder, hit the longest home run in baseball history, off the Cardinals' left-handed pitcher Curt Simmons. Post's teammate Jay Hook, an engineering student, calculated the ball's distance, if it hadn't smashed into the scoreboard clock, as 569 feet—four feet farther than Mickey Mantle's 1953 shot in Washington DC's Griffith Stadium.

We were there in 1962, on the 18th of July, when Bob Gibson struck out twelve Cubs on his way to a three-hit shutout. We were there in 1963, on the 23rd of April, when the Cardinals scored 15 runs against the Houston Colt .45s.

This time around, in 1964, the Cardinals beat the Giants, 6–4, on their way to winning their first National League pennant since 1946, the year we were born. Stan Musial had retired the year before, but the Cards still had Gibson, Curt Flood, Kenny Boyer, and Bill White, who got three hits that day, and the newcomers Lou Brock and Mike Shannon. And we got to see Willie Mays slam a home run for the Giants in the seventh inning.

Between St Louis and Independence, Missouri, we stopped in Jefferson City, the state capital, to watch a drive-in movie on the outskirts of town—*Strait-Jacket*, starring Joan Crawford as a woman who spent 20 years in a psychiatric hospital after axing her husband and his mistress to death.

On the way out of town the next morning, we couldn't find the highway, so we asked an old farmer in bib overalls for directions. He pointed to a hill.

"Just go toward that rise in the road," he said, "but turn just before you get to the top, and you'll get to the highway."

"Whatever you do," he said, "don't go over that hill." He paused. "Make sure you don't go over that hill."

Being smart alecks, we thanked him, rolled up the windows, and said to each other at the same time, "Let's go over the hill."

And that's what we did. And a few minutes later, when we inched back again toward the farmer and turned left to get on the highway, we saw the poor man still standing there, shaking his head at the two biggest dumb-fucks he'd ever come across.

CHAPTER 4

The Old Bray of My Heart

Every night on the way to Denver, we slept in sleeping bags in the back of the Rambler, with the rear seat folded down and our jeans rolled into pillows. Nobody hassled us till we got to Independence, Missouri. There, we found the local tennis courts, under lights, and challenged anybody and everybody to take us on for a few dollars a set. We wore our sailor caps and kicked ass for three or four hours. We took our winnings to the Independence McDonald's for hamburgers and fries, then found a quiet spot on a dark street to sleep in the car. But just after midnight, Danny shook me and pointed at a pack of evil-looking white boys strutting our way, toting wooden clubs and baseball bats. They'd probably sized us up as a couple of smart-aleck homos, and they were half right. I jumped over the seat and got behind the wheel, and we hightailed it out of Independence, without looking back or slowing down till we got to Nebraska.

The reason we were going to Omaha instead of straight to Colorado was that Danny's uncle, a priest known as Father Steven Deaver, lived in Nebraska. I knew Father Steve from a fishing trip we'd taken in August 1960—me, Danny, our dads, and Father Steve—from Tuscola to Lac Seul, a big lake in northwestern Ontario.

Before the fishing trip, Danny and I sharpened our casting skills for hours outside the Deaver house, aiming our lines at the base of a big linden tree in the side yard. Our shared goal for Canada was to catch as many walleye and northern pike as our canoe would hold.

That trip to Canada hadn't started well. Dr Deaver had decided to stop drinking—to go on the wagon—leaving behind in Tuscola all the beer and wine my dad had purchased to pass the time in the lakeside cabin. He didn't find out what Dr Deaver had done till we got to International Falls, on the Minnesota–Ontario border, when we pulled into a gas station run by the hulking Bronko Nagurski, the old running back for the Chicago Bears. Bronko was considered by many to have been the best player in NFL history. He lumbered out to fill our tank, and as Dr Deaver paid the bill and got his autograph, my dad and Father Steve took turns testing the gas cap to see if it was true—could Bronko really twist the caps so tight that his customers couldn't get them to reopen? It was true. You had to come back to Bronko's station for a refill so he could get the cap off.

My dad said he wanted to toast the crossing of the international border, and that's when Dr Deaver confessed that he'd left the beer and wine behind. So they drove to a local bar in a seedy part of International Falls, and the three of them—my dad, Dr Deaver, and Father Steve—went inside while Danny and I stayed in the back seat of the car. It was scary. Drunks kept tapping on the car windows and making rude remarks and gestures. We tried to distract ourselves by playing word games and setting off fake farts with a whoopee cushion.

When our three grownup companions came back to the car, about an hour later, our dads were soused but Father Steve hadn't touched a drop, so he drove us across the border.

In Ear Falls, Ontario, we met up with two guys from Tuscola, Eddie Schultz and his dad, Big Ed. The Schultz's car caught my attention—a 1940s Nash Suburban with real wooden panels on the sides. Eddie Junior was a Catholic boy like Danny and me, a year older than we were, one of those guys who nobody paid much attention to, except that one day in catechism class Sister Mary Walter asked if anybody could name the Seven Deadly Sins, and Eddie rattled them all off before anybody else could think of any. Pride, greed, lust, envy, gluttony, wrath, and sloth. Phil and I were impressed.

I never could figure out if this rendezvous with the Schultzes in Ear Falls had been pre-planned or was a coincidence, but Danny and I joined Eddie Junior in casting off from a long wooden pier, and each of us landed our first walleye.

In those days, you had to take an amphibious plane from Ear Falls to get to Lac Seul. After our plane landed on the water, a Chippewa Indian guide named Vic rowed us to the shore and led us to our cabin. He told us to be on the lookout for deer, moose, and bear. He made them sound like kittens.

Each night the loons lulled us to sleep, and each morning Danny and I played "bottlecaps" outside the cabin as the men cooked up a huge breakfast. Danny pitched as I stood at an imaginary home plate with a long wooden broomstick. Instead of baseballs, he threw bottlecaps that had been left behind by previous campers. The bottle-caps were hard to hit—they curved through the air like tiny frisbees. To have any chance at all of making contact, I had to keep a close eye, from Danny's hand to the broomstick, on his curve balls and sliders. Then we'd switch positions.

Dr Deaver was in charge of making the scrambled eggs. He'd crack the eggshells in style, one by one with a single hand. "Surgeon's fingers," he joked. After breakfast, we'd portage along a trail through the woods with canoes on our shoulders, from the cabin to the water, with Vic leading the way and keeping a lookout for black bears. One morning, he bent down to the trail and scooped up a fresh pile of shit with his fingertips. He raised the goo to his nose and said, "Bear." We picked up our pace that day, and every day for the rest of the trip.

Danny and I caught even more fish than we'd anticipated. We had to throw most of them back even though they were big enough to eat, because there were too many to carry back to the cabin. Our dads and Father Steve were pretty useless when it came to fishing. For some reason, they preferred horsing around, stripping down to their underwear and taking turns with two of them kneeling in their canoe holding the other one by the heels as he dipped his torso into the water to fumble around for some booty. Whenever one of them emerged holding a 20-cent lure or an old coin or a tent peg, Danny and I could hear them whooping it up like they'd just hit the jackpot, all the way across the lake.

We weren't very proficient at casting, despite all of our practice in Danny's front yard, and one time Danny's cast didn't even make it out of the canoe. That's because the hook got stuck in Vic's back. Vic reached over his shoulder and calmly wiggled the hook out of his flesh.

Vic didn't talk much, but this time he explained. He said he had "no nerves" left in his back and arms. He couldn't feel pain. We asked him why. He said he'd been in a car crash that left him that way, with no feelings. It happened as he and his wife were driving away from a church on their wedding day. She went straight through the windscreen and was decapitated.

Danny and I took care to cast high above Vic's head for the rest of the vacation.

Forty years later in his poem *Lac Seul*, Danny—now Philip Deaver—remembered the "moose moving in the black shadows" of the woods nearby, the "cold nights with the bears," the Chippewa guide "in the corner / of the cabin away from the woodstove, / watching in another language." He still dreamt about his "earliest initiation / first utter absence from my mother":

> We'd find an inlet and fish for hours
> pools turning, twist of currents,
> not a word said. We'd build our fire
> at noon for lunch, pike and beans,
> scrape it all away like it never happened,
> climb back in the boat and fish till dusk …
> Lac Seul, what a gift you were.

CHAPTER 5

Fill the Unforgiving Minute

IN AUGUST OF 1964, when we got to Omaha, I was looking forward to seeing Father Steve again. He'd checked into a cheap hotel in a bad part of town, and we met him there. At first everything was light-hearted. He took us to a McDonald's for burgers and fries, but they wouldn't let him pay because he was wearing a collar.

"That's on us, father," said the boy at the serving counter. About a quarter of the people in Omaha seemed to be practising Catholics in those days.

On our way back to his room, Father Steve handed the money he'd saved at McDonald's to a drunk on a stairway in an alley and told him not to buy alcohol. Back in his room, the three of us sat around and talked. I remember Father Steve making a joke about not needing a wife because he had his Catholic breviary, which wasn't very funny but Danny and I laughed anyway because he was a grownup and we weren't.

It suddenly dawned on me that I was the odd guy out, and what Father Steve really wanted to do was to be alone with Danny so they could talk about his dad—Father Steve's brother—and the crash and the future. So I excused myself and went down to the hotel lobby to hang out for a while. There was a Cardinals game on a small black-and-white TV, so it was okay. An hour or so later Danny came down, and he and I slept in the Rambler in the hotel parking lot.

The next morning, we joined Father Steve for breakfast and then said goodbye. There were tears in Father Steve's eyes, and Danny's too, but they didn't hug each other because guys didn't do that in those days. They just shook hands, Nebraska style. I shook Father Steve's hand too, and Danny and I set off across Nebraska for Colorado.

The rest of the trip took about 12 hours, with a few stops. We kept our eyes on the horizon, waiting for the Rockies to show up in the distance. We didn't have to wait long, and when we rolled into Denver we snaked around the streets till we found the Brown Palace Hotel on 17th Street.

The Brown Palace was our idea of living it up. Before we left Illinois, my grandfather told us that it was one of the great hotels in America, and he'd stayed there a few times in the 1920s when he was touring with the Schubert Jazz Orchestra. (By coincidence, my grandfather's name, like Danny's grandfather's, was Lester.) So we drove the Rambler into a multi-storey car park next to the Brown Palace and checked in.

I bought a postcard in the lobby to send to my grandfather. My message wasn't very creative: "Having a good time. Staying at the Brown Palace." On the front of the postcard was a picture of Mark Twain sitting in a rocking chair next to Tom Sawyer. The photo was taken at the local wax museum.

We were tired after our long drive and the late night with Father Steve, so we ate in the hotel restaurant. On the way back to our room, a guy in a beige suit stopped us at the top of the stairs and asked us if we wanted any girls. "Cheap," he said. It's hard to believe now, but we really didn't have a clue what he was talking about. We were both virgins, in mind and in body. We politely declined and figured it out later.

Over the next few days, we went to the wax museum on Brannock Street, the Denver Mint, and Elitch's Amusement Park. For some reason we also drove down to Colorado Springs to have a look at the Air Force Academy. Looking back, I can't imagine a more boring set of things to do, but that's what we did. We spruced things up by using aliases whenever we introduced ourselves to anybody. I was Buzz Talbot; he was Bob Reid. Years later, in his story "Arcola Girls," Phil recycled those same youthful aliases for his boy characters.

When we got back to the hotel from the Air Force Academy, things got a whole lot more interesting. As we entered the elevator, there were four guys already in there. They were wearing suits and had the same dopey haircuts. One of them reached for the "up" button. I looked at him, and looked again. It was John Lennon. I looked at the other three. They were the fucking Beatles—John, Paul, George, and Ringo.

They got out before our floor. Danny and I took the elevator back down to the lobby, and the concierge told us the Beatles were playing the next night at the Red Rocks amphitheatre, ten miles west of Denver. It was the sixth stop on their first American tour. Seven thousand tickets had already been sold, but we were able to buy a couple from a scalper at double the price. He was the same guy who'd offered us the cut-rate girls.

On the amphitheatre's outdoor stage the next evening, the Beatles looked tiny, and the sound system was awful, but it was a great night anyway, and it got better in our memories as the years passed. In 1964, they weren't the Beatles of the White Album and Sergeant Pepper, but they made us feel good. They played "I Want to Hold Your Hand," "She Loves You," "All My Loving," "A Hard Day's Night," and a few more songs. We got our money's worth.

Half a century later, it seems amazing to have seen the Beatles in their early days. But at the time, we thought they were just another English band, like the Dave Clark Five. Frankly, we were more impressed with Lois Lee & the Rockets from Danville, Illinois, the Shattertones from Bloomington, and Jim Easter & the Artistics from Champaign, three bands that rolled over to Tuscola every few weeks to play for our Saturday night dances at the community hall, known as "the Wick." They were among the bands Phil immortalised in his 1986 short story, "Arcola Girls." When we thought of rock 'n roll, we thought of gyrating to their music with our best Tuscola dance moves—the Jerk, the Stroll, the Mashed Potatoes, the Swim, and the Monkey.

The trip back home to Illinois was a blur. We just kept swapping the driving duties every few hours, stopping only to pee or grab a bite to eat, and we made it to Tuscola in 18 hours flat. I dropped Danny off at his house, waited to make sure the lights came on inside, then drove back home. The summer of 1964 was over.

CHAPTER 6

Truths That Lie Too Deep for Taint

P HILIP FINTAN DEAVER JR was born in Chicago on 14 August 1946. His parents, native Nebraskans, had moved there so his father could complete his medical studies. His mother, Althea, was a registered nurse.

One of the nurses in the maternity ward nicknamed him "Danny," after the Rudyard Kipling poem, *Danny Deever*. Although it had a nice alliterative ring, it wasn't the most propitious choice of names. Kipling's Danny, a young soldier, had been sentenced to death for murdering a sleeping comrade.

After Dr Deaver completed his internship at the Illinois Central Hospital in Chicago in January 1947, the family moved downstate. Danny told me a story later that seemed unlikely, about how they chose Tuscola. According to Deaver family lore, his parents placed a map of Illinois on their apartment wall and Dr Deaver, blindfolded in the style of pinning a tail on a donkey, stuck an old suture needle into Douglas County. Tuscola was the county seat.

After establishing his practice during the next four years, Dr Deaver was drafted into the Army Medical Corps. He'd been rejected for military service during WWII because of a broken back suffered while playing high school football, but now the army needed doctors in Korea. He was stationed on an island near Pusan (now called Busan).

The Battle of the Pusan Perimeter, from 4 August to 18 September 1950, had been one of the first major engagements of the Korean War. An army of 140,000 UN troops, most of them Americans, rallied to defeat the invading North Korean army, 98,000 strong, but the victory was costly. Around five thousand US soldiers were killed, and another twelve thousand were wounded. Pusan and its surrounding islands became campsites for Korean refugees for the remainder of the conflict.

While stationed with the 64th Field Hospital near Pusan, Dr Deaver initiated a campaign for children's clothing to be shipped from Tuscola to the island where, he wrote, kids wandered around "naked from the waist down and blue with cold." Many, he said, were "no older than my own children," Danny (5) and Maureen (3).

As the Korean War drew to a close, Dr Deaver completed his military service and returned to Tuscola to pick up where he left off with his medical practice and his marriage, and to raise his two kids. It was the era of small town hospitals—Dr Deaver often worked at Tuscola's Jarman Hospital from 7am to 7pm—and frequent house calls, with the Deavers' home phone ringing at all hours of the night. It was a party line. Everybody knew everybody else's business.

Dr Deaver was a man of few words. He liked to take his young son Danny with him to Chicago, a city he knew well from his 10 years of medical studies. They'd travel by train to the 12th Street station, walk north to the corner of Roosevelt and Michigan Avenue, and make their way past the lion statues into the Art Institute.

Even at that tender age, Danny was entranced by the Art Institute's paintings. He and his father would find a particular work that took their fancy, and stop and stare at it for a long time. One of Danny's favourites was Edward Hopper's *Nighthawks*, a rendition of 1940s urban loneliness. Somehow Danny connected with it at the age of nine, despite the big gap in time. He came back to *Nighthawks* repeatedly during his life and in his writing, for as long as he lived.

Danny loved these weekend getaways with his father. Even though Dr Deaver was quiet and reflective, Danny liked it when just the two of them were together. They were pals.

In the autumn of 1957, Danny Deaver's life was altered by the arrival in Tuscola of a new family, outsiders from the Mississippi River side of Illinois. My dad had lost his job at Quincy College, and he'd accepted an offer to be Tuscola's new high school basketball coach. It was a backward step. At Quincy College, he'd led his teams to state championships and national tournaments, all the while pushing hard for the civil rights of his African-American players at a time when they weren't allowed to drink from white water fountains or eat in white-owned restaurants. He wouldn't put up with discrimination. He played his best players on the court regardless of skin colour and he refused to stay or eat at any place that wouldn't accept every member of his team. But he ran afoul of the Quincy College president, a Franciscan priest named Julian Wood, who didn't like the negative publicity.

Father Julian believed that people should know their place. Martin Luther King and Rosa Parks were not yet household names. Quincy's population included a hard core of white racists. James Earl Ray, a Catholic, was still living in Quincy while we were there. In 1955, he was convicted of mail fraud after stealing cheques across the river in Hannibal, Missouri. He was sentenced to imprisonment for four years in the federal penitentiary in Leavenworth, Kansas. Fourteen years later, he assassinated Dr Martin Luther King Jr.

In Quincy in 1957, my dad was suddenly out of work with three young kids and he couldn't afford to bide his time. So he took the first job that was offered—high school coaching in Tuscola, Illinois, on the other side of the state.

I entered Mrs Marguerite McDaniel's sixth grade classroom in Tuscola's South Ward Elementary School. It was the first non-parochial class I'd ever been in, and I had trouble adjusting after five years of nuns. The first time Mrs McDaniel called on me, I stood up as I'd been taught to do at Quincy's St Francis Solanus Catholic Elementary School. The Tuscola kids laughed. They'd never seen any kid stand up to answer a teacher's question. I soon became the butt of their jokes, and decided my best play was to become the class clown.

Like a chicken in a pecking order, I looked for someone down the line. And I found her in Marcella Gasaway, a hillbilly child with a surname that invited ridicule.

"Gasaway," I whispered to her from my desk.

"Gasaway," I whispered over and over again, until she'd had enough. She chased me to the front of the classroom with her fist clenched. I lost my balance and lunged headfirst into the sharp corner of Mrs McDaniel's wooden desk.

I sat on the floor with my mouth bleeding, touching my fingers to the hole in my upper lip, and that was when Danny Deaver came into my life. He sat down next to me and tried to make me feel better until my dad arrived to take me to Dr Deaver for some stitches to close the wound. Danny's eyes were the sharpest blue, and his brown hair was parted on the side, unlike the rest of us boys who sported crew cuts or flat-tops. He looked sort of beautiful. He looked like an angel.

"It went clear through," I said to Danny.

I showed him the open gash in my lip, and he peered through.

He said he could see my front teeth on the other side. Half an hour later, my dad arrived, and Danny was smitten. He wrote to me about it half a century later:

> That day you made fun of Marcella Gasaway and she retaliated and pushed you head-first into Mrs. McDaniel's desk and your lip got gouged, you sat dazed at your desk right in front of me,

turned to me and mumbled, holding one of those awful paper towels to your mouth, 'It went clear through.' About that time, your six-foot-three thirty-something-year-old star quality dad in a letter jacket that wasn't Tuscola's strolled into the room to take you to get stitched up. The room got quiet. He was bigger than life.

It stayed like that for the rest of the year in Mrs McDaniel's class. I kept getting into trouble, and Danny kept trying to bail me out. He was the teacher's pet.

One day, Mrs McDaniel gave us a science quiz, with multiple choice questions and fill-in-the-blank answers. She attached a few essay questions to test our writing skills. Danny's essay was about dinosaurs, and it was so good that Mrs McDaniel read it out loud to the class the next day.

"I felt like I was right there with the dinosaurs," she told us.

"Danny has a flair for words," she said. "One day, he's going to be a famous writer."

CHAPTER 7

Gleams of Half-Distinguished Thought

F OR THE NEXT couple of years, I was in Danny's orbit, but we weren't yet the best of friends. He already had an established circle of Tuscola boys he'd known as far back as he could remember— Billy Adkisson, Andy Jolley, Alan Forsythe, Clayton Harriss. I was an outsider and my family was in turmoil. My dad's Tuscola basketball teams couldn't win. He wasn't used to failure. He'd had the golden touch in his first eight years of coaching. Now he went deep inside himself, and sometimes he lashed out at anyone within his wingspan. It wasn't pretty. And we were poor. Our family's dysfunction gnawed at our happiness and self-esteem, compromised our social standing.

Parallel lines of railroad tracks ran through the centre of town, east to west, and we lived on the wrong side of them, in the northeast corner in a shabby rented house near the trailer park. My first Tuscola friends were the town's poor kids—the three Bishop boys with their reclusive single mother and their father in jail, the feral Stablers with their three-generation reputation for trouble, fellow newcomer Bobby Green and his wayward family of transplanted rednecks.

On the south side of the tracks, where the Deavers lived, the streets were paved with bricks of red. Manicured lawns as crisp as golfing greens were graced with sturdy maple trees and oaks. The Deaver house was, to my eyes, a two-storey white mansion on the corner of Scott and Niles, the epicentre of the town's respectability and wealth. In Tuscola terms, the Deavers were royalty. They weren't stuck up about it. They just carried it around with them, naturally, wherever they went.

In 1959, at the age of 37, my dad was fired by Tuscola High School. He would never coach again. He took what he could get after that—a brief principal's job at Pesotum Elementary School, just up the road, then teaching school in Champaign, Illinois, for the rest of his working life. To give you an idea of what was lost, one of his successors as Tuscola's basketball coach—Bob Arnold, a guy whose team went 22–3 with the building blocks my dad had put in place years before—took me aside when I was a high school senior and said: "Do you know where your dad belongs?"

I said I didn't know.

"He belongs in big-time coaching," he said. "That's where he belongs." He meant in the top collegiate ranks, or maybe the NBA.

Near the end of primary school, there was a change that cemented my friendship with Danny Deaver, which was to last in one form or another till the day he died. A new kid moved to town from Montezuma, Indiana. His dad had been transferred to manage Tuscola's Panhandle Eastern Pipeline station, four miles west of town. His managerial job came with a big on-site house not far from the Panhandle station.

We first noticed the new kid during a basketball game in the North Ward Elementary School's cracker-box gymnasium. Danny and I were on the grade school team, the Hornets, and the new kid, a reserve named Herb Budden, was sent in to play late in the second half. Danny stole the ball from the opposing team, and Herb galloped down the court ahead of the pack, looking for a pass so he could score an easy layup. With his floppy arms and jerky legs, he reminded me of the scarecrow in *The Wizard of Oz*, but somehow his quirky set of movements seemed just right, almost like poetry in motion. Danny's pass came to Herb, who bounced the ball in the general direction of the hoop. When he got to the basket, he stopped underneath and stood alone for what seemed like an eternity, with his eyes fixed on the net above. Nine other kids were racing toward him, five of whom were bent on his destruction. Herb closed his eyes and heaved the ball straight up, underhanded. It clanged against the bottom of the steel rim and bounced back into his face. He fell to the floor.

It was by far the worst basketball play Danny and I had ever seen, or ever hoped to see. Our eyes met in admiration. We had discovered our missing link.

Herb was more intelligent than any kid in town, and very sophisticated from an early age. He knew everything, and he was funny as hell. By the time we entered high school, the three of us were inseparable, and satellites gathered round us—Craig Sanderson, Billy Matthews, Eric Pflum, Billy Adkisson, Dennis Stewart—together with a group of fast-developing pre-adolescent girls who intimidated us—Patti Jenks, Dorinda Knapp, Sarah Kegley, Bonnie Powell, Janet Ochs, Teresa Little, Judy Hanners, Joyce Newlin.

Herb's arrival in town didn't help my sporting ambitions, or Danny's, but he was good for our souls. The three of us just fucked around, non-stop, for five years. The basement of Herb's house in the country had one of the town's only fallout shelters, stocked with everything a family would need when the nuclear bombs hit. It was never used, although we had convinced ourselves that Tuscola was among the Soviet Union's prime bombing sites because of the pipelines and a big chemical plant located three miles west of town.

We gathered in Herb's living room, reading books and playing records and flexing our infantile brains. Herb was the first to find out about everything—the Beatles, Bob Dylan, the Rolling Stones,

Barbra Streisand, soul music. He was light years ahead of everyone in Tuscola.

He was a mystery. Montezuma, Indiana, wasn't exactly an intellectual hub. It was, in fact, worse than Tuscola, with a population of only 1,000. Herb's parents weren't worldly. They were salt-of-the-earth, working class. Where he got his knowledge and style from, nobody knew. It just came naturally. He was born cool.

CHAPTER 8

The Beauty of Inflections

B ASEBALL WAS DANNY DEAVER'S thing. On defense, he liked to play the infield positions, especially shortstop and third base, and he had a good throwing arm. But as a kid, he couldn't hit for shit.

Tuscola didn't field a high school baseball team. Football, basketball, and track were the traditional high school sports back then. Baseball was a community game and drew a different mix of kids. With no baseball in the schools, the option was to join the Little League, and later the Pony League or an American Legion team, and to organise our own games of sandlot ball in Ervin Park.

The league coaches weren't from the high school staff. They volunteered to coach after they finished their day jobs. One came from a local gas station, another from a dairy, two were farmers, and another was on his way to becoming the county sheriff. One of the coaches, Bob Hastings, was the editor of *The Tuscola Review* newspaper, so we got lot of free press even though our teams weren't part of the local school system.

When we weren't playing in the leagues, Danny and I arranged most of the kids' pickup games in Ervin Park. We phoned around so many times that even half a century later we could remember most of our friends' phone numbers. Danny's was 463. Mine was 841-W. You went through an operator in those days.

If we managed to put together a group of eight we could get a good game going, because we played a variety of baseball called "Indian ball," which was designed for fewer players. Eight was the perfect number, four per side.

Everybody had a chance to be a star in the pickup games. We'd meet at the park on a summer morning, pick sides by the hand-over-hand ritual—up the length of a bat—to determine first choice of a teammate, and play till suppertime. For breaks, we'd ride our bikes downtown and eat hamburgers at old Gus Flesor's Candy Kitchen, then ride back to Ervin Park. When our wooden bats broke, we nailed them together. When our baseballs started spilling yarn, we wrapped them with black tape. When we got thirsty, we cupped our hands and guzzled water from the taps next to the dugouts.

Being from a sporting family, I hung in there with basketball and track all through high school and played baseball in the summer. But I was never much good at any of them. I lacked confidence and I was skinny, and every time I played in front of people I got self-conscious and my hands started to shake. My dad told me an attack of nerves before a game was a good sign—it meant I was focused, and the shaking would stop once the game got underway. But it never did for me. I was nervous the whole time. My superstardom was limited to sandlot baseball games in Ervin Park or shooting baskets in my own driveway, when no grownups were watching.

So we continued playing our games, year after year, but after Herb arrived our hearts were torn between sports and the art of fucking around. Danny and I had decided that we were gifted with extra-sensory perception, and if I sat in the bleachers on one side of the high school's gym and drew a picture, Danny could rub his temples on the other side and receive my message via invisible brain waves. Then, he could duplicate my drawing. Crowds of hangers-on gathered at each of our posts to watch the magic unfold and to verify outcomes. It would have been easy to cheat by giving each other clues beforehand, but we didn't do that. We had a sense of integrity.

So there I was, drawing a set of barbells or a triangle or a stick-cow, and there was Danny on the other side of the gym floor, eyes closed, rubbing his temples. The amazing thing was that we actually hit way more than we missed. Our classmates were spooked. They thought we had powers. And we thought so too. Years later, Phil was still writing about extrasensory perception in his stories "Arcola Girls" and "Cassadaga."

We invented something called "the Layer System." It's hard to explain, even now. It applied to everything, but the best examples are probably the dozens of poems Danny and I co-authored midway through high school. We billed ourselves on the title page as Philip "Greenleaf" Deaver and Garrison "Brown Nose" Forrester. Our slim volume carried a Whitmanesque title, *Leaves of Mud*, and we circulated our photocopied poems to our classmates. Here's a sample, which Danny named *Furrowed Fields*:

> I'm a gangster, yessiree,
> And everybody shoots at me.
> Bang bang bang,
> Here comes a gang.
> Of cops.

Or this one, *The Good Dog*:

> Run, dog, stop.
> Stop, dog, run.
> Good dog.

Under our Layer System, at Layer One, these poems were breathtakingly stupid, and that's exactly what most of our readers thought. But at Layer Two, the poems were incredibly funny, even profound. The difference was that Layer Two came with a subtext, along the lines of knowing exactly how dumb the poems were, which made them not-dumb. But then came Layer Three, where people who were more advanced than Layer One and Layer Two still thought the poems were dumb, because they were. The difference was that the Layer Three people knew what the Level Two people were up to but didn't give a fuck, while the Layer One people didn't have a clue to begin with. It went on and on like this, back and forth in ascending layers of one-upmanship, ad infinitum. Each layer was another level of superior consciousness that trumped the previous layers.

Our Layer System was harmless when used as a simple analytical tool. Lots of things were so stupid they were funny. But when we used it to put people in categories, the Layer System could rot your brain. We kept at it for a few years during high school but had to drop it upon re-entry to planet earth. Even then, it lurked around in our heads, and Danny never quite got over it. A quarter of a century later he asked, in reference to a grownup poem I'd written, "Do you ever get bad dreams about what a disease that Layer System was? It's interesting to see how it has come out in the wash in someone besides me, for whom it is a psychosis and I am not exaggerating."

CHAPTER 9

The Sea Which No One Tends

AND ALL THIS time, all through high school, Herb Budden was our real master of ceremonies, weaving his endless cool into the fabric of our lives. He was our tireless watcher, our judge and jury, our real or imagined listener to every conversation. His standards were our standards. He was the glue that held us together.

With a group of classmates, we broke the Guinness world record for non-stop talking from one phone booth to another on Highway 36. We set another record, since broken in South Africa, for the most bodies (24) crammed into a phone booth. One winter's day, we rolled hardboiled eggs from the north end of town to the south end with our noses, down on our hands and knees in the ice and snow, to establish another world record. Our photographs appeared in *The Tuscola Review*. Our names were on the radio. We felt like celebrities.

We watched movies in the Strand theatre on Sale Street and told each other what the actors' next lines would be before they were spoken. We predicted outcomes at basketball games, sometimes play by play. When a guy named Hahn from Oakland made a last-second shot from half-court to beat our varsity team, Danny and I looked at each other in disbelief, because we'd just said to each other, moments before, that the guy we called "Hood Hahn" (because of his duck-tailed hairdo) would win the game exactly like that. We collapsed dramatically to the gymnasium floor in mock amazement, feigning simultaneous comas, for no reason other than being dumb fucks. The head coach, a slow-witted bully named Don Rumley who operated exclusively in Layer One, pulled us up by the collars and slapped us silly. We were idiots.

In the last semester of our senior year, Danny and I found a vacant patch of land across the street from his home, where we engaged in impromptu wrestling matches over a couple of months, just horsing around. Neither of us ever got hurt, and the bouts seemed harmless to me, but they had lasting consequences for Danny. I developed a trick move. Somehow we'd scramble until he was manipulated into a face down position, then I'd reach over and grab hold of one of his ankles and bend his leg back till it came to a right angle. And then I tugged it inch by inch toward his butt till he finally gave up. I got him every time. It seemed that he wanted to lose.

Danny took to calling my tactic "the leghold." Even before we started the next bout, he knew how it would end. Although it was just a dumb trick, he decided it was some sort of metaphor for bigger things and kept writing to me about it off and on for the rest of his life. In 2004—forty years later!—when he was experiencing frustration with his unpublished novel *Past Tense*, he wrote out of the blue: "let me say that the leghold was a spectacular and foreboding metaphor for my life, and I think I knew it even then. I'm not going to say more, because to face these things is to announce one's whole life failure."

I didn't understand how a childhood wrestling move could be a metaphor for anything. I couldn't even remember the fucking thing till he brought it up time after time.

The only places where we could channel our energies productively, other than in Herb's rural sanctuary, were the high school's English classrooms. Miss Naomi Claassen was an unconventional teacher, young and bright, and she thought we were precocious—Herb and Danny and I, and Craig Sanderson too. We wrote essays and stories and poems, we read everything she assigned, and she gave us good grades for being grammatically correct and occasionally original. We knew where to place a comma, when to use an apostrophe. We knew when to write "it's" and when to write "its." We knew not to say "between you and I." For Miss Claassen, that was a lot. And in her English classes, being weird and thinking strange thoughts were advantages.

All the other high school classes—mathematics and science and history and Latin—were boring as hell. They made you follow rules. They came with right and wrong answers. In English class, you could follow yourself into a world of your own imagining.

CHAPTER 10

Mud-Luscious and Puddle-Wonderful

WHEN DANNY AND I weren't in school, we were either playing ball games or running around in the woods. About ten miles east of Tuscola, near the village of Camargo, there was a forested area with a small lake fed by the Embarras River (pronounced Am-braw). The lake and its surrounds were known as Patterson Springs, named after a guy who bought the area in 1880 and built a house next to the lake. In the early 20th century, Patterson's property hosted Chautauqua assemblies, which were Christian-fuelled education and entertainment events that spread across rural American communities until the mid-1920s. The Chautauqua gatherings brought a measure of culture to such communities, featuring teachers, musicians, preachers, long-winded speakers, and specialists of the day. Forty years after the last Tuscola-area Chautauqua, the Deavers bought a block of land near the old Patterson homestead, with the vague idea of eventually building a lake house of their own. At that time, there were only a few houses at Patterson Springs.

The Deavers took to driving me and Danny out to their plot and leaving us to fend for ourselves in the woods. During our first time out there, Danny produced his grandfather's ancient Buck hunting knife and said it would be "neat" to be blood brothers. He'd seen the technique on TV in an episode of *The Lone Ranger*. So we each scraped a layer of skin from an index finger and pressed the bleeding wounds together, just the way Tonto had done with the Lone Ranger.

"Brothers for life," Danny said.

"Yeah," I said. "Brothers for life."

During our final two years in high school (1963–64), if you can believe it, Danny and I spent hours at Patterson Springs, at the ages of 16 and 17, playing fucking army. This was at a time when boys about our age were getting shot up for real in the jungles of Vietnam. The US already had about 17,000 soldiers fighting over there; 122 were killed in 1963 alone. But I doubt if either of us had ever heard of Vietnam at the time. There we were, ten thousand miles away from the real action, carrying on like twelve-year-olds.

Herb didn't join us on these escapades—he was way too sophisticated. Usually it was me and Danny, along with Andy Jolley, Billy Adkisson, and Craig Sanderson. We'd split up into teams. The first group of two or three would head out from the Deavers' property into the forest, and after counting to five hundred, the second group would march out looking for them, with military-style manoeuvres.

Everybody had fake rifles and guns. If you were in the first group, the hiding group, you tried to find a spot behind a tree or a clump of land, from which you could ambush your stalkers. If you were in the second group, the hunters, you and your partner(s) kept eyes peeled for any signs of movement or fresh tracks, so you could pick off your enemies before they got you. When we spotted somebody, we actually said, out loud: "Bang." And sometimes there would be a big argument about who said "Bang" first, and who was dead and who wasn't. One time after I shot him, Andy Jolley got so mad he started throwing rocks and hit me in the head, which brought that day's conflict to a bloody end.

Our hiding places could be crafty—high up in the branches of tall hickory trees and oaks, or buried under piles of sticks and rotting leaves and acorns. Billy Adkisson took the cake for the best covert operation ever. Danny and I were stalking him down by the springs, tiptoeing along in the marshes, when he popped up from under the water and casually shot us both dead from behind. He'd been submerged in the springs, breathing through a hollow reed, waiting all the while to kill us.

Phil wrote about Patterson Springs in a number of his stories—"Wilbur Gray Falls in Love with an Idea," "The Kopi," and a few others. In "The Kopi," he regretted that by the turn of the century Patterson Springs "had been divided into lots and developed into a housing area. Fairly nice houses, but the karma was off." In 2009, he walked with a friend through the built-up area, stopping every now and then to tell stories about his favourite burr oak and the make-believe games of army. There were tears in his eyes as he spoke. The wild woodlands existed only in his memory.

I'll tell you a secret. In the 1960s, when we were young, playing army in Patterson Springs was loads of fun.

During those last years in high school, before the car wreck, I started hanging out at Danny's house quite a bit, sometimes for sleepovers. Even at home, Dr Deaver wore expensive suits and ties and smoked a pipe, like the intellectuals of the day. Althea added a mystique of glamour. She played the grand piano and chain-smoked cigarettes like Ava Gardner and dressed more elegantly than any other woman for miles around. In Tuscola, she seemed to be the epitome of carefree style and casual beauty.

Danny's sister, Maureen, was two years younger than Danny. She had the same blue eyes as his, the same chestnut hair, the same preternatural self-assuredness.

Inside their big white house was the grand piano, a spinet organ, stylish furniture made of real leather and wood, and a home library with lots of books—bestseller hardbacks and classics. On the living room wall, above the fireplace and opposite Dr Deaver's favourite lounge chair, was Salvador Dali's *Christ of Saint John of the Cross*, a huge print of the original oil on canvas, in an ornate golden frame.

If you stood across the room and stared at the Dali, as I was wont to do whenever I snuck into the Deavers' living room alone, you could imagine being seated next to God the Father Almighty, looking down at His Son from a vestibule of heavenly light. Jesus, head bowed, was suspended on a wooden cross against a backdrop of threatening skies above a twilit body of water. An empty fishing dinghy was moored below. A tiny fisherman, standing next to the boat, was stretching out his nets to dry.

The face of the Son of God wasn't visible in Dali's painting. Just the top of his head, uncrowned by thorns. His hands and feet rested softly, even comfortably, against the wooden cross. No nails. No ropes. No blood.

There were no Salvador Dalis in my home on the other side of Tuscola's tracks. There was no home library. There was no fine furniture, no stylish clothing. There were hardly any books or magazines, except for outdated Reader's Digests.

Many years later, I heard about W B Yeats's attack on a group of politicians in Dublin. They were the sort of people, he said, "who do not have books in their houses." For Yeats and erudite Irish—and my family was half-Irish, descended from the Conway clan—it was hard to think of a greater insult, whether aimed at people with money or people without. But that was who we were—people without books in our house.

One time Danny came over to our home for dinner, which was unusual. The table conversation turned to the latest Otto Preminger movie, *Anatomy of a Murder*, which had finally made it to the Strand theatre on Sale Street. It starred James Stewart as a small-town lawyer and Lee Remick as his client's wife. My sister Nancy, then 13, asked Danny what the movie was about.

"Rape," said Danny.

The worldly Deavers, with their medical sangfroid, discussed such things openly in their home. At our house, sex didn't exist and had never existed. My dad nearly fell out of his chair.

I wasn't jealous of the Deavers. I was in awe. They were urbane. They were knowledgeable They were charming. They were blessed. They were perfect, all four of the Deavers.

Except they weren't.

Dr Deaver was a gentleman, schooled in every grace. He was wealthy by Tuscola standards. He was a war hero. He was married to the most glamorous woman in town, and they had two beautiful children. But the Deavers guarded a dark secret, close to home.

Dr Deaver was an alcoholic—and, in the privacy of his home, a mean one. A guy who would drive his wife and kids from the house when he got drunk. A guy who caused his wife to seek refuge in the nearby Forty Martyrs Catholic Church, the only place she could think to go. But every time she ran to the church, the local priest, Father Casey, told her to go back home to her husband.

While Danny and I were locked in that car in International Falls, Minnesota—two teenage boys waiting for our dads to come out of that seedy bar so Father Steve could drive us across the border for our Lac Seul fishing trip—Danny told me a story. Once upon a time …

… Danny was twelve years old. One night, his dad returned home late, breathing heavily and smelling of alcohol. It was all too familiar. Althea had run, yet again, to Forty Martyrs Catholic Church to ask Father Casey for help.

Danny and Maureen, who was ten, watched as their dad stumbled across the ground floor of their home. He couldn't keep his balance. He bumped against the furniture and walls. He groaned. Then, seeing his young children, he turned away and wobbled to the back porch. Everything was quiet.

Danny and Maureen listened for a while. Then, when they thought he had fallen asleep, they snuck out the front door and ran to

Forty Martyrs. Danny knocked at the rectory door and Father Casey appeared. The kids could see Althea standing behind him in the hallway, dishevelled, downcast, holding back her hair from her face.

She ran to them. The three Deavers huddled together at the doorway.

Father Casey told Althea to take her children home to her husband. He said she shouldn't file for divorce. If she did, neither she nor Dr Deaver would ever be allowed to receive any of the sacraments of the Catholic Church. Besides, a divorce would cause a scandal in the community. Father Casey said she needed to think of the children. He placed his hands on the little heads of Danny and Maureen. "The disgrace," he said. "The shame."

Althea, Danny, and Maureen walked home in the dark. Dr Deaver was nowhere to be seen. They could hear him snoring in the master bedroom upstairs. That night, Althea and Maureen slept together in Maureen's room. Danny lay down on the living room rug, next to his pet dog, and cried himself to sleep.

For years after that, Danny regularly combed through the pantry and the cellar and the attic above the garage to round up his father's latest stashes of booze. Several times, he lined the bottles up against a wall in the cellar or the garage and crouched on the floor, military style, with a .22 rifle. One by one, he shot the bottles till each one was shattered. Then, he left the shards of broken glass and the trail of alcohol for his father to discover. Time after time.

A few years later, just before we left for the Lac Seul fishing trip, Dr Deaver finally confronted Danny. It came after a baseball game in Tuscola's Ervin Park. Danny had been playing shortstop for our Pony League team and Dr Deaver was in the stands—not falling-down drunk but way too loud. When the game was finished, Danny rode his bike home and climbed high into the rafters of the garage to wait for his dad. An hour later, Dr Deaver parked the family Buick in the garage and unloaded a box of Old Fitzgerald bourbon from the boot, which he hid in a corner before limping into the house. Danny climbed down and grabbed his .22 rifle. He fired away at the box. Then, for good measure, he blasted a hole through the windscreen of the Buick.

Just before bedtime, Dr Deaver slipped out to the garage for a nightcap. He saw what Danny had done. Back in the house, they passed each other on the stairway. Dr Deaver grabbed Danny by his shirt collar. "Watch yourself, Junior," he said. "I'm not perfect. I never said I was."

To his credit, Dr Deaver went on the wagon for six months. Till he went into that seedy bar in International Falls, Minnesota, with my dad and Father Steve. When he got back from Lac Seul, he started drinking again, heavily.

Sixty years later, Danny/Phil fictionalised this traumatic car-shooting incident in his final work, *Forty Martyrs*. A teenaged girl from Tuscola, Misty Wagner, is embarrassed because her father Lowell turned up drunk at her afternoon softball game. That night, Misty sneaks into the garage and fires a round of bullets into Lowell's hidden stash of Jack Daniel's Tennessee Whiskey and—for good measure—blasts away at the family Corolla. Lowell, drunk, sleeps through the whole thing. In the morning, his wife Veronica—Misty's mother—stares at him. "The car was just a metaphor," she says. "You know that, right? You really pissed her off."

Not to be outdone, in 2018—shortly before Phil died—his sister Maureen wrote a piece of "creative non-fiction" called "Running in the Dark," which was published by *Flying Island*, an online journal of the Indiana Writers Center. Her story recounted, nearly verbatim, Danny's story about their father—"a bad drunk." It was clear that, despite outward appearances, the two Deaver kids had internalised a few layers of family secrets and a lot of grief—they were damaged, and their damage could only be softened by telling their stories, in writing, to a public audience. Their private writing rooms were their confessionals, and their imaginary readers served as their all-forgiving priests, granting absolution.

CHAPTER 11

To Touch Things with a Lighter Hand

AFTER HIS FATHER'S fatal car crash in 1964, and after our summer trip to Denver and back, Danny and I were off to college. Herb Budden enrolled at the University of Illinois, naturally, where the best education around was available. I went at Eastern Illinois University, a glorified teachers' college south of Tuscola, which was the only place my parents could afford. At least I had a scholarship. Danny went north to St Joseph's College in Rensselaer, Indiana, a town of 5,000 people. His dad had made the arrangements during Danny's senior year in high school.

With a tip of the hat to our Tuscola High School teacher, Miss Naomi Claassen, each of us was determined to major in English literature.

Danny left home first, and I joined him and Althea for the ride to St Joseph's College. Danny drove, in another Deaver family Buick, from Tuscola to Rensselaer, a trip of about two hours. When we arrived, I helped him transfer his bags into his dormitory room, which was in an old red brick building with creaky hardwood floors and high ceilings. Other students and their parents, strangers with funny accents, were doing the same.

Then, we sat at a picnic table on the campus green, Danny, Althea, and I, with a young English professor named John Groppe, as he held court about the past and future glories of St Joseph's College. Groppe was a priest, a Catholic intellectual, a liberal. He used the word "provincial" to describe the kind of thinking that annoyed him. I'd never heard that word before. Althea had to explain it to me.

He told us there were over 30 priests and brothers on the faculty, and most of them, like Groppe himself, were "progressive." He spoke proudly of the college's commitment to the civil rights movement, and of its most famous alumnus, Gil Hodges, the son of an Indiana coal miner, who later played first base for the Brooklyn Dodgers in their bittersweet years from 1943 to 1963 when they were the celebrated "Boys of Summer." Danny was rapt. He was about to try out for the college baseball team and he fancied himself as a defensive specialist, like Gil Hodges. He was beginning to think that St Joseph's College sounded like a good fit.

Then, Groppe told us a story about the Chicago Bears football team. Every year, since 1944, the Bears had held their pre-season training camps on the fields of St Joseph's College. In 1963, they'd been NFL Champions—their first championship since 1946, the year we were born. They were expected to repeat in 1964, but on 27 July 1964, everything changed.

"After practice," Groppe told us, "Willie Galimore and Bo Farrington went out to buy some takeaway pizza for their teammates, who were getting together at the country club west of Rensselaer. Willie the Wisp, the great running back, was driving his brand new Volkswagen convertible."

I didn't like where this was going. Groppe continued.

"When the party was finished, Willie was speeding back to the dormitory to make Coach George Halas's ten o'clock curfew. Normally, there was a warning sign up ahead for the road's last sharp turn, just before reaching the Iroquois River. But earlier that day, a mowing crew had knocked the sign down and they didn't put it back in place."

I looked at Danny. His folded hands were white-knuckled on the picnic table. He was looking straight into Groppe's eyes. His face gave nothing away. Althea closed her eyes and turned her head.

"The police report said Willie was speeding. He got thrown out of the car. Bo's neck was broken. They both died at the scene."

He paused. "It was the worst day in the history of the Chicago Bears."

Althea stood up, bent her head, and walked away slowly in the direction of Danny's dorm. Groppe turned to me.

"Did I say something wrong?" he asked.

I said nothing. Danny cleared his throat.

"That happened to me," he said. "That happened to my dad and my grandfather," he said.

"It happened in July," he said. "The same month as those two guys," he said.

Groppe's eyes welled with tears. He reached across the table to cup Danny's hands in his. Then, they stood and walked together across the campus green, stopping beneath a big burr oak, a stone's throw from the baseball diamond. I watched them talk quietly for half an hour, until twilight. When they came back, Althea put her arms around Danny and said goodbye. It was time to leave him behind.

CHAPTER 12

Anecdotes and Eyeball Kicks

O N T H E W A Y back to Tuscola, something happened that, in later years, caused a problem. Actually, nothing happened, but it caused a problem anyway. Although the trip from Rensselaer to Tuscola was only a couple of hours, Althea decided to stop for the night, halfway home, at a small roadside motel in Kentland, Indiana. No frills. She checked us both in—me in one room, her in a room next door. I crawled into bed and started to go to sleep.

Half an hour later there was a knock at my door. Althea asked me to come and sit with her for a while. I followed her into her room and took a chair next to the motel's chest of drawers. She sat on the edge of her bed and told me how unbearable everything was for her, with her husband and father and mother dead, and now Danny leaving home. She was crying. I handed her the box of tissues that was sitting on the chest of drawers. She felt all alone, she said, as alone as a person could possibly be. She feared she was losing her mind. She said she was sleep-deprived. She was frightened. She was worried about Maureen.

I didn't know what to do or what to say. I was 18 years old and stupid, and her level of grief was unimaginable for me. I just sat there and listened.

After an hour or so, her words came more slowly, so I got up to say good night. She thanked me for listening and showed me to the door. As I was leaving, she lowered her head and laughed softly and said she felt embarrassed. She said she'd be all right now, and she'd see me in the morning.

And that was it. But years later, when I'd become even more of a jerk than I was then, I told Danny about that mysterious encounter with his mother, after he was left alone at St Joseph's College. I joked that she may have had some designs on me that night, which was so ridiculous it never would have made it past Layer One in our Layer System.

Danny was perturbed. He hated me for telling him this story. He thought it was weird that Althea had stopped at a motel during the two-hour drive from Rensselaer. And he said he remembered something: he and Althea had gone to see the movie *The Graduate* a few years later. Dustin Hoffman was a college boy, Benjamin Braddock, and Anne Bancroft was Mrs Robinson, a middle-aged woman on the prowl. Danny said that, during the movie, Althea got up and walked out when Mrs Robinson made her move on young Benjamin.

Actually, it wasn't all that weird for Althea to stop on her way back from Rensselaer. Her life was in ruins. Her son had left home. She didn't want to drive at night. She was sleep-deprived. Groppe's story about the death of Willie Galimore had been deeply upsetting. She wanted someone to talk with before she slept, and dumb and skinny and ugly as I was, I was the only person within earshot. So she talked to me.

Later, I was sorry I'd said anything at all about it to Danny and wrote to tell him so: "Your mother did nothing in that motel room except be the wonderful human being she always was. Nothing happened and I was just blowing smoke when I mentioned it." If she walked out of a cinema when Mrs Robinson slithered across the big screen, it had nothing to do with me.

But Danny never forgot. Thirty full years later, he unloaded in a letter: "If what you said about my mom was true, what were you hoping for by telling me … if you just meant it as irony, maybe I was just too dumb to catch it, you think?" And in his 1992 story, "Cassadaga," his character Skidmore is accused of having an affair with Beth Landen, the wife of the narrator's late father, John Landen, the doctor who "died a few years back in a wreck." In the story, Skidmore replies to his accuser, a "psychic counsellor" named Janet, "This is bullshit. I never slept with Mrs Landen." But Skidmore, like me, was not entirely trustworthy.

And even near the end of his life, in 2015, Phil Deaver was *still* banging on to a woman who knew us both—Lora Goodnight—about me "and his mom on a road trip from Rensselaer."

"I tried to explain to him that you were still kids," Goodnight said. "It was fifty years ago and surely he could let it go. But he couldn't let it go, even then. He held you responsible for the entire episode."

"But you gotta remember how raw and vulnerable they were at the time," she said. Althea's loneliness, her completely broken heart. And Danny was a mess too, with his development in the process of arrest. And he was still stuck there, 50 years later.

A common hallmark of grief is misplaced anger. He had to put it someplace, any place that would take a load off, so that's where he put it. Onto me.

"I promise you," Goodnight said, "what haunted him most was not what you said—it was that you said it and then she walked out of *The Graduate.*"

Phil Deaver had a talent for nursing a grievance.

But those bumps in the road were way ahead of us. In September, 1964, Danny and I settled into our new homes away from home and began a lifelong correspondence. And I saved everything he ever wrote.

CHAPTER 13

Before Your Mind Like Rocks

O UR COLLEGE CORRESPONDENCE picked up where our high school poetry, and all the other dumb things we did, left off—with layers of immaturity recorded in words. Sometimes Danny tried to be cute with his envelopes. Addresses became "Abraham Lincoln's Hall" instead of Lincoln Hall, or "Wherever you are, EIU"; the addressee's name morphed from mine into "Dear Abby Forrester." One envelope arrived covered with pink fingerprints. Somehow these envelopes all found their way to my dormitory room at Eastern Illinois University.

I'm not suggesting that our letters were the building blocks for great literature, or even lousy literature. But they do show where our heads were during the first couple of years in college, and they show Danny's early gift for "suspending disbelief like nobody's business," as he put it many years later. All we were trying to do was to make each other laugh.

His first small envelope was postmarked "Collegeville, Ind. Oct 5 1964." It was addressed to me in conventional terms, at "Lincoln Hall, Rm 351, E.I.U., Charleston, Ill." The handwritten letter inside was about our favourite baseball team, the St Louis Cardinals, who had just reached baseball's "World Series" for the first time since the year we were born. His phrasing, repetition, and alliteration were intended as Layer System humour:

> Insomuch as the Saint Louis Cardinals won the pennant, I should like to congratulate you on account of you are a Cardinal fan as I, of course, am also, and it seems so nice to have the team we root for go to the World Series in the first year of many when we can't afford to miss any school to attend.
>
> Therefore I wish to pass on my sympathy when you can't go to the World Series to see yours and my favorite ball team play there cause you can't afford to get out of school on account of you have to keep getting good grades.
>
> Consequently, I would like to tell you how happy I am for you because you are getting such good grades at good old EIU which you shall attend during the long awaited days when your (and my) favorite baseball team (the Saint Louis Cardinals) got to the place they have aimed at for such a long time through rain sleet snow and etc.
>
> In conclusion, I'd like to close by bidding you a conclusive closing comprised of a common conclusive closing such as:
>
> Common conclusive closing,
> Danny

A couple of weeks later, he adopted the persona of a kid at a boys' college, raving on about imaginary friends, non-existent violin lessons, and make-believe difficulties in adjusting. Nobody really beat up on him, and he never played a violin in his life. "Dear Mommy," he wrote:

> I do not like it here. All of the boys here I do not like. They are bad boys. (One said "dam.") They yell also. And they eat with their mouths open sometimes. They play games which are rough. (Like football.) And spit.

They beat up on me because I tell them I don't know what things mean when they ask me what they mean sometimes. Why did you have to send me to a silly boys school? I do not like it here. It is so gruff!

Marissa Spolgf was a better friend than the friends I have here. Wally is a good boy and he doesn't play football except once (when he was 8) (years old) (but it was 'touch') (where you touch them instead of push them onto the ground). He (Wally) says he doesn't like it here too. He too does not like it in this place.

College life is great except for I do not like it here, like Wally. Can I go somewhere else like to where Marissa is going to? She is my best friend. Wally says he doesn't like girls.

My violin lessons are nice. I learn in them to play it better (yes, much better) than before. I like my teacher better than Peter, my old violin teacher. He had a son who played football and other such rough games like that.

Welp, I guess I better go.

Your son,
Freemont

In November, he asked me to revisit our high school past by performing "a mental telepathy at 10:00pm Thursday evening":

You transmit your design by mail. Don't fail. Not only is it important, but we (you & I) would become highly exalted by the cream of the St. Joseph crop. Great Experiment. Date: Nov. 12, 10:00pm. Send the figure you use as soon as possible, for proof. Ho Ho. Deaver.

I did as he asked, but our drawings looked nothing alike. We'd lost our touch.

His disappointment was short-lived. His next letter was another joyride from reality, in handwriting that pointedly scribbled off the bottom of the page, as if his fictional writer had fallen asleep or dropped dead. By this time, he was under the spell of the American humourist Robert Benchley (1889–1945), but if you compare this letter with his 2016 story "Vasco and the Virgin," you'll also see traces of Philip Deaver's grownup voice.

Dear Cousin Alfonse,

Regarding the matter of the time of your arrival at Kennedy Airport next Tuesday, I should like to point out that your time would be considerably hastened if you planned your arrival to be by aeroplane. Folks have been flying them for years now and there is no need to be frightened. Besides.

Now, in concentrating my mind upon our family problems, I would suggest for your approval that you secure a passport and a divorce (in that particular order). Having waited on tables for several years at the Little Brown Jug in New York, I have found that there are only five different categories of people. Your wife falls into none of these categories and I suggest you secure a divorce and a passport (in that order particular). Besides all that she doesn't drink and we can't allow her to break family tradition. The passport is so that you can be admitted into the US without having red tape all over your knuckles which also would break family tradition.

> Sincerely
> Cousin Freddie

He was just warming up. In April 1965, his "Dear Abby" envelope arrived. The real-life Abby was a woman named Pauline Friedman, who wrote a popular newspaper advice column under her pen name, Abigail Van Buren. Pauline's twin sister Eppie did the same thing, under her pseudonym "Ann Landers." They were all the rage in the 1960s. Inside, Danny's letter was typed for the first time:

Dear Abby,

I'm sorry to bother you at such a time as 2:00 am in the morning but I simply can't sleep. You see, I have a problem. That I must tell you about. And maybe you can give me aid. In my time of trial. And fortitude. I work for the park service in Cordial, Bremman County, Texas. I plant trees and bushes and grass.

My technical name (that is, the title by which I am called in the business) is Landscape Engineer, but my technical title is Marshall of Law and Order, Park Bureau. As you can see, my job is one of complexities and vast importance. Though I am paid a meager wage for my salary and efforts, I am a hardworking man who loves the outdoors.

My problem is that my wife thinks that I and my job are insignificant. I must have a way to prove to her that I am NOT insignificant. I must prove to her my significance. In order to save our marriage. We can't afford any pets. We can't afford to rent a car or a home. So we live in my father's one-room trailer with him and my two sisters and their husbands, and the three children that have come from those two unpleasant marriages. My wife and our six children are a happy family. But I must prove to my wife that I can handle any financial problems that might one day arise. I have tried to do this several times and each time I have failed.

As I look around the trailer right now, I see all nine children, frolicking, having fun, smiling, stomping on Grandpa and the bed. My wife and my two sisters are taking their turn at sitting outside so that the trailer won't be so crowded (there is a space problem but we are dealing with it). They are cooking on the camp fire that I built when it was my turn to be outside. I am very proficient at building campfires, since I love the outdoors, the great outdoors. We take turns doing everything around here so that everyone gets a chance to do everything and no one gets left out. Grandpa is taking his turn at sleep. In an hour he will wake up, and my oldest sister's second youngest son will sleep.

Next Tuesday, according to the schedule, I will get to sleep. In an hour I must go to work, my wife gets to come in the house and warm up. Rarely does anything ever go wrong with this kind of schedule. We had only two fatalities so far this winter. Grandma froze during her turn outside and we had to pull off one of Jani's toes (the piggy that went to market) when it got slammed in the toilet lid during a mix-up in the bathroom schedule. All of this I organized. This I think shows great promise for further advancement in the business world of the Park Association. I am not insignificant. How can I convince my wife? According to the schedule I won't see her till December 19, just ahead of the Christmas rush. (Incidentally, I also have the job of providing the Christmas tree. Is that insignificant?)

At the bottom of the "Dear Abby" letter was a handwritten note:

Dear Abby

I am the 'wife' spoken of above. I found this letter in the typewriter when I came in from outdoors. I see nothing wrong with my husband consulting you. Please give him the expert advice he so sorely needs. I trust our peril is evident.

Mrs. William Prendergast

That spring, just before Easter break, he tried out for the St Joseph baseball team. He was just a freshman, so it wouldn't be easy. He wrote about it in a letter, after letting off steam about a tragicomic mental breakdown that may or may not have had some connection with things that really happened to him. For example, the "Patti Jenks" and the "Dave D'Avignon" he mentioned in his letter were real people. The parenthetical comments in the letter below were in Danny's original:

I want you to know that since the last time I was at home I have gone quite mad. Now you are probably thinking, "Why, that silly goof. He hasn't gone mad. He is just using 'mad' as an expression to show his frustration." But no. I have gone crazy, absolutely incoherently ravingly mad, so to speak.

You may have noticed that I haven't written. Your last letter implied that possibly you had noticed that I haven't (have not) written. Well, you are (you're) right. I sure (certainly) have not (written). Well, here I am. And I'm going to tell you how come I haven't writed. And you simply bear with me while I tell you a story that honestly truly did happen to me, by me. It shows you that I am crazy, as I have said before (that I'm crazy).

One night last week (a MOnday night) (my capital 'O' was an accident) I got a call from Patti Jenks (on the phone, you know) and she caused it all. She said nothing for three minutes then hung up on me. I was completely crazy before this, but it was a dormant type of insanity. Now it manifested itself. It was 1:00 am by the clock, and the shutters were shut and the doors were closed and all of the kiddies were in bed when there came a clank and a clatter of me in my blue jeans, suspenders and fake moustache. I came running at a dash down the hall yelling with no bars held, quite as loudly as could have the next fellow.

"Move those cannons out of the way. Make your way for the Fifth Cavalry Unit on the flank. Sergeant, where is my right flank? Dammit, Sergeant, where are you?! Jones, where's the sergeant?! Move that flank … prepare to move across that draw, keep low! Sergeant, where are you?!! I'll kill him, I swear I'll kill him!! Major Jones, the Fifth will have to lead the charge! The Sergeant has disappeared!! Move that right flank. Dammit, get out of there or we'll run you down!! What?! Dead?! But how? He was on our flank … our flank. God, Lee's flanked us. Lee has flanked us!!!! Prepare for hand to hand …here they come!! Charge across that draw. Make for the round-top. God … (Here there is a slight break in the dialogue, a bowing of the head for the commemoration of the death of General George Pickett, whose fatal charge this is a betrayal of.)

I've been hit … This is it (so to speak) (Here the prefect entered to ball me out for yelling out the window, down the hall in the bathroom and in my room at such a rotten time of the morning.) (However I was dying on my bed with a bullet hole in my spine so he had to wait until I had passed away.) (He then bent over the broken body of General Pickett, Gettysburg 1863, and yelled at him for having made such a noise.) (In a British accent, I looked up to him and spoke, also in a British accent), "Is it that time already, James? Call the carriage and I'll get ready as fast as I can.") (I got into vast amounts of trouble for all of this.)

It should be pointed out that the latter part of my performance was not without an audience. Many tired and curious boys who had been slumbering (so to spike) stood in the hall and watched the death scene. These boys were not laughing. They were distressed as to my mental health. Of this I am not kidding. They were tired, it was late, and I was fighting the battle of Gettysburg, dashing up and down the hall yelling for the sergeant and for the flank to be moved, rolling open my window and yelling completely across the campus that we had been flanked and to charge. They were not laughing. They were sickened by the sight of an absolute madman. Since they all look at me with an eye of complete and total suspicion, and they laugh behind my back. I've been trying to keep up the image by doing silly little things every once in a while. That's the distressing part of it. I'm finding keeping up the image remarkably easy.

Yesterday in baseball I was playing center field and a ball dropped in for a hit. I picked it up and decided to really heave it to third base (whereat a man was dashing about). I slipped on wet grass, did the splits and the ball landed six feet behind me where an outfielder on my right or left picked it up and disposed of it while I labored at moving from my assumed position. I'll be cut sometime next week. As you can see I have entered upon a new phase of life where I no longer have to create humor in my mind. I create it every time I move, quite naturally, quite embarrassingly. Wait till you hear some of my stories. At Easter I'm bringing home my roommate and a kid from Cincinnati named Dave D'Avignon (an ace punner). It should really be fun but I don't know when I'll work in the girls. I'll have to sometime. I'll simply have to. My typewriter has gone crazy.

> Bye.
> Deaver

Maybe he did have a crack-up of some sort at St Joseph's College. I don't know. What I do know is that he had therapy at St Joe's and he wasn't cut from the college baseball team. As I found out the following summer, he kept getting better and better at baseball, as a glove man and as a hitter, far away from the distractions of me and Herb Budden.

A month after his General Pickett breakdown, he sent me another "Dear Mommy" letter, wrapping up the end of his first college year:

> Welp, school is almost over. I must warn you that my grades aren't too good. Oh, they aren't failing. But they aren't too good. I think the problem was slow adjustment to college life. You know I always have been a slow adjuster. Even in high school I was a slow adjuster. But I can make the grade now. Just wait till next year. Next year I'm going to really buckle down!!

> Love from your boy,
> Danny

That summer, back home in Tuscola from EIU, I got a job at the Kraft Food plant in Champaign, stacking bottles of salad dressing onto wooden pallets, eight hours a day. Herb worked there too, in the mustard department, and Danny went back to his summer job in Tuscola, baling hay.

He and I played baseball together on the same team for the first time, in Tuscola's American Legion league. We'd always been opponents before, on the town's Little League and Pony League teams, Danny as a Cardinal and me as an Indian. Now we were teammates. I was amazed at how much he'd improved during that first year at St Joseph's College. Somehow he'd gained a big dose of baseball acumen and the confidence that went with it. He hadn't quite developed a swagger, but he was getting close. He was still a slick infielder, and now he had a bit of pop in his bat as well. Once upon a time, he'd been an automatic out. On our Legion team, he moved up in the lineup, from batting dead last at the start of the season to second or third by the end.

When the summer of 1965 ended and we went back to our colleges for the second year, his fanciful letters continued, with that same familiar voice. "Children," he wrote:

> Today is a momentous time in the lives of you, each and every one. You have reached 12 years old. You have gone beyond childhood, and all those punky eleven-year-olds and you are twelve. This is indeed momentous.
>
> I once knew a twelve-year-old named Carlotta. Ah, and she was very beautiful and she had a wicked stepmother too. Her wicked stepmother was always hitting Carlotta and pinching her pre-adolescent pimples. Sometimes the wicked stepmother even cleaned Carlotta's ears with a hairpin and a strand of sheep's wool. Carlotta was helpless. Carlotta was sad. So she killed her mommy. With a hat pin. Then she went dashing out of the house, a twelve-year-old out into the world of fellow adults, and sought shelter and comfort from all of her friends, who hated her because she had jabbed her mommy in the forehead with a hat pin.
>
> They said, "Go home, Yankee. Turn back, you dirty cheater."
>
> Poor Carlotta cried her eyes out. Poor Carlotta bawled her head off. And then she fainted right there on the ground and behold a beautiful goddy mud-feather appeared with these words of good advice for her.
>
> "You are sad, Carlotta. You are forlorn. You are sad. You are forlorn. You are, sad, and, also, forlorn, in any case. Go forth to

the palace of the King and give him your rooster, your cow, and the body of your father's favorite gold fish which he flushed down the toilet because of old age."

Carlotta said: "Oh dear."

But the fairy had disappeared into, no doubt, the wilderness, gone for ever and maybe for Everett.

Off into the Forest of the Forlorn went Carlotta, in search of the home she had lost and the animals she had left there. One day while experiencing many adventures she found her home and the animals she had left there.

"Oh, my. The animals I have left there," quoth Carlotta.

So she set out to the palace of the King who lived in the village of Middleberg-on-Avon, an island city in the middle of a door-bell that said, "Ding-dong-ding, Avon cawlink." She went up to the King, an economy-size spray can of Avon hair deodorant and cuticle softener.

"My father flushed a goldfish down the toilet because it was white from old age and had a ripped tail fin from when mommy tried to kill it by putting it in the butter churner. I have to have my fish back and also a cow and a rooster, and they are lost and I can't find them anywhere because of it."

"Tough luck," said the official interpreter. "What good will all of that do you? You got a plumb bum steer."

Carlotta dashed away and fainted again, at which time there appeared to her another fairly.

"Don't run away. Don't faint. We'll take care of everything." This fairly had a big plaque on his chest that said, "Go Cosa Nostra."

He pulled out a tommy-gun and shot her head back on and her eyes back in from that time way back there when she was crying. Then all of her worries were over. So she went to the movies and paid adult prices.

Yours,
The management.

I was writing back to Danny along similar lines. There must have been something Freudian going on.

CHAPTER 14

In All the Shrouded Heavens

IN THE FIFTH chapter of my 2014 novel, *More Deaths than One*, I wrote that on 26 November 1965, I travelled from Champaign to Chicago by rail, on the *City of New Orleans*, with "my friend Deaver" to see Bob Dylan in concert.

That was a lie. It worked okay in the novel, where neither "Deaver" nor the narrator was completely real. But that was fiction.

Now I've got to come clean. Danny wasn't there.

I did try to talk him into going with me, but it was too awkward for him to get to Chicago from St Joseph's College on short notice. So I went to the Dylan concert with Herb Budden and Craig Sanderson. All I could do was report to Danny afterwards and then, 50 years later, make up a load of codswallop for my 2014 novel.

Danny didn't get to see Dylan in concert until October 2010, when Bob rolled into the University of Central Florida for the latest instalment of his never-ending tour. By then, his voice was shot, and he'd taken to performing in a wide-brimmed white hat and a string tie. Danny—now Phil—still found him "wondrous," adding a qualifier—"if you happen to live in the past as intensely as I do":

I wanted my friends from back then to be with me, and I wanted that me to come back again and hang out for a while. The past is present at a Dylan concert. We can't go back except maybe just a little, and when the music takes off, something very big I can only call (with reverence) the past comes up the tunnel to meet us half-way.

But in 1965, the past wasn't past. Dylan's concert was at the Arie Crown theatre in old McCormick Place, before it was destroyed by fire. Bob had amped up at the Newport Folk Festival in July, electrifying half his audience and electrocuting the minds of the rest. His tour later in the year cemented his new direction, combining folk and rock. With him that night at the Arie Crown theatre were Al Kooper on the keyboard, Harvey Goldstein on bass, Robbie Robertson on lead guitar, and Levon Helm on drums.

Bob was still hedging his bets. He opened with a solo acoustic set, songs that had made him legendary as a folkie. "Gates of Eden," "She Belongs to Me," "Love Minus Zero/No Limit," "Mr Tambourine Man." We had good seats, up close, but Bob looked small on Arie Crown's stage, all alone with his guitar and harmonica. He was scruffy, folksy, earnest.

Then came intermission, and the audience grew restless. Herb and Craig and I looked around. We were the straightest-looking guys in the crowd. Everyone else was dressed like proto-hippies, in flowing clothes with lots of floral patterns, two years ahead of San Francisco's Summer of Love.

When Bob came back on stage with his full band, Paul Revere's horse was being reincarnated. Jezebel the nun was knitting a bald wig for Jack the Ripper. A geometry of innocent flesh was on the bone, causing Galileo's math book to be thrown—at Delilah, of all people. The beauty parlour was filled with sailors, the circus was in town. Everyone was making love, or else expecting rain.

The second set opened with "Tombstone Blues," and it was loud! One of Dylan's biographers, Bob Spitz, wrote afterwards that the audience response was along the lines of, "Dylan, you're deserting us!" He added: "We nearly shit our pants."

Dylan gave a sly grin and someone backstage turned up the volume. Gypsy Davy and his blowtorch were burning out the camps. His faithful slave Pedro was tramping behind him. Then, Dylan sat at a piano and played "Ballad of a Thin Man," but even his Mr Jones didn't know what was happening. And neither did we.

CHAPTER 15

Cold Polished Stones Sinking

I F THE DYLAN concert was a watershed moment for me, Herb, and Craig, as it should have been, it didn't show up in my correspondence with Danny. I sent him the usual garbage in early 1966, and he replied from Layer 2, 4, or 6 to someone he called "Dear Emma":

> You don't understand. I ask you, please, let me in the house; we could talk. Surely we could settle something. It's not over, I know it isn't. Give me another chance. Please.

> It's awful cold out here. And during the daytime I have to hide in the only thick bush in the yard, the evergreen tree next to the front walk. You don't know how miserable that is. Yesterday, there was this dog … And soon it's going to snow.

> I'll freeze for sure. I already have a cold. In the garage, I found the grass sack that attached to the lawnmower, but it doesn't cover very much of me.

> Yesterday, to eat I had grass and sparrow, and it wasn't too bad. But I can't live out here all winter, Emma. It's been over a week now. Couldn't you reconsider, and, at least, let me come in and get my clothes? I'll freeze.

I have already conceded the entire argument. I will clean my own ring out of the bathtub. What more do you want? I love you, Emma. Please let me back in the house. I can't go to work without my clothes. I can't live without my clothes. I'll freeze. And if I don't go to work there will be no money. Then what of the baby, Emma? What of our child? You must. Let me in the house (emphatically).

Please.

If you should reconsider and come to a favourable verdict, I'll be either in the garage or in the bush by the front walk. Or I may be en route from one to the other, dashing timidly from tree to tree with the lawnmower sack around my body and goosepimples here and there about my body which is freezing. If you do not reconsider, I do not know what I shall do. I will spend the majority of my time moping about the lawn freezing. But since I love you, I'll never leave you until you give me my clothes.

Remember, I can offer you comfort. Remember the lot that I own four miles west of San Francisco. The climate there will be good for your health. I have the money to do this. If you turn away from all this that I have to offer for your state of health and your independent financial stature, you too will freeze and starve.

And remember our child. Don't you want the best for Alfie? If I freeze out here, he will never live through his next birthday. He will have died at the age of thirty two without ever having had a chance to live. Then you'll be sorry. Now c'mon Emma. Open up. I'll freeze out here. You make me so mad I could just spit. Please?

Love from your hubby,
Francis

Bear in mind that this nonsense came at the very moment that a jury in Champaign was mulling over the deaths of Dr Deaver and

Lester Samples. Danny had created a bubble for himself, and I was happy to crawl inside.

His next letter, the following month, was to "Dear Mrs. Gerlacht." He'd regressed from typing to handwriting:

> In answer to your last letter, and on the subject of your son's psychological ependyma, I would like to point out that, regarding the last few generations of mankind, actions such as your son's were proved to be beneficial to those who have partaken. It proves to be a very effective buffer, preparing the child for later traumatic experiences.
>
> In a way, I realize, such actions, used as preparatory therapy, seem diabolical. The profound aspects of your son's problem reflect a prolific, if not lethargic, attitude toward his surroundings. To correct this in the manner I prescribed earlier will, I'm sure, be a great aid in your son's ability to retain what he has learned through the therapy for many years thereafter.
>
> Regarding your son's right to change his name, I would say let it go. 'John P. Gerlacht' simply doesn't give him the distinction he strives for. Adolf Hitler Gerlacht gives him this. I don't feel this is an accurate reflection of the boy's violent tendencies. I feel that his dynamiting of the dog house is sufficient evidence of this, but, rather than being a vicious tendency, it is more of a barbaric one, which is additionally supported by his eating of baby birds and his sharpening his fingernails on the elm tree.
>
> Please do as I ask, and have him report here next Tuesday. Tell him he can wear the leopard skin under his toga if he wishes.
>
> Thank you,
> Phil Deaver

This letter was notable for Danny's change to "Phil Deaver" in his signature, which mirrored the change of name by his fictional John Gerlacht. For the first time, he took his father's name, which he would carry for the rest of his life, regardless of what Tuscola folks may have continued to call him.

His last two letters from St Joseph's College, late in our sophomore years, contained no alter egos or dramatis personae. They were addressed to me, and me alone. He had a proposal:

> I have been thinking about next summer and how you hate me and all [which of course I didn't]. So, I decided 'Let's do something next summer.' Of course, what I say will likely as not be rejected (careful).
>
> I think you and I, who will be 20 years old next summer, and who will have such illiteracies as our Canadian fishing trip and one 'I'm Buzz and he's Bob and we're taking this trip' to Denver under our belts, should grab up our guitars and go on tour. I could take my car this time. What fun we would have! I know you are more musically inclined but I could learn some stuff and we could make up some songs. (I've made two up). No kidding. We could do anything on this trip. I'm even learning rhythm!!(?)!!
>
> Ha Ha Ha. Ha. And maybe while we were gone you would drive me just as insane as you are!!(?)!! Or maybe I could make you just as dumb as me!!
>
> We could set a date to go right now for two weeks simultaneous to the end of school. We could make up a program, almost a concert. (God what a dream). Really, what do you think?

I couldn't tell if he was serious about a musical tour. Neither of us could play the guitar when we were 19, and we'd never sung a note together. But I guess his idea wasn't any dumber than calling ourselves The World's Greatest Tennis Team. "God what a dream" indeed.

On 12 March 1966, he followed up by suggesting an Easter concert in Tuscola as a warmup for his proposed summer tour:

> I have just been re-reading one of the letters you sent first semester. It was funny. You may think it remarkable but I

have not yet ceased working on our Easter concert. The way I see it, it will be good practice for the summer trip. Isn't that remarkable? Bar Harbor, Maine. Murphysboro, Illinois. It will be nice to have a repertoire.

This summer is going to be great. If you have thrown off the shackles of everyday existence in favour of your own mind, how about a trip to the western country, say, Denver. We could stay in the Brown Palace and lose the car keys again. And besides, we've already done Murphysboro, right? Ducks on the pond, cows in the margin release.

George Barber will set up a sound system in the Forty Martyrs school building. We will do it Easter night and all the ladies will wear their Easter bonnets-on-it and the men will wear suits of bright colors like eggs.

Say, that reminds me. If you have thrown off the shackles of everyday existence, want to work on a rich dude ranch showing beautiful rich girls the countryside for a while? Tucson, Arizona! We start when we get there. 'Hello, I'm your guide and that is a waterfall tumbling thirty feet to the lake below where we will now swim while resting afterward on this here blanket while the horses get a drink. From my hat. That is a famous mountain range. That is, a famous resting spot for guides and pretty guesses. The cactus is 300 years old if the weather holds.' Oh … brother?

'Hello, is this Mrs Harry German? We would like to wish you a Happy Easter in a very (space) special way, ok? I'm your guide for today. We will go look at the mountains and a thirty-foot water fall into the water fall into the waterfall.'

Ha!

Deaver, blood running from between his teeth, stared up at Forrester on the cliff above, "Don't just do there, stand something," he said. Forrester, on his horse, threw down his rope. 'Fool,' I said, 'why didn't you keep one end of the rope you

throo down?' Forrester laughed heartily/hartily/heartly/hardly
hahahahahahahahahahahahahahahaha!

Danny foresaw the end of our youth, and longed for one last round:

> Tucson would be neat. Besides, in a few years things like that
> will be gone. We won't be able to be idealistic. We will be
> ordinary screwed-up married folk, with smiles on our faces
> and no shoulder holster which I have just bought and put
> a cheap but realistic cap pistol in and fooled a teller at the
> Chicago Conrad Hilton by casually showing it as I reached
> for my billfold in the breast pocket of my suit, it is funny!
> I did that. Get a shoulder holster! My gun cost one dollar,
> silencer included! Married folks don't have blood running from
> between their teeth standing on ledges with poor harassed girls
> all around that are beautiful and like horses. Right?

> Why did it rain today? Where is the cow (on the pond) (margin
> release)? Lead me to my victors, sir. We've had our subtractions,
> but right,

Phil

We never arranged that Easter gig, and we never made that
summer tour. It was just as well.

But after the summer of 1966, things would never be the same.

PART TWO

CHAPTER 16

Now and Hence Forever

IN HIS STORY "Infield" from his first book, *Silent Retreats*, Phil Deaver becomes Carl Landen, the son of "the doctor that died." He and his erstwhile friend Skidmore, both infielders, play Pony League baseball together, with a lot of dysfunction. Says Landen about Skidmore: "He's brilliant, and can be very funny … For some reason I even liked him back then, but he had a terrible mean streak that used to rise up out of him like a second personality—lying, evil, angry, driven."

Once again, like the Skidmore who denied having an affair with Mrs Beth Landen in Phil's story, "Cassadaga," I was the Skidmore in "Infield," thinly camouflaged at Phil's border between reality and fiction. Phil, a/k/a Carl Landen, relates the following anecdote to anyone who would listen, and to anyone who would read:

> In college, in 1966, two years after my father was killed in a car wreck, Skidmore and I had a major falling-out. It was simple why. At a party which I did not attend, he'd quietly passed along to those who were attending that my father had had, in earlier days, an affair with some woman in town. I never knew

the source of this rumor, but always suspected Skidmore's dad was somehow at the root of it.

The next morning I was in bed when my mom yelled that I had a phone call.

'Hi, it's me.' It was a girl named Kitty whom I'd sometimes dated.

'Last night,' she said, 'your old pal Skidmore said something I think you ought to know about. He said your dad had an affair a few years ago, with the lady Mrs Stowe, at the hospital.'

I sat there. Something like that had never occurred to me. In fact, it took me a laughable ten seconds to imagine what Kitty meant by the word 'affair.' Then my initial reaction was that this was another vicious thing Skidmore had dreamed up to say, being mean in a lot of ways. But then I realized something about him—that his meanness was rarely in outright lies, more often in brutally administering the truth.

'He said there might even have been a child,' Kitty said.

I knew Mrs Stowe's youngest daughter, who was then about nine. By subtraction, we came to the summer of 1957.

The trouble with this episode from "Infield" *wasn't* that it was fiction. Everything Phil Deaver wrote, even his poetry, was fictional. The trouble was that it wasn't based on fact, but it had real-life consequences.

I'd been at that party all right, at Eric Pflum's place in Champaign in the summer of 1966, with Herb Budden, Craig Sanderson, Patti Jenks, Andy Jolley, Sarah Kegley, and a host of other ex-classmates from Tuscola High School. I knew "the source of this rumor," and it sure as hell wasn't me. And my dad wasn't "at the root of it" either. If anyone, living or dead, was defamed by "Infield," it was my dad. He was still very much alive when the story was published in 1988, and everybody who mattered knew he was "Skidmore's dad."

The source of the rumour was Herb Budden. I was standing in the circle as he held court, telling one funny story after another. When he came to stories about the Deavers, he said there was, indeed, a secret third sibling, a "love child," as he put it. He paused to explain what he meant by "sibling" and "love child." Then, he named the child, Mona Froman, and her mother Myrtle—a former nurse at Tuscola's Jarman Hospital.

"Did you ever take a close look at Mona?" Herb said, referring to Deaver's alleged half-sister. "Her eyes are just like Danny's!"

Herb's own eyes were full of mischief as he told his tale. I didn't think much about it one way or the other. Herb was always bullshitting at the highest comedic levels, saying outlandish things about anyone and everyone, famous or obscure, the more hyperbole the better. That was his style. His humour was based on exaggeration and shock value. I didn't have a clue whether what he said was true or not, and I didn't think he was being malicious, and still don't. He seemed to have picked up a thread of gossip somewhere and juiced it up before passing it along at a party. A bit of wicked fun.

But by the time the report got back to Danny, by way of Patti Jenks ("Kitty" in Phil's story) and Andy Jolley, it was *me* who'd defamed the late Dr Deaver, and my own dad might have been the original source. A multi-generational Forrester conspiracy against multiple generations of Deavers.

In real life in 1966, Danny phoned my dad the next day and told him what I was supposed to have said. My dad told Danny he didn't know anything about it and passed it on to my mother to deal with.

"Doctor Deaver's dead," she said to me. "How could you do such a thing?"

I phoned Danny to tell him the facts of the matter, and repeated them again and again in coming years, but he couldn't accept my account. It wasn't easy for him to believe Herb was responsible. Herb was never a baseball rival. He'd never tricked Danny into a leghold.

My edgy side was well known to Phil and to everyone else in town. I was a cleaner target.

Twenty-four years later, in a letter dated "Spring Equinox 1990," Phil wrote to apologise:

> This is the last thing I'm going to say on this topic, unless I forget I said this sometime later on, and say it again. In fact, I may have said it before and said it was the last I'd say of it. But this really is, unless I forget. Thanks for telling me the background on the thing about my dad. It put to rest a demon of some years upon which the entire story 'Infield' hangs, and it does hang. I know I've ripped and shredded at you over the years on that item, and I'm sorry.

But that apology was years ahead of us. In 1966, our correspondence stopped, and stayed stopped for the next decade.

A lot happened around us from 1966 to 1976. The whole country was going crazy. In Vietnam, LBJ built up the US troop levels to half a million and more, with 60,000 dead Americans before the USA ended its war crimes.

Back home, there was rioting in the streets and paranoia in the air. Dr Martin Luther King Jr pointed out the obvious link between America's moral decay at home and its violence abroad. The press, goaded by FBI director and serial racist J Edgar Hoover, screamed for King to shut his mouth about Vietnam and stick to civil rights. They said he was getting uppity and didn't know his place. Finally, he was repaid with a bullet to the jaw—from the rifle of a loser from Quincy, Illinois—and right-wing Americans gradually started thinking King was okay as long as he stayed dead.

His assassination happened just as Phil, Herb, and I were wrapping up our senior years in college. A blond guy at the reception desk in my dormitory at Eastern Illinois University said what a lot of white folks thought at the time.

"He had it coming," he said.

Two months later I was sharing a rented house with Herb in Champaign, where we both worked at the local Kraft Foods plant. Herb and I had never talked about that 1966 party, where the rumour about Phil's dad caused such a problem. From my perspective, I'd straightened it out with Phil, and if he took it up with Herb, that was their business. I was all for letting sleeping dogs lie.

Herb was still way ahead of everybody in everything to do with popular culture. He'd introduced me to the Beatles' Sergeant Pepper album in 1967, and in 1968 he was the first to know that they were in India writing a batch of psychedelic songs. He passed such bits of information along as if they were insider trading. He made it sound like he was on a first-name basis with George Harrison.

On the fifth of June, I came home late from stacking bottles at Kraft and switched on the black-and-white TV in the living room of our rented house. Bobby Kennedy had won the California primary, and he was giving a victory speech at the Ambassador Hotel in Los Angeles. There was a glimmer of hope that somebody who wasn't an asshole could still become president. A few minutes later, he too was gunned down.

In August, the Democratic Convention was held in Chicago to crown Herbert Humphrey as the nominee for president. Craig Sanderson and I rode *The City of New Orleans* to Chicago again, but this time we got our heads cracked in Grant Park by Mayor Richard Daley's goon squad. Everybody around us was chanting, "The whole world is watching"—with the assumption shared by most Americans that their country and the world were one and the same. All I could think of was Fuck This Shit.

America's slow, 50-year decline to Donald Trump and beyond began in earnest that week. Craig and I wore our scabs and bruises like badges of honour for a while. But like all injuries, they healed one way or another, and we got interested in other things. We travelled together to the Grand Ole Opry in Nashville, Tennessee. The Opry's broadcasts on WSM had reached our Tuscola radios throughout our school years, so we wanted to have a look before the next phases of our lives began, whatever they might turn out to be. But when we got to the Opry's Ryman Auditorium, I felt like that kid in James Joyce's *Dubliners* who is disillusioned by the shabby "Araby" bazaar—all I could see was a parade of grinning cornpones in sequined cowboy costumes, and all I could hear was those same yokels explaining the meaning of hillbilly life in three chords. Every few minutes a big sign would light up above the stage, saying "APPLAUSE," and old Roy Acuff would raise his hands, as if in prayer, to make sure we all clapped and whooped for the radio audience. Needless to say, I couldn't bring myself to join in all the fun.

By late 1968, Tuscola's local draft board had me in its sights for shipment to Vietnam. My student deferment had run out, and I was ordered down to St Louis, Missouri, to take a physical exam so I could be classified for the draft.

My physical exam didn't go well. Not only was I declared 1-A, ripe for the plucking, but I managed to piss off several of the examining officers. All of the potential draftees, hundreds of us from all over the Midwest, stripped down to our jockey shorts and joined an assembly line. One officer, an African-American with a thick southern drawl, noticed that I'd ticked "poor vision" on my intake form. I was near-sighted. I wore glasses. No big deal.

"What's wrong with your ahs, son," he said, looking up and down my pathetic skinny frame. He meant to say eyes, but I honestly thought he said "ass." I turned my head and looked at my rear end, hoping I hadn't shit my white underpants. Nope, all clear. I stood at what I thought was attention.

"There's nothing wrong with my ass, sir," I said, staccato-like, like I'd seen soldiers do in B-grade movies. It infuriated him.

"Your ahs, stupid," he said. "Your ahs!"

Then, in disgust, he shoved me along to the next booth. By that time I'd developed a powerful need to urinate, so I asked the next officer if I could please go to the bathroom. This guy was a wormy white guy wearing horn-rimmed glasses.

"Number one or number two?" he asked in a tired monotone, without looking up from his paperwork. It was an indelicate question, and nobody had asked me such a thing for a long, long time. I couldn't remember which number was which.

"I don't know, sir," I said, in my soldierly way. He put down his pen and raised his eyes.

"Number one is when you piss, boy," he said. "Number two is when you shit. Just exactly what is it you are aiming to do?"

I thanked him for his explanation and said I had to do number one, and he excused me from the line. My military career was not off to a great start. In fact, it had gone downhill since the glory days with Danny Deaver and Billy Adkisson, playing army at Patterson Springs.

After the physical exam, I returned home and applied immediately for the Peace Corps. If I got accepted, it came with an automatic two-year deferment. The war might even be over by the time I got out. I didn't care where they sent me, so long as it wasn't Vietnam.

My application was approved, and in the same week that Neil Armstrong set foot on the moon, the same week that Teddy Kennedy killed Mary Jo Kopechne by driving off a bridge at Chappaquiddick, I was flown from Champaign to Philadelphia to begin training for my two-year stint as a Peace Corps volunteer in Guyana, South America.

CHAPTER 17

Emptiness over Emptiness, but Flying

PHIL'S COURSE DURING the war years had more ups and downs. After graduating from St Joseph's College in May 1968, he taught English for a year at St Francis High School in Wheaton, Illinois—at a whopping annual salary of $6,600 per year.

In December, he entered into a good Catholic marriage with Cynthia ("Cyndie") Walan, whom he'd met in 1964, not long after he began his studies at St Joseph's College. She was a student at Rosary College in River Forest, Illinois, where she earned her B.A. degree in English literature. In addition to intriguing Phil with her fetching appearance, she'd impressed him with her knowledge about writers and writing, especially her obsession with John Updike. Phil became a lifelong fan of both Updike and Cyndie.

But seven months after the wedding, in July 1969, Phil was drafted into the army. The local draft board in Tuscola hadn't looked kindly on his stream of letters to *The Tuscola Review* newspaper, criticising the war. In the dead of night, he and a small group of other local boys were hauled off by bus to a Chicago warehouse for their induction physicals.

A big piece of good news soon outweighed the bad. For reasons he never understood, Phil was one of the very few draftees in the years after the Tet Offensive who were assigned to Germany instead of being sent to Vietnam. He didn't know why he was so lucky. He was placed in a top-secret NATO unit in Frankfurt, at a time when the American death toll in Vietnam was climbing day by day. ("Begging the question," he put it later, speaking of himself in the third person, "why he was drafted into the Vietnam War and not assigned to the war.") I always wondered if the local draft board in Tuscola, aware of the devastating losses the Deaver family had already suffered in 1964, pulled some strings to keep him out of harm's way. If so, I'm eternally grateful to those dimwits. For once, they did something good.

Phil hated the army. He described it as "fat, corrupt, and stupid." His own drill sergeant tried to sell him amphetamines during rifle training. But he counted himself lucky, working as an army clerk in Germany and playing shortstop for his post's softball team instead of dodging bullets in faraway rice fields.

The closest he came to Vietnam was in March 1971, when he wrote a letter to *Time* magazine about a military book that had recently been published. *Time* printed his letter—possibly the first published words of Philip F Deaver, award-winning-writer-in-waiting (unless you count his anti-war letters to *The Tuscola Review* and *The Champaign News-Gazette*, or his photocopied high school poetry). On the cover of that issue of *Time* were colour portraits of Muhammed Ali and Joe Frazier, "The $5,000,000 Fighters." *Time* provided a headline for Phil's letter—"Another Union":

> Sir
>
> The reviewer of Ward Just's book *Military Men* [Feb 8] ended with the question: 'In the complex, chaotic America of today, can a citizen's army really work?'
>
> The answer is implicit in Just's book. It is that military men are not citizens of the U.S. They live 'on post,' a country on the other side of guard gates and cable fences, a land with its own doctrine and traditions, its own norms for dress and

grooming, its own schools, its own ideas of the past and future, its own newspapers with their own ideas about the present, its own ideas about management and labor and democracy, its own social circles, its own churches and chaplains, its own hospitals, even its very own five-sided capitol. And to regulate it, a separate code of justice. Sometime in the last 20 years, the military men seceded from the union, and Ward Just is one of the rare souls who has noticed.

> SP5 Philip F. Deaver
> Frankfurt, Germany

This letter had a strong whiff of anti-military sentiment. When Phil's commanding colonel, a WWII veteran, got wind of it, he ordered Phil into his office. He held a copy of *Time* in his hand.

"Specialist, is this you?" he asked, tossing the magazine across his desk. Phil hadn't seen that issue and didn't know his letter had made it into print. When he saw it, he felt a sense of pride, even as trouble was brewing.

"Yes sir, that's me," said Phil.

The colonel rebuked him for 15 minutes. "A soldier with this kind of attitude probably doesn't belong here," he said. "Exposure like this, inside the covers of a magazine distributed worldwide, well, it's not good. Furthermore, it's an embarrassment, to me. I could have you shipped out to Vietnam, tomorrow."

(And how do I know the words of this conversation? Because Phil wrote about it in his introduction to *Scoring from Second: Writers on Baseball*, the book he edited in 2007. A story of mine, "Begotten, Not Made," appeared in *Scoring from Second*.)

Phil's colonel changed the topic from Vietnam to softball. Phil was the best shortstop on the post's softball team. He was indispensable, and the colonel knew it. No other soldier could match his nimble glove-work or his rocket arm. Plus, he was batting .482.

The colonel relented. "We need a shortstop on the softball team," he said. Phil remained in Germany till his tour was done.

Cyndie had followed Phil to Germany, and whenever he got leave they explored as much of Frankfurt and the surrounding areas as they could. Frankfurt still showed signs of WWII, with its bombed-out opera house and its ruined castles along the Rhine. These images hardened Phil's anti-war sentiments, which he maintained for the rest of his life.

When his active duty was complete, he and Cyndie drove to St Moritz in a new blue Volkswagen Beetle and slept in a tent on the side of a mountain. In the morning, they walked higher into the mountains until the meadows were filled with snow, then back down, making plans for their future. They saw Barcelona, Rome, Vienna, Venice, Dubrovnik, Sarajevo, London, Amsterdam, Luxembourg. Phil turned 24 in Paris. Everywhere they went, Phil was moved by Europe's reminders of the century's two world wars, especially the expanses of battlefield headstones in France.

By the time he was discharged from the army, I'd come back home from the Peace Corps in Guyana and, once again, my number was up for the draft. I submitted an application to be reclassified as a conscientious objector. It wasn't automatic. You had to make a case for it, and I cited the Father, Son, and Holy Ghost: i.e., St Augustine of Hippo Regius, North Africa; Reinhold Niebuhr of Lincoln, Illinois; and Bob Dylan of Hibbing, Minnesota. I raved on about the theory of just war, the Serenity Prayer, and "Masters of War." It wasn't much of an essay, but the Tuscola draft board was sufficiently buffaloed to give me a C-O classification. I suspect they realised I'd be useless as a soldier, and decided not to waste everybody's time.

CHAPTER 18

Between the Rocks and the Vapour

A FTER PHIL AND Cyndie got back to the USA, he worked briefly in a "model cities" program in Indianapolis, followed by ten months of unemployment. With help from our old friend Herb Budden, he found work in August 1972 as a "community education coordinator" for the Indianapolis public school system.

During 1972, Phil applied successfully for a Mott fellowship, named after Charles Stewart Mott, one of the co-founders of General Motors. The Mott grants were based on financial need, and Phil had plenty of that. He used two consecutive Mott fellowships to pursue a master's degree in education at Ball State University in 1974, then a doctorate in education from the University of Virginia. His Virginia dissertation sounded soporific: *"A study of community education process through an analysis of the work of Paul Goodman."* Not exactly a page-turner.

In 1976, he used his experience and education to line up an administrative job at Murray State University in Kentucky, with the unpromising title of "Director of Continuing Education/ Administrative Assistant to the President." His job description called for him to "coordinate programs and workshops in the office of continuing education." The appointment included a non-tenured faculty post as "assistant professor in instruction and learning." Phil had just turned 30. He and Cyndie were to stay in Murray for the next eight years.

Phil arrived at Murray State when its creative writing program was blossoming under the English department chairmanship of Delbert "Deb" Wylder, who had an eye for fresh literary talent. Wylder brought many exceptional writers and teachers to Murray State at the beginning of their careers, such as the award-winning poet Mark Jarman and the future Pulitzer Prize winner Jorie Graham. At Phil's first faculty meeting, he stared across the room at Graham, Wylder, the poet Jim Galvin, and the novelist Joe Ashby Porter.

Phil was a writer, but not yet a published one. He volunteered to help coordinate the Jesse Stuart Writers Workshop, and through those efforts he met lifelong friends William Matthews, Bobby Ann Mason, and Charles Wright. He took writing classes from Wylder, from the British poet Ken Smith, and others. Later, Smith helped Phil find a publisher for his first story, "Silent Retreats." Wylder would help him place his second one, "Fiona's Rooms."

All but two of the stories in Phil's *Silent Retreats* collection, published in 1988, were written for his Murray State writing classes. He never ceased to be astounded, and grateful, that Deb Wylder and his colleagues welcomed an administrator like himself into their literary fold.

Meanwhile, I'd abandoned the USA again, this time for Australia. Phil and I crossed paths a couple of times before I left. In November 1971, we both showed up at Herb's home in Indianapolis. Herb had avoided the draft and married Bonnie Powell, the smartest girl in our high school class. Already they'd begun to settle into Indianapolis for the rest of their lives, with their knack for social climbing and domesticity. That evening, Herb prepared a chocolate fondue, something I'd never even *heard* of, and Bonnie served up a gourmet meal with a table setting that included finger bowls. I'd never seen a finger bowl before, so I drank the contents. Herb and Bonnie thought that was pretty funny because Sylvia Plath's character in *The Bell Jar*, Esther Greenwood, had done the same thing. Phil and I still didn't have much to say to each other, but we joined Herb and Bonnie to watch a new thriller on television, a movie directed by a young hotshot named Steven Spielberg—*Duel*, his first film, made for black-and-white TV.

Another time when Phil and Cyndie were visiting Althea in Tuscola, they popped down to see me in Charleston. I was studying for a master's degree in English and trying unsuccessfully to be an American again. My experiences in Guyana and the Caribbean had left me non-anything, non-everything.

Unlike Phil's experience in Europe, my two years in Guyana weren't on an American post with a lot of fellow countrymen. I'd been sent by the Peace Corps to the rural town of New Amsterdam, across the wild Berbice River, where I lived alone in a wooden house on stilts and taught mathematics at the local Teacher Training College.

There weren't any televisions in Guyana, and I didn't bother reading the news. America disappeared from my mind for those two years, except when I hitched a ride to the capital city, Georgetown, to engage in some solo anti-war protests in front of the US Embassy.

During my second year in New Amsterdam, the civil rights activist Stokely Carmichael came to town for a nighttime Black Power rally on the esplanade. I stood there, one white guy in a sea of black faces, all of us stirred to righteous anger by Stokely's rap. It seemed like the most natural thing in the world for me to be in that crowd. After two years in Guyana, I couldn't even think white. I came home alienated from everything I'd ever known.

When Phil and Cyndie came to Charleston, it seemed to all of us like a visit to a zoo, with me inside the cage looking out at them.

We exchanged monosyllables for a couple of hours, then they left. It was the first and only time I ever met Cyndie.

After getting my master's degree in English, I decided to go to law school. I was under the charming delusion that a lawyer could help make the world a better place. My heroes were Thurgood Marshall, who'd argued *Brown v Board of Education* before the US Supreme Court and later became an Associate Justice, and William Kunstler, who'd defended the Chicago Seven after the 1968 riots at the Democratic Convention. In the early 1970s, after Wounded Knee II, Kunstler represented the American Indian Movement. His motto was, "I only defend the people I love." That sounded good to me. I wanted to be like William Kunstler and Thurgood Marshall.

But by the time I finished my legal studies at the University of Illinois in 1975, Kunstler and Marshall seemed like distant memories. I'd achieved a good class ranking and got offers from the best law firms money could buy. Still, I knew they weren't good fits for me, and I wasn't a good fit for them. I would only have caused trouble if I'd taken one of their offers. I didn't quite know what I wanted to do, or what motivated me, but it wasn't money. So I worked for a while as a law clerk for a federal judge in Danville, Illinois, then moved to Australia in May of 1976. I didn't know a soul in the country, but it seemed like a good idea at the time. I wanted to get as far away as I could before the American bicentennial celebrations hit their stride in July.

In September 1976, when I was safely overseas, Phil sent me a letter, the first he'd written to me in ten years. His return address was 1109 Circarama, Murray, KY. He seemed to have been moved to write by a "rare appearance" of Bob Dylan on television. He said Bob's fans weren't the same as they were when I'd seen him in Chicago's Arie Crown theatre in 1965, and he wanted to give me an update.

Dylan had just released his great albums of the mid-70s, *Blood on the Tracks* and *Desire*. With his flair for the telepathic, Phil sensed that Dylan was due for a new persona, three full years before his born-again Christian phase:

> He's actually very well packaged by now, perpetually to remain whatever it was that he always was—like the unburied body of Lenin. It wasn't him that made me write to you—it was the flashes of his audience. I got existential neuritis when I saw what we had become. Three hundred yards from Bob, they stood on tip-toes, waving their children at the stage, evidently hoping for consecration. Bob, wrapped in cellophane, just kept on singin'. My old psychiatry professor, James Kenny, once told me that 'there's nothing more pitiful than an old hippie.' I hated him for saying that, still do.
>
> Dylan, I think, should have fooled them all by changing media again, like he did when he zapped the purists by picking up a wired guitar. This time he should have just read the poems, with the old hippies in the cellophane standing behind him, phalli in hand like the statues of the immediate past they insist on portraying in their lives. It would have been better than just submitting to the existential nostalgia.
>
> His performance was the end of me in a way—at least the part of me that still wants me to be back to the way I seem to have always been, a subjective judgment filtered through a clouded perceptual field. There used to be some clarity.

He implored me to resume our correspondence:

> You've got perspective and brains and you're free and far away, and everyone here is listening and laughing at how you address your letters from Australia. I'm sincere when I say I'd really like to read a letter in which you take a crack at telling us what to do, what we are, where this is all going.

Almost immediately, he had second thoughts:

> Mind you, I don't advise it. There seems to be such a thing as abstract rot. You'd see how it works if you tried to put such a thing down. You would know from experience that

whatever you were writing would be worthless seconds after being concretized on paper, because it would be frozen and everything else would be moving and shifting and revealing itself in a new light and shedding old skin and metamorphizing and swelling and shrinking.

At Murray State University, he was writing stories with little ambition other than satisfying his colleagues and his own personal need to express himself. As he was to tell the *Kenyon Review* in 2006, he'd "written in isolation from other writers and from *any* readers for years" before *Silent Retreats* was published in 1988.

"The stories were written in the middle of the night," he said, "in the dark without many expectations except to keep writing them."

I replied to Phil's 1976 Dylan letter with a ridiculous poem, since (thankfully) lost. I called it *The Disco Duck is a Crow: An Exercise in Profundity*, after a song by Rick Dees, a Memphis disc jockey, and his band, the Cast of Idiots. The song, which was as bad as my poem, was number one on the Billboard Hot 100 for a week in October 1976. All I remember is that I was inspired to write *The Disco Duck* by some Aboriginal rock carvings in Tasmania, and that the poem erroneously suggested that Ernest Hemingway shot himself in the bathroom of his home in Ketchum, Idaho. In fact, as Phil pointed out, Hemingway died in the foyer, near the front door, in a patch of sunlight.

With acerbic insight, Herb Budden declared my duck poem "a passing gas," but Phil was intrigued by its self-obsessed energy. He said it displayed "a destructive air-lock of a situation and I don't suppose you'll ever get beyond it. It probably accounts for the Nazi that emerges out of you in interpersonal relations. But you do emit pearls from time to time also."

Phil guessed, correctly, that I'd be coming back to the USA for a visit soon, and he wanted to get together after all these years:

Maybe you and I could drive into St. Louis and catch a Cardinals game and talk some. It would be tough for me and you'd have a fucking field day with one-liners and obscure references.

Or maybe we could race from my house to the nearest bar on foot—it's eleven miles south of here. I've run there twice. The first time I averaged nine minutes a mile, but the second time was slower because I stopped to take the hugest shit I've ever taken in my tight-assed life. Honest.

I did fly to Illinois at the end of 1976, for Christmas with my extended family, but I didn't manage to catch up with Phil. Murray, Kentucky, was too far away. In the meantime, I'd sent him another poem, again lost to eternity. It was about a dog I had in Quincy, Illinois, when I was ten years old—Skeeter, a fox terrier, who got killed by a car.

I learned about Skeeter's death as I strolled home from Cub Scouts. My dad led me to the back yard where he'd dug a shallow grave. He'd already placed Skeeter's little brown-and-white body in the grave, but he hadn't covered him up yet. Apparently, he thought it would give me an early dose of Midwestern manhood to bury my dog. So he handed me the shovel and I scooped up a pile of dirt. But then I noticed that Skeeter was twitching.

"He's still shaking," I said to my dad in my high voice. I tipped out the shovelful of dirt next to the grave. My dad looked at Skeeter, then looked at me.

"It's just nerves," he said. "He's dead."

I didn't believe him, but I covered my quivering dog with dirt. I had bad dreams for a long time after that, about being buried alive. I always wished my dad hadn't made me do that.

Then, the same poem segued ahead six years to a Forrester family secret that was every bit as dark as Dr Deaver's alcoholism—a secret I'd never shared with Danny, notwithstanding his private disclosures to me. In my poem, I sat at the dinner table in my Tuscola home one evening as my dad whispered softly to my mother, in a sinister voice, that in the morning she would wake up in a puddle of blood. All I knew was that this scared the bejesus out of me, and I ran into the night across the tracks to the Forty Martyrs Catholic Church and knocked at the door of Father Casey's rectory. There was nowhere else to go. I was only 16. I told Father Casey my dad was going to kill my mother.

He brushed it off, the same way he'd brushed off Althea and Danny and Maureen. He told me to go home.

"Your dad comes to daily mass," Father Casey said. "He doesn't chase women," he said. "Don't worry, my son." And he placed his hand on my head.

So I walked back home in the dark, from the south end of town across the tracks to the north, and crawled into bed. And when I woke up the next morning, my mother was still alive.

Some poem.

When I got back to Australia after my 1976 Christmas visit, Phil wrote that my stream-of-consciousness prose poem about my dog and my parents was "the best writing of yours I have ever seen," but he described it, fairly, as "confessional art." He said his positive comments were "kind of like praising a dead bullfighter for a really great afternoon of entertainment."

Phil's guarded praise motivated me to start a longer piece, which I grandly described as a "novel in the works." I gave it a working title, "Low Gravity." In reality, it was nothing more than a few slices off my psyche. I was under the delusion that whatever spilled out of me and onto the page was literature. I cranked out around 60 pages and sent them off to Phil with a note saying I was burning with creative fire.

This time, Phil's feedback was more severe:

> If you persist with this project, would you please give a little thought to whether you really want to write a 'novel,' however you choose to define the term? If so, why? A novel tells a story. Maybe you just want to pass it around to your friends in

Melbourne, but that doesn't let you off any hooks. If you want to tell a number of people exactly the same thing in exactly the same words, that's enough. There has to be a reason for those words, over and above the level of a one-way conversation with piano accompaniment, and that's saying quite a lot.

For starters, there has to be significance in the form. You can put that in by what's happening, and that's probably the easiest, or you can put it in by the balance in the words, and that's been done about twice in the history of the world (see James Joyce and Virginia Woolf), and I wouldn't count on it happening again—at least not in *Low Gravity*.

I'm not asking you to write my kind of novel. I'm suggesting it's a helluva lot easier, which it is. I'm saying that whatever kind of novel, whatever kind of whatever you write, the odds are immense against it being any good, and you're going to have to be prepared to criticize it harshly. You're the last person in the world who should like it. If you can't see what's wrong with it, you're not doing your job.

Phil's letter also reported that he and Cyndie were "doing fine." Cyndie had given birth to their first child, Michael, in 1975, and Phil was polishing off his University of Virginia doctorate. He took the opportunity to name-drop the French anarchist Pierre-Joseph Proudhon and the Russian anarcho-communist Peter Kropotkin, who were somehow connected to his dissertation.

Then, he returned to *Low Gravity*, applying our old high school Layer System:

Do you ever get bad dreams about what a disease that Layer System was? I can see it in Low Gravity and you might believe it is a mirage. But there is an 'out' at every point at which a person might care to engage, and you have kept yourself so wiggly that you managed to hide your inner heart from vulnerability while driving a stake through it. We don't get to look at you. We get to look at you in a hall of mirrors in which all images are reflected likenesses but none are flesh and blood.

It's the first I've seen any of you at all in writing, except for a couple of poems. It's interesting to see how the Layer System has come out in the wash in someone besides me, for whom it is a psychosis and I am not exaggerating.

He was talking from experience, because he continued to write stories at Murray State University.

"Writing is the only sane thing I do," he said. "The rest is crap." Then he spoke of himself in the third person:

Not that my writing isn't crap, he said, working toward Layer 7 on a scale of one to ten; I'm not speaking of the product of writing but the act of it, conceding Layer 5 by anticipating a counter of Layer 4, 6, or 8.

Over the next ten years, from the mid-1970s to the mid-1980s, he kept slogging away at his stories without much to show for his efforts. And finally, just as he was hitting rock bottom, he received his first rewards.

CHAPTER 19

Curved Like a Road through Mountains

P HIL'S SPOT-ON CRITICISMS of *Low Gravity* made the world a better place, because I packed it in. The only good that ever came from my 60 pages of expiation was that a handful of one-liners became useful later on.

In 1977, as Phil was putting the finishing touches on some of his earliest works and I was settling into life Down Under, he sent me another letter. He said he had no idea what would become of him, and he was stuck in a series of dead ends. His working life was in a rut, which he described as "existential neuralgia," apparently a cross between the neuritis and nostalgia he'd experienced after Dylan's TV appearance a year earlier:

> We live in Murray, Ky. I always knew I would end up here if I ever knew there was such a place because this is where I've been going. Cyndie and I are happy here, if we could only keep the TV off.
>
> I'm an assistant professor in adult and community education. I'm proud to say that in five weeks I'll have run about 18 miles a week for a year, give or take a day, and I could philosophize on that a little if my poor stomach, tired from a day's work and this

terrible attempt to write to you, could stand one more sortie into my memories under the category 'Tuscola Community High School.' Pitiful, pitiful, I'm so pitifully sad.

He wrote that he didn't know what to say to me:

> You keep moving. Being fucking crazy. How does one know the persona to adopt with you? It's like, even though you will probably protest, our Layer System is in your bones and you can't quit; or else it's in me and I can't quit suspecting you think you're running a gambit, aiming to be three layers above me.

Phil seemed to be having an early-onset midlife crisis, which must have been hard for Cyndie. He acknowledged that he "might be defensive because I have a baby and a house. If I am, I wish I could throw myself upon my sword, oh Lord, till gored." He still had modest expectations for his writing but lacked confidence even to pursue those. He was writing, but he didn't know why.

He reached for another metaphor, this one capturing his literary ambitions—of all things, a 20-storey building:

> All that remains of me is what I always seem to have been— and this is an assessment of my existential neuralgia just subsequent to admitting my state of mind—the utopian fool who doggedly planned a 20-storey building. Not that I would speak in terms of a 20-storey building, or in fact in terms of anything so concrete as to be vulnerable to practical application or other vulgarities. I merely mean to admit that everything I can think of is a little fast for me, a little too complicated, or a little too simple, or a little too wiggly—I plan only to cope, and not (anymore) to bore you or others I know with my plans.
>
> Plans are to the 1970s what plastics were to Benjamin Braddock in *The Graduate*—attempts to change the facts through manipulation (failing to realize that the facts are hinged to the stars and electrons and every single fucking thing in between).

His letter's next sentence, although directed at me, gave an insight into everything he was trying to do, and everything he would do for the rest of his writing life. He told me I should write a book, "where truth and fiction bleed together so the author's confessions are amply expressed but camouflaged."

That line was prescient. Phil Deaver bled truth and fiction together in everything he ever wrote. Every paragraph held camouflage and confession. Every story was a descent into some sort of purgatory, every denouement a momentary absolution. His stories bared his soul, if you knew where to look. His stories were the remnants of his youthful religion and the embodiments of his arrested development.

In a small scene from his story "Wilbur Gray Falls in Love with an Idea," published in *The Florida Review* in 1986 and later included in *Silent Retreats*, he captured the inadequacy of his childhood religion to help him with his midlife conflicts:

> I caught [Father] Casey at the end of confessions when no one else was there. He opened the little window and waited. I could see the Roman collar and the ceremonial stole. I tried to think how to begin. I was trying to separate sins from duty. He waited several minutes, neither of us saying anything. Finally, he slid the window closed.

In his "Wilbur Gray" story, his first-person character finds a better spirituality, a better road to absolution. Wilbur, beset with his own brand of middle-aged "existential neuralgia," goes for a run through Patterson Springs to mask his depression. He reaches his halfway point, "the old Chautauqua ground"—still "a place of solitude" in the mid-1980s:

> It's familiar to me from when I was little—I used to play there, and later Skidmore and I would camp there. I rejoice at the wonderful existence of this forest. I take it personally. I marvel at the patience of these oaks. You imagine their roots, reaching down, holding tight. They are my reward for making it this

far—the rich fragrance of hickory, white oak, their rotting leaves and cracking acorns, renewal of sprouts.

The old Chautauqua ground is located where a deep-running network of pure-water springs suddenly wells up out of the earth. The pioneer Virgil Patterson built his place among these oaks and so honored the blessing of cold, pure water that he built a shrine, not dank and moss-covered, back in the trees where the water presents with a deep rippling sound coming straight up out of the black loam.

The hush of the wind here, blended with the windy brushing sounds of my footfalls in bent grass momentarily absolves me from, rids me of, my depression, even though I know this absolution is nothing but the arrival of my second wind, the sudden alignment of energy, circulation, and chemistry that produces a moment of strength and optimism. I've learned from experience it arrives at three and one-half miles, deep in this forest on the path that leads to the fresh-water springs and, beyond that, the Chautauqua ground. During this fleeting moment I can hallucinate God and Peace, I can envision my own reincarnation, I can summon a sense of relative innocence and well-being. In this moment I realize that this moment is the whole reason I'm running.

Substitute "writing" for "running," and you've got Phil Deaver, just as Hemingway used fishing-as-writing in *The Old Man and the Sea*: if Hemingway's Santiago kept his lines taut and true, his faith would be rewarded and the great fish would come.

Phil, like Wilbur Gray, may have been able to "hallucinate God and Peace" by running or writing, but at home he was struggling. He was earning just $22,000 a year at Murray State University, which "in this economy," he believed, was "the rough equivalent to the $6,600 I made teaching high school in Wheaton in 1969." The best thing he could say about his job was that it came with "a big office with its own toilet."

He said his marriage to Cyndie was now "surviving"—a low bar—but he had rationalised that disappointment by concluding that marriage "was not a natural state of affairs."

"Our house sometimes rattles like the Friendship 7 spacecraft upon re-entry," he said.

He and Cyndie now had two young sons, Michael and Daniel, and he said those two kids were "about all" he had. In saying this, he left out Cyndie, although in earlier letters he'd claimed that she was his best friend. She had a way of distracting him when he got into these downward spirals. She could sooth him by saying something like, "Hey, remember that place we went to back in 1969," and she would recall a full, beautiful memory for him, something from their past together. Even though he knew what she was up to when she did this, it worked every time, and he loved her for it. It showed him how well she knew him, how well she understood more than anyone that the past was where he spent a lot of time.

He felt, almost certainly without justification, that he was "friendless" at Murray State University and attributed it to his sense of being "fucking boring."

> I am the unleavened bread of persons. Bland. I had one friend, but he was a photography professor and one day he just went out of focus, so to speak.
>
> Believe me, being a nice guy, in my hypocritical way, hasn't paid off any more than your tactic of being a professional asshole. And yours is one hell of a lot more fun, if only you weren't so soft and fleshy underneath it all.

He said he'd written "about eighty witty letters" to me in the last year but hadn't sent any of them because he was "pissed off" about being unable to rise above the levels of discourse I imposed. It sounded like yet another struggle with the old Layer System.

"I was engaging you right at the layers you hate the most and handle best," he wrote. "I couldn't muster anything that would surprise you or make you laugh or make you back off. For me, you are totally out of control."

Unsurprisingly, the leghold came back again, more dire than ever:

> I've been meaning to make some observations to you about patterns I discerned in the old days when you really loved me and were my friend, before the rigors of the latter 1960s drove us both outside-the-nine-dots in respective directions.

> We used to wrestle, and the very hold I hated most, the leghold, was the one you always got me on—time after time. It was a personality thing—dominant and submissive. It had nothing to do with skill, of which you had some I'll grant, or intelligence, okay okay, but I learned some things about myself at that time which really helped later.

> Not that I was able to avoid the same thing happening, but at least I had it diagnosed, old pal! I had it figured. I knew exactly what was happening and where it fit into the big picture!

> I've been in that leghold ever since. Don't worry, I'm speaking metaphorically.

> Other patterns of that period would also serve as well as our wrestling matches—my utter athletic failure despite having all the necessary tools; my utter academic failure despite having, well, the basic things I needed. My social failure, a story in itself.

> These patterns are still in place, exactly as you knew them when you knew me. I AM the 48th percentile. I embody that position on the bell-shaped curve, whether in the leghold or sitting in my Murray State office, with its bathroom, fancying myself to be a writer and never, ever, ever, DOING IT.

He was way too hard on himself. He was already "a writer," and he was most assuredly "doing it," but he had yet to find a publisher. Writing was already something he couldn't have stopped doing even if he'd wanted to. As he said in a Christmas letter, "[t]he only thing that keeps me quasi-sane is my voluminous output of fiction."

He took a bit of sardonic pride in his rejection letters. They could be cruel. One reviewer wrote back, "James Joyce could get away with this, but James Joyce you ain't." Another said a manuscript written along Southern Gothic lines had "creeped us out." And *The New Yorker* rejected a single story twice. Phil had waited a few years before resending the story, with a different title, to a different editor at the magazine. It didn't work. The story was returned again with a note that said, "We didn't like this any better than we did last time."

Phil was still aiming to construct his imaginary "20-storey building," and wrote that his goal for the coming year was "to generate 150 pages of short fiction, seven stories in all." He'd also begun a first novel, with the working title "Warm Values of the Interior." He described it as a tale about drug abuse, but it was also about Skidmore's Tuscola:

> I've tried to include all the comings and goings of Tuscola in those days. It revisits a time you will remember very well, the time Mr Kelly the coin collector came to town, roughly, by slamming into a bridge abutment. You and I both got into coin collecting that year, as I recall. I think, unless you hoodwinked me, that we actually lost a 1909 penny on the lawn of Jarman Hospital after a visit to Kelly. I remember our great argument over a 1927-S dime, which you claimed you got as change when you bought a hot dog at a football game.

> I've included old pre-development Patterson Springs, Gus Flesor's Candy Kitchen, Gabby's Tavern, Camargo, and that great caper the deputy sheriff pulled where he faked his own death and turned up in Santa Fe with his new girlfriend. Fun to write, hell to hold together. Oh yeah—I grafted a college campus to the southwest corner of town, down at the end of Scott Street. Picture the 'Old Main' building at EIU.

At the same time, he was completing his "Forty Martyrs" story, which was destined to become the title piece for his very last book. His *Forty Martyrs* novel-in-stories, published in 2016, would be based in Tuscola, with a made-up "college campus to the southwest corner of town."

Phil's gloom was off the mark. He didn't know it, but he was on the cusp of receiving some of the best news of his life. In 1983, *Puerto del Sol*, a literary magazine run by graduate students in the English department at New Mexico State University, published his story, "Silent Retreats." He credited this first success to the poet Ken Smith, one of his mentors at Murray State University.

Phil was as relieved as he was happy to see his name in print after all those years alone in darkened rooms. That first publication was quickly followed by "Fiona's Rooms," which found a place in *South Dakota Review* with the help of Deb Wylder, and "Long Pine," which was published in *Sou'Wester*. At long last, he was on his way.

In 1984, our high school class had its 20th reunion in Tuscola. As it happened, I was in the USA at the time, but I didn't go. No one would have been happy to see me anyway. Phil attended, now in his persona as a newly published author. But his writing was still unknown outside a small circle of acquaintances, and he lamented the fact that our high school class had yet to produce anyone of significance. After the reunion, he ran into a couple of ex-classmates at a nearby bar, who told him some dirty jokes while updating him with gossip. These random barroom conversations made their way into several of Phil's short stories, including "Infield."

He wrote to me, disingenuously, that "we must make an effort to forget Tuscola completely." Anybody who knows anything at all about Phil Deaver knows that that was among the dumbest things he ever said. Tuscola was everything to him, just as it was nothing to me. For the rest of his life he spoke of his hometown as "the middle of the middle"—the place where things may have fallen apart, but where the centre still could hold.

Although I avoided that 1984 class reunion, I did take the opportunity during my American visit to drop in to see Althea.

She was still living alone in the Deaver family home in Tuscola. We chatted about old times and about her kids and grandchildren, avoiding mention of the 1964 car crash and its aftermath. She seemed to be doing okay, but there was a faraway look in her eyes that I didn't remember, as if she had difficulty engaging in this or any other conversation.

I learned later, from Phil, that Cyndie was eavesdropping in another room of the house while I was talking with Althea, but she never came out to say hello. She was probably standing guard, ready to pounce if things went haywire. Needless to say, there was no mention of that weird 1964 encounter between Althea and me in that motel room outside St Joseph's College, because there was nothing worth mentioning. Nothing had happened.

Sometime after my visit to America in 1984, Phil and Cyndie left Murray State University for Longwood, Florida, on the outskirts of Orlando. Phil had accepted a job as a director of something called "The Tutoring Center," but it turned out to last only 18 months. In January 1986 he was laid off. For half a year, he was unemployed. Broke and far away from his bearings in the Midwest, he was facing financial ruin, "with children old enough to know what going down the drain meant." The only thing that was holding him together, psychologically, was his writing.

Cyndie could be forgiven for wondering what the fuck he was doing in the first half of 1986, clickety-clacking on his favourite Smith Corona typewriter, alone again in some other room. She had given birth to their third child, Laura, and Rome was burning as Phil fiddled around. But those six months gave him time to fine-tune several of his stories and to submit them to potential publishers and writing competitions.

He wasn't clickety-clacking for hypothetical readers or reviewers, or even for his family. He was writing for his sanity. And he did manage to put a couple more runs on the board: "Wilbur Gray Falls in

Love with an Idea" was accepted by *The Florida Review*. "Arcola Girls" came next, in *The New England Review*.

In mid-1986, Phil finally found another job, with an Orlando-based outfit called "Wilson Learning." Wilson Learning was a "human performance" corporation, and Phil was hired as one of its many "consultants." The company's mission statement must have been laughable for someone with literary ambitions: "Helping People and Organizations Achieve Performance with Fulfillment." When asked several years later what he did at Wilson Learning, Phil said, with a straight face, "We helped companies select executives."

In the Wilson Learning psychobabble he adopted for his day job, he said he "designed assessment centers," testing applicants' "management skills" using "role-play situations" under the guidance of a "trained observer." He coordinated with prospective Wilson Learning clients about his "assessment designs."

His goal, and Cyndie's, was to save enough money to buy college educations for their three children when the time came. But Phil's salary at Wilson Learning was a modest $35,000. He and Cyndie put $10,000 down on a $100,000 house in Longwood, with a monthly mortgage floating at just under $800. Their monthly payments, and their debts, rose steadily.

Talk about paying your dues. Phil Deaver, company man, was not his idea of self. For the next decade, during the heart of his child-rearing years, the demands of his Wilson Learning job squeezed and strangled him so that his kids' soccer games and gymnastics classes and school conferences became high-pressure ordeals. His writing dropped to third place in his priorities, behind his kids and his job.

But he reassured himself that lots of writers were moonlighters. Edward Arlington Robinson supported his writing with a sinecure at the New York Customs Office. Wallace Stevens was an insurance executive in Connecticut. William Carlos Williams was a paediatrician when he wrote that "so much depends / upon / a red wheel / barrow /

glazed with rain / water / beside the white / chickens." As a medical man who found time to express himself in verse, he believed in "no ideas but in things."

And as Philip Roth once declared, "it's all material." Seeing the bright side when he looked back at his years with the Wilson Learning corporation, Phil remembered how the relationships he formed in his otherwise mind-numbing work influenced his stories. "Human relationships are endless," he said. "It's absolutely endless what you can write about."

After working at Wilson Learning during the day, Phil wrote stories at home from 10pm to 2am, averaging five hours' sleep before reporting to Wilson Learning in the morning like a zombie. "Sweat equity," he called it.

He described his life as being "exactly split between what I do to make a living and what I do to justify myself for living."

CHAPTER 20

Long Journey Towards Oblivion

N EARLY A QUARTER of a century after the awful car crash that killed his father, Phil Deaver achieved what was, by general acclamation, his greatest success as a writer. At the beginning of 1987, he wrote to tell me that "[t]he University of Georgia Press will publish my first collection of short stories, 12 in all, due out in the Spring of 1988." Phil was 40 years old, a few years shy of the age his father had reached before his untimely death.

Some of the stories had been published previously in literary journals. In the end, only eleven stories appeared in *Silent Retreats*, not twelve. "Forty Martyrs," one of Phil's earliest and best short stories, was left out because it made the book too long for the publisher's liking. Phil hoped to use "Forty Martyrs" later, to launch a second collection of stories, but as it turned out that would take another 30 years.

Silent Retreats won a Flannery O'Connor Award, and with that award came a publishing contract with *The University of Georgia Press*. Before he fully realised what had hit him, he was giving a reading at the Harvard Club in New York. And on a single day in June, 1988, his book was favourably reviewed by both the *New York Times Book Review* and the *Chicago Tribune*'s *Sunday Book Review*.

The Flannery O'Connor Award (named after the short story master of the Southern Gothic style) was, and remains, a prize given annually to two relatively unknown writers of a short story collection. The award promotes the work of talented newcomers to a wider audience of readers and reviewers. In addition to publication contracts with *The University of Georgia Press*, the recipients are given a thousand bucks.

Phil was one of two winners in 1988. The other was a young Texas woman named Gail Galloway Adams, who never wrote another book. There had been twelve recipients before them.

In addition to the Flannery O'Connor Award, Phil's story "Arcola Girls," which was to be included in *Silent Retreats*, was recognised in 1988 as one of the year's twenty *O. Henry Prize Stories*. The first-prize winner of the *O. Henry* prize in 1998 was Raymond Carver, for the last story he ever wrote—"Errand," a semi-biographical retelling of Anton Chekhov's last days in a German hotel room. By any objective criteria, Phil's story was better than Carver's; but Phil didn't have Carver's fame, and his name didn't sell books.

Other *O. Henry Prize Stories* in 1988 were by Ann Beattie, John Updike, Jane Smiley, Bobbie Ann Mason, Joyce Carol Oates, and Andre Dubus. Phil was tossing the dice with some very high rollers.

Silent Retreats is a fine book, comparable to early Fitzgerald or early Hemingway, as good as some of Alice Munro's finest, at least as good as Carver's tales of hardscrabble gloom. *The New York Times Book Review* described *Silent Retreats* as "full of blurred time and half-lived dreams. Written in vivid, spare prose, the best of these stories linger, sad and profound, like songs you sing to yourself."

Publishers Weekly agreed: the stories were "[p]ermeated with finely crafted writing," making for "a wise, quietly provocative statement about commonplace tragedy and the ironies and fragility of relationships" (including a "pointless death by car").

The St Louis Post Dispatch observed that "Deaver's characters have stood as close to ground zero as men can and live." Its review said that his "portrayal of their longings, their impetuous actions and their hard-won understandings is impressive."

Kirkus Reviews offered cautious praise for "a noteworthy introduction," describing the writing as "middlebrow poetry that recalls Saul Bellow's greatest character, Henderson" (i.e., *Henderson the Rain King*).

Puerto del Sol said that most of the stories were:

> ... sad, funny, carefully crafted, quiet, smart. They bespeak an author who cares about his characters, who allows them to speak the kind of crisp dialogue that defines them, who writes skilled narrative which furthers the story without being flashy, who is confident enough of his themes to let them emerge without authorial highlighting.

Among the characters he "cared about" most was Skidmore—the same guy who was recalled by the fictional Wilbur Gray during his solitary run through Patterson Springs. In his menacing way, Skidmore meanders through half the stories in *Silent Retreats*. In later years, Phil would claim that Skidmore was a "composite character," but if so, the ratio was about 97% me and 3% somebody else—probably him, or at least the parts of himself he saw in me. This ratio was fluid from story to story, based on Phil's mood as he wrote and on my most recent behaviour.

As late as 2013, in a post on his blog, *Long Pine Limited: Philip Deaver on the Craft of Fiction*, Phil mentioned a book I'd sent him from New Zealand, *Hemingway's Boat*, by Paul Hendrickson. On the blog, Phil identified me as Skidmore, who "turned me onto [the book] a few months ago." There was no mention of my real name, and there didn't need to be. Everybody in our world, from Tuscola, Illinois, to Orlando, Florida, knew that I was supposed to be Skidmore.

There I was, camouflaged in Phil's *Silent Retreats* stories, where truth and fiction bled together. Like Phil's anti-hero, I'd developed an irritating Australian accent by the time his stories were finished, having lived in Melbourne for many years. Like Skidmore, I'd spent six years on Indian reservations in the American West, working as a legal aid lawyer for various tribes.

Phil sent me a hard copy of *Silent Retreats* in April 1988, with a cryptic note in his familiar handwriting: "I hope you like these stories, or at least can understand." I was amused by the "at least" part. I did understand, and I did like the stories.

I wrote back from Australia, saying I was proud of him, and that he'd written a fine book, even a courageous one, filled with insights into the human condition, mistrustful of the conventions of language, impatient with the publishing industry's expectations for what a story should be. I confessed to being a bit jealous and thanked him for inspiring me to follow his lead by getting serious about writing something of my own.

This adulatory feedback from his cantankerous old friend took him by surprise. In June, he replied:

> Let me say that nothing I have ever known about you prepared me for your letter. I am glad you like the book. Some of the reviewers are going after the structure of the stories a little, the apparent plotlessness, etc., and your letter did buck me up. Quite honestly, I would rather have you like the book than the *Chicago Tribune*.
>
> I know there's a lot *you* could say critical of it (and you would be right), but you controlled yourself real well and I appreciate it. For me it was a hall of fame letter that made me happy for days.
>
> Going around as Continuing Education Director for Murray State University made me feel real blando with my kids. Having no real profession, I've had to navigate through the paper swamp of the service economy attaching myself where I can for a living. These days my kids know me and identify

me by one word—'writer.' That makes me, long in search of an identity, real happy.

I'll write more later. I'm busy as hell right now. Thanks, many thanks, for that last letter.

He signed his letter "Danny."

It took him a few years and a few more successes, but the confluence of these three events—the Flannery O'Connor Award, the O. Henry Prize, and the publishing contract with *The University of Georgia Press*—gave Phil his ticket out of the wasteland of Wilson Learning into his new life at Rollins College, where he would become writer-in-residence and a creative writing teacher for the last 20 years of his life.

When the bell finally tolled for Philip F Deaver in 2018, not too many remembered him as a human resources consultant at the Wilson Learning corporation or as a Murray State University administrator, or even as a person with a doctorate in education from the University of Virginia. He was remembered as a guy who'd fulfilled his own dream of becoming a published writer, a teacher of writers, and a member of an exclusive club of people who earn their crust by their creative work.

CHAPTER 21

Whose Walls Are Mirrors

NOTWITHSTANDING OUR SMALL window of mutual admiration in 1988, Phil's portraits of Skidmore in *Silent Retreats*, by any measure, were pretty savage. But the truth is I didn't mind. It stoked my ego to be a character, real or imagined, in a book, any book, Deaver's book.

The Champaign-Urbana News-Gazette quoted me this way, from an interview during a visit back to Illinois: "'They're not very flattering portraits,' says Forrester, a/k/a Skidmore. 'But Phil and I are best friends, so what the heck.'"

I wrote along similar lines directly to Phil, when he expressed concern that he might have hurt my feelings. "Your characterisation of Skidmore was never objectionable to me," I said, "and never gave me any pain. I revelled in it."

The New York Times took aim at my alter ego: "Skidmore, a once high-minded attorney living in a small Nebraska town just off an Indian reservation, seems perpetually on the run." Change Nebraska to South Dakota and stick Skidmore in the middle of the reservation, and that was me.

Publishers Weekly noted Skidmore's "genius for meanness." *The St Louis Post-Dispatch* wrote that "Skidmore, guilty over a failed love affair and his incompetence as a lawyer for the poor, writes mean, late night letters to his friends." The real me wasn't incompetent as a lawyer for the poor, and I didn't think my real-life letters were all that mean-spirited.

The Champaign-Urbana News-Gazette focused on the tension between Skidmore and his creator:

> Skidmore is the best friend of the narrator in several stories, and the protagonist in two others. As a friend, he's kind of bad news, even if the news is true. ... As a public defender and the last hope for Indians in a small Nebraska town, he doesn't even much like the clients he helps all the way into jail. Skidmore isn't much good to himself, either.

For what it's worth, the truth was that I cared a great deal about my Indian clients, and did a good job representing them in tribal courts, state courts, federal courts, and before the US Congress. But I understood and accepted Phil's portrayal of Skidmore as necessary in achieving the "emotional core" of his stories.

When he spoke publicly or privately about Skidmore, Phil was happy to confirm that Skidmore was his old friend from Tuscola, Illinois. In this way he not only fictionalised me, which was fine, but he was also able to hide his own less savoury characteristics in his Skidmore character. He could take the moral high ground as Skidmore floundered. It was a good trick and it was good therapy, and it worked. He was on fire.

He transmogrified several of my letters into communications that met his fictional needs, and attributed them to Skidmore. The results were way meaner than my originals. Here's one from Skidmore to Wilbur Gray, the Deaver character who discovered nirvana while running through the old Chautauqua grounds at Patterson Springs:

> Dear Wilbur,
>
> I read some of the poems you sent me, and I want you to know they are the most worthless, pitiable utterances I've ever known

to be authored by an adult. They're abstract and escapist and have very little to do with you.

All I want to know about is your pain, Wilbur, and if you can't write about it, then hang it up. I'm telling you pain is all that motivates and everything you write should be an extended paraphrase of the word 'Ouch.' Stop mulling over abstractions and keep running, is my advice. If it hurts, run faster.

I didn't like that guy any more than Wilbur Gray did. Who would? The Skidmore letter may have reflected how Phil *felt* when he read some of my correspondence to him, but my words were never that harsh.

Curiously, Skidmore's advice about running in that "Wilbur Gray" letter—"[i]f it hurts, run faster"—was destined to be transformed into a mantra about writing that Phil passed along to hundreds of his students. As the writer Diana Raab was to note after Phil's death, one of his favourite admonitions for struggling writers was "when it hurts, write harder."

Phil and I had grown accustomed to writing to each other without restraint, without pulling our punches. In later years, a woman who knew us both—Lora Goodnight—said we were like "old friends who were trying to kill each other literarily." But we were usually able to laugh at ourselves, eventually, as we continued to pound away.

Skidmore makes his first appearance in the book's title story, "Silent Retreats." His childhood friend Martin Wolf, a lapsed Catholic experiencing a midlife crisis (hint hint), discovers that his once-safe harbours have disappeared. Church retreats, for example, have deteriorated into encounter groups. Martin is cornered, with nowhere to run. In desperation one night, from a lonesome room in Chicago's Drake Hotel, he telephones Skidmore, who is living out west on an Indian reservation. Skidmore picks up the phone but pretends to be the receptionist at the fictional "South Ridge Legal Services."

"We're closed," he says.

Martin Wolf smells a rat but plays along. "I just wanted to tell this guy Skidmore what to do with a red-hot poker," he says. "Tell him this is your old pal and worst enemy from when you were twelve."

They both laugh. Martin drops the pretence and tells Skidmore his letters are "meaner than usual lately." Skidmore, in character and in denial, says he isn't mean.

Privately, Martin wonders if this will be the last time they ever talk. "Letters were easier than phone calls," says the narrator. "Nowhere in this world could Martin quite find the Skidmore he knew a long time ago ... Always, on the brink of making a call to Skidmore, he noticed his motivation. It was always a wave of feeling alone, wanting to be friends again."

They exchange pleasantries about the St Louis Cardinals, and unpleasantries about Martin's wife and child. Then Skidmore metamorphosises into Beelzebub by the magic of Phil Deaver's fiction, saying the kind of thing to Martin that only a dark and damaged soul could utter.

"God," he says. "What a laughable jerk."

Martin, stunned and saddened by these hurtful words, can only mumble to himself.

"I always think," says Martin, "if I could just put together the right set of words or something." But his lost pal is having none of that.

"Outgrow it," says Skidmore. "It's pitiful."

And Martin Wolf recognises, in that bloodletting scene between truth and fiction, what to him is obviously true.

"There isn't any friendship anymore. Or something."

Except that, in real life, there was. Phil wasn't Martin Wolf, and I wasn't Skidmore.

In *Silent Retreats*, Skidmore really came into his own in two related stories, "Fiona's Rooms" and "Long Pine." The Skidmore in those stories was a big drinker, with a softness for Jack Daniels whiskey.

Unlike Skidmore, I don't drink, and I didn't drink then. Skidmore was a serial and equal-opportunity womanizer, regardless of race, creed, or social class. I wasn't. Skidmore loathed his Indian clients. I didn't. But these were minor quibbles around the edges of Phil's portrayal. His Skidmore was self-centred, manic, insensitive, borderline autistic—these descriptions were closer to me, and to the "emotional core" that Phil aimed for in everything he wrote.

My only real criticism of *Silent Retreats* had to do with the stories' occasional racist references, which were attributed to Skidmore. In "Fiona's Rooms," Skidmore talks about "goddamned drunken Indians" and refers to his clients as "drunken Indian braves." I hated those descriptions of Indians. I'd been on reservations long enough to know how damaging such stereotypes were for the Lakota people and others. In the story "Silent Retreats," Skidmore was living in a trailer that doubled as his office—same as me—but he tells Martin Wolf, on the phone, that he just saw an Indian woman "go by the window here a minute ago, chasing a blue jay with a goddamned tomahawk." At least Phil avoided the word "squaw." But this image of a crazy Indian woman sporting a "tomahawk" was the kind of racist rhetoric Indians had been putting up with for hundreds of years.

I don't believe Phil had a racist bone in his body, but I always wished he'd run these descriptions by me, or by someone who was familiar with reservation life, before they made it into print. It probably didn't matter much. Phil's stories didn't have a wide audience. In all likelihood, I was the only reader who was rubbed the wrong way. And the reason he didn't let me preview *Silent Retreats* was because, given my track record, he thought I'd be upset about Skidmore, not about Indians.

Since 1976, I'd been sending him letters from Australia and the Indian reservations, which he snuck into his work. I gave him his character "Fiona"—that was the real name of an Australian friend of mine. Phil lifted her heavy eye makeup, her literary ambitions, her singing voice, and placed them in *Silent Retreats*. I gave him "Yank," Fiona's boyfriend, a Vietnam veteran who was my best American mate in Australia. Yank and Fiona and I took a road trip in my 1965 VW Beetle, north from Melbourne to a farmhouse in Grafton, New South Wales, where, during a bout of cabin fever brought on by a biblical downpour, they slipped some magic mushrooms into my rice and kept me high for two days straight. Phil was intrigued by my tales about Fiona and Yank and dropped them into *Silent Retreats*.

I gave him "McFarland," a bit player in "Long Pine" and "Silent Retreats." I went to law school with the real Patrick McFarland at the University of Illinois. He practised zen, stood on his head a lot, prized his Swiss army knife, loved Robert Ardrey's books on human evolution, and had an Australian girlfriend named Eva. I gave Phil a law student named "Blondy," Skidmore's ex-girlfriend in "Long Pine." I gave him an ex-nun I once took on a date in real life—she crawled her way into his story "Cassadaga" and into his unpublished novel, *Past Tense*. I gave him my 1964 Martin D28S dreadnought guitar to pass along to Skidmore—as Phil noted in his story "The Kopi," it was "formerly owned by Paul Stookey" of Peter, Paul, and Mary fame.

And most of all, I gave him Skidmore.

I should emphasise that I don't give two hoots about plagiarism, and I don't think Phil was plagiarising. It doesn't bother me that Hemingway didn't attribute "we owe God a death" to Shakespeare, or that neither Eliot nor I acknowledged that "il miglior fabbro" came from Dante, or that Bob Dylan didn't give credit to somebody else's online notes for his mail-in Nobel Prize lecture, or that Doris Kearns Goodwin pilfered other writers' words for her book on the Kennedys. The scholar Keith D Miller, observing that Martin Luther King Jr often cribbed, verbatim, words and sentences from the sermons of the Reverend Harry Emerson Fosdick and other famous theologians, noted that in those days "words were shared assets, not personal belongings."

Australian Aborigines don't plagiarise—they don't even have a word for it. Lakota don't plagiarise, or at least they didn't used to. The Egyptians made appropriation an art form for 3,000 years, and none of them attributed nuthin to nobody.

Some reductionists hold, with little imagination and less joy, that every thought we have, every word we say, every gesture we make, every feeling we experience has been thought, spoken, made, or felt by other sentient beings, a hundred thousand times before, a million times before. From this perspective, even our precious sense of self—that construct that deceives us into believing we're somehow unique—is entirely crafted from a hotchpotch of social, cultural, and ancestral norms.

(During his occasional flirtations with the popularised words of the Buddha, Phil came to believe that the brain constantly creates narratives to interpret reality. Even as he exploited such false self-narratives in his fiction, he was on guard—with mixed success—not to mistake them for reality. He understood the individual sense of self as more akin to a fictional character than to a real thing—an illusory by-product of incessant internal chatter. The Buddha had a word for this concept—"anattā"—which is often translated as "no self." I.e., there is no me.)

An old Lakota custom, dating back to long before the white folks drove them west to their horse culture on the plains, was to hand over, to anyone, anything he or she coveted. After a rodeo in South Dakota in 1982, I complimented Cheeto Mestes, a Lakota friend, on a fine fox pelt he had hanging on his wall. I didn't want it, I just admired its beauty. But without a word, Cheeto took it off its hook and handed it to me, for keeps.

"Take it," he said. "It's yours."

For Lakota, such an emptying of material wealth enhances the giver's place with Wakan Tanka, the Great Mystery. But white folks and their lawyers came up with the bright idea that abstractions can be personal possessions, and they like to get outraged and threaten "intellectual property" litigation at the drop of a hat. Pay up. It's mine. Gimme credit.

Everybody borrows stuff, and everybody always has, but some people disguise it better than others. To be clear, anybody can take anything I've ever written and, if they think it's good enough, slap their name on it without attribution, turn it in for a class assignment, publish it, stick it up their arse. I don't care. If they make some money in the process, more power to them.

I was happy for Phil to take as much of my correspondence as he wanted. He didn't really plagiarise anyway. He just borrowed some of my stuff to spark his imagination, the same way he used to borrow my baseball bats and basketballs when we were kids. He didn't have to ask. I didn't care. And I still don't.

In "Fiona's Rooms," he took the elastic strip from my Jockey underpants, which I'd converted into a headband when I taught at the Melbourne University Law School. Phil wrapped it around Yank's head. Like me, Yank "held back his long hippie hair" with an "elastic waistband from his Jockey shorts around his head."

I sent him a photograph from that farmhouse in Grafton, New South Wales, where Fiona and Yank got me got high on mushrooms and we cowered during that thunderstorm, and in *Silent Retreats* he described it to a T:

> Fiona is standing straight, even under the weight of Yank's left arm, which she seems to have shouldered in order to hold him up. There is a blur through Fiona's face, like a question she didn't know she had. The picture was taken on the front porch of the farmhouse …

It's not easy to write a description like that from a photograph. Phil was fascinated with two-dimensional renderings of stories in photographs and paintings, and from his earliest days he was gifted at seeing the 3D story that was behind a pictured scene. From Phil's childhood to his death, Edward Hopper's *Nighthawks* carried him from the painting's cast of four lonely people in a city diner to a reflection on an "unspeakable truth" about loneliness:

> Hopper, born the same year as James Joyce and Virginia Woolf, those other two masters of stream of consciousness, fiction's fourth dimension, shows us but will not tell us the unspeakable truth I know, from this picture and many of his others, that he knew—how beautiful, sweet, and awful loneliness is even if we're with someone, even if it's our wife, a lover, or our own happy curious little boy. It might be possible to be alone and silent by being a painter or by being a writer—don't we crave it most of the time?

In a similar way, Phil's poem *The Vanishing Point* remembers a photograph of his father with his "hand on my shoulder," and dissects the image for analysis: "See how the lines of this picture / seem to pull the two figures / along a rail receding to the distance? / … See the way his eyes / stare directly into the camera? He's waiting / for the flutter behind the lens / that signals the moment is over."

Fiona's face in my photograph may have revealed a question, but it took Phil's insight to put her expression into words, and to intuit from her body language that she was "holding [Yank] up."

I gave him Jolinda, the Lakota woman in "Fiona's Rooms" who tried to kill herself by drinking from the same bottle of Pine-Sol I had once snatched from her hand. And I gave him another attempted suicide, by Skidmore's ex-nun in "Cassadaga"—but sadly her attempt was her final act, in the story and in real life.

I was the Skidmore in "Long Pine," the guy who, during the Vietnam War, "wrangled CO status and wimped out the sixties in the Caribbean." I was that conscientious objector, ducking the draft for two years in the West Indies.

Phil was a sponge, soaking up words and images from anywhere and everywhere, and squeezing them into his fertile imagination. All credit to him. I'm glad he found something in my letters he could use.

When I visited him in Orlando in 2004, he was still introducing me to his groupies as "Skidmore. This is Skidmore." And I wore the mantle proudly, even as I paraded around Rollins College with Phil and his friends Connie May Fowler, Darlyn Finch (later Darlyn Finch Kuhn), and Hoyt Edge. Instead of the elastic band from my underpants, I sported a coonskin hat with a long stripy tail.

Connie May Fowler was flying high with the success of *When Katie Wakes*, a memoir exploring her descent into and escape from an abusive relationship. She and I trotted over to the Rollins College Bookstore where I bought two of her novels, *River of Hidden Dreams* and *Before Women Had Wings*, a favourite of Oprah Winfrey's. In my copy of *Before Women Had Wings*, Connie May scribbled: "To Forrester—Be forever kind and good to my dear friend Philip F. Deaver. And thank you for inspiring his fiction. I wish you abundant joy and wonder! Stay in touch!" In *River*, her inscription was to Skidmore, not me: "To Duane Skidmore—in praise of your inner studness!"

As early as the late 1970s, Phil had started addressing his letters to me as if I were not only a Skidmorian monster, but hydra-headed as well. I wrote to him that I was training for the Melbourne Marathon and had run nine miles in 58 minutes. He wrote back to my collective persona, "Dear Forrie, Fiona, and Yank," that I was a "goddam liar" about my running time, and expressed a bit of apprehension about our next get-together, even though he was "somewhat beginning to relax" with me being ten thousand miles away:

> I love thee for the rascal that thou art. And for how you manage to communicate that underneath that schizoid/coral-reef exterior there is a tender-sweet-cute little guy whose sensitive nature was harmed by the world unbeknownst to he, a fuckwit [an Australianism I'd introduced to him].

Whose brain, by its very IQ and internal dimension, was a sponge, bound for better things, but alas, careerus interruptus, the darned world made him into a complex hotshot poet/cynic grand circular social commentarian with unique insight ... but not the supreme/obliterating cosmic power he might have been, had the cards been dealt another way.

He imagined me on a TV show:

The soap operas have been trying to catch your character for years. They know you are in vogue. You are what's happening, cooking along on a semi-even keel, hatching d-r-a-m-a with your every move. I can see it. It would go:

'Genetical Love Albeit Confusion,' starring Forrie and Yank, as existential nihilists caught in the pragmatic web of law school, forced by reality itself and their hungry passions to OD on mushrooms and many other less common but somehow chic DRUGS!!!! A show for the young set.

The harshly intelligent if uneven tale of true passions construed by harried nihilists lost in a world of harsh data processing and public relations stunts. It charts the course of a young man who once played baseball for the Tuscola Indians, as his arm developed!!! Faced with insanity because of sheer intellectual power and complex personality traits, he takes up Zen and Jogging!!!

Also featuring Fiona, chic Aussie broad out for a GOOD TIME!!! With Yank, who, while waiting for seconds, keeps himself in shape by giving himself IQ tests and cutting up underwear for when the pictures are taken!!!

Young anarchists, crazy, fun-loving, existential, liberated, AND artsy, going around saying 'dig' and 'far-out' and adopting ALTERNATIVE LIFE-STYLES!!!

And featuring, in cameo appearances ... Forrie's daddy, as the coach who did his best but was caught short when he accidentally fathered a young nihilist radical who, when bearded, looked like Carlos the Cross-Eyed Lion!!!

Don't miss this extremely original yet somehow interesting tale of true confusion and Layer System zaniness. See a great classic character created before your very eyes: FORRIE, zany old wild-ass letter-writing world-travelin' guy!!!

He even gave my imaginary TV show a couple of sponsors: "Brought to you by Proctor and Gamble and chewy Bike's Bananas!"

CHAPTER 22

Door in the Mountain, Let Me In

L IKE MOST GOOD things, Phil's breakthrough with *Silent Retreats*, in 1988, came with a downside. On the one hand, the publication led to a flurry of good reviews and speaking engagements, as well as what, with the benefit of hindsight, was his destiny: escape from the drudgery of meaningless work in the business world to his Rollins College career. As Phil told an interviewer 20 years later, he assumed "that's the way it would go from then on."

The publication of *Silent Retreats* must have been a revelation for him, opening his life to an expanding circle of literary-minded friends and admiring fans (including, not incidentally, many women admirers). And yet, as time passed, the demand that he continue to develop as a writer and (more importantly) the growing expectation that he find publishers for his work lingered in the background like an undiagnosed illness.

He had always written in spurts and was easily distracted. Short stories continued to be his genre of choice—he could complete a short piece, set it aside, pick it up weeks or months or even years later. And small literary journals across the country were always available to publish short works. But he felt pressured to produce a novel, which, in coming years, seemed increasingly overwhelming and insurmountable—the sense of "haunting" (identified by Richard Goodman) that Phil experienced as he was "weighed down" by his "burden of promise."

He relished the opportunities to read his material to appreciative audiences. In addition to the Harvard Club, he gave readings close to his roots in Illinois and Florida. In Daytona Beach, he read the entirety of "Fiona's Rooms" to an audience of 150 aviation students on the campus of Embry–Riddle Aeronautical University.

"Skidmore appears in all my work," he told them. "He jumps out at everyone. But this is the only story, so far, in which he's the main character. Sadly, Skidmore takes more than he gives."

He was asked by one of the aviation students why he named his leading man Skidmore.

"I don't know," he said. "It just popped into my head."

It was probably more than that. I always assumed that "Skidmore" referred to a guy on a downhill trajectory. If a guy is on the skids, the only thing worse is more of the same.

Another student asked him if he started writing a story with a firm idea of how it would end. Phil answered that he was "a great believer in the subconscious."

"When I start writing with an idea," he said, "what I really want to write about comes out in the end and the original idea falls to the side."

He gave readings at Tuscola's Carnegie Library, where he signed stacks of copies of *Silent Retreats* for former classmates and other locals, and at the *Pages for All Ages* bookstore in Champaign. With the hyperbole that goes with the "small-town-boy-makes-good" riff, *The Tuscola Review*'s headline stated, "Author comes home to autograph best seller." *Silent Retreats* may have received good reviews, but it wasn't a best seller.

Phil was asked about his séance scene from "Arcola Girls"—was it "fact or fiction?"

His answer went back to our mental telepathy days in the Tuscola High School gym: "Mysterious things happened that I've always wondered about, so I just made the whole thing up."

What he said about making up "the whole thing" wasn't quite true. He may have cut the séance scene out of whole cloth, but the exotic Arcola girl who catches his young narrator's fancy, Rhonda with her "dark brown hair and strange, blue catlike eyes," wasn't made up. She was my first girlfriend, Susan Johnson, from nearby Villa Grove—like Rhonda, the daughter of a truck driver and his wife of easy virtue.

Herb Budden was back from Indianapolis for Phil's reading at Tuscola's Carnegie Library. "*Silent Retreats* really touches me," he said to a Champaign reporter. "I know the tone and can feel the atmosphere from back then. Some of the stories are very evocative of the time, the early 1960s."

I received the ongoing news about Phil's successes by international snail mail, in my home in Melbourne's seaside suburb of Williamstown. My first two kids had been born, and I had a job shuffling papers in the Australian public service.

My reaction to the attention he was getting was a mix of admiration and jealousy. My first thought was, Jesus Christ, if Deaver can do this, so can I. But there was a big difference: he'd actually done it, and I hadn't. After Phil thanked me for that "hall of fame letter" in which I expressed pride in his accomplishments—the same letter that made him feel "happy for days"—his next letter, in mid-1988, unloaded.

I'm not quite sure what prompted his sudden change. He'd sent me an early draft of another story, "Vasco and the Virgin," which wasn't to be published until 1995, and I'd mentioned that I'd drafted some chapters of my own with a couple of common threads—which had no life at all except as counterpoints to Phil's stories—and that my chief protagonist, like his, would be named Skidmore. I'd given Skidmore first and second names that Phil had omitted: "Duane" and "Leonard."

I told Phil I'd picked up where he left off in *Silent Retreats*. I'd resurrected scraps of my novel *Low Gravity* from their 1970s graveyard. I was aiming for 75,000 words, and my new working title was "Skidmore's Revenge." I sent him three random stories in draft form—"Skid," "Duane Leonard Skidmore and the Limits of Solipsism," and "Abraham Lincoln in Australia."

"Skid" was told in the voice of Duane Leonard Skidmore's female companion. It named names:

> Duane's gone crazy again. It's probably that goddam Deaver, sending him another manuscript from Florida. Every time Duane gets one, he goes crazy. This one's the dumbest of all, called 'Vasco and the Virgin,' all about some small-town college professor in the American Midwest who has a visitation from the Mother of God.

"Skid" rolled on about the disconnect between Duane Leonard Skidmore and his aging parents, which left Duane longing for a visit from Jesus himself. The beleaguered female narrator concludes:

> He knows he's going crazy, but he tells me he can't stop it. He prays for Jesus to come into the room and talk to him.
>
> 'There was this Russian archbishop,' he says. 'I read his book. When he was about forty, Jesus came and sat across the table from him. He said he never had any doubts about the resurrection after that.'
>
> Sometimes I wish Jesus would come and visit Duane. Maybe it would make things easier for a while.

The next story, "Duane Leonard Skidmore and the Limits of Solipsism," was told in third person limited, and it wasn't any better. Duane was keeping a crazy secret:

> All his life, he had known, more than he knew anything else, that he was alone and had always been alone and would always be alone. He was mind, for want of a better expression, his

mind, pure mind and nothing else, mind forever. He tried to imagine that other people, some other people, felt like this from time to time.

He could remember before his children were born, and he reasoned that there must have been a time before he was born as well, but he didn't really believe it. He was absolutely certain that he would never die. He had no sense of place. There was no dynamic to alter his central perception of reality—that he was an immortal consciousness without external references.

In "Abraham Lincoln in Australia," the female narrator returns. Duane has grown a full beard and proposes to shave off his moustache for a framed-face look, like Lincoln's. The narrator is worried: "I don't think he just wants to *look* like Abraham Lincoln. I think he wants to *be* Abraham Lincoln." In the story, Duane has been reading and re-reading histories of the Civil War, and he weeps each time he comes to the death of the Lincolns' beloved ten-year-old son Willie.

"We loved him so," Duane/Lincoln says, time after time.

As I was writing "Abraham Lincoln in Australia," some people living in the cabin next door to my family—hippie members of a religious sect—circulated a theory that each person has seven hundred reincarnations before reaching nirvana, which prompted my female narrator to declare:

> Don't get me wrong. I don't think Duane *is* Abraham Lincoln. But if the neighbours are right, if you're *really* good in an old life you can jump ahead and don't need to put in your full quota of seven hundred before getting to the good stuff. Who knows? Nirvana for Duane may be just a heartbeat away.

In addition to these snippets, I told Phil that I was busy writing songs for my Australian bluegrass band. I outlined my song-writing method: start with random guitar chords, hum a wordless melody to follow the changing chords, then wait patiently for the humming to shape itself into words that suited the rhythms and the sounds. A series of chord changes might, for example, suggest a story about a frontier woman in a log cabin. Yes, there she was. A couple of percussive downstrokes on the guitar might give her a name: "Hannah." By that stage, no other name could possibly do. No Jacquelines. No Ramonas. No Christines. And the rest of the story about Hannah and her cabin would fall into place. All I had to do was to keep it ripping.

Phil's reply to all this new information started well. He was bemused by my new Skidmore stories and didn't quarrel with my new first and middle names for his most memorable character.

"You have a schizoid way about you," he wrote, "that drives others mad—in that you can be disarmingly warm, and then you can be an absolute murderer of the psyche."

He observed that my would-be novel struck him as "an exercise" rather than art.

"If you were to really pour in on something," he wrote, "and give it at least five months of steeping time, there would be no stopping you."

Those backhanded compliments aside, he liked the idea of telling Skidmore's story from a woman's point of view:

> That keeps some of the venom in check, but still gets some manageable emotion going from a purely fictionalized point of view. I tell people this all the time. If you are writing a story that is close to the bone, the trick will be to manage the material and not simply argue the points & let the rest of it throw you around the room.
>
> One great way to manage the material and in fact even to therapeutically (almost) further explore the issues is to change the point of view to some slightly more objective party. In the 19th century, the solution for many authors was the invention of pure omniscient narration, the ultimate objectivity. Your choice in two of your three chapters works for you.

He also expressed some fascination with my song-writing method:

> Jung would flip over it, how you tap the unconscious with that process. If that's what you really do with songs, I think THAT'S the way you should write your novel, instead of beginning with your rather contrived set-ups, which have the end-point of your chapters leadenly in sight.

> I was amazed that you could open yourself up so wonderfully in the rendering of song, then close your mind entirely with a pre-fab construct for your novel. My advice is to apply your song-writing technique to the rendering of fiction.

So far, so good. But then he got downright tetchy.

Although he was later to apologise for clinging to the false rumours that my dad and I were responsible for Herb Budden's party gossip and that something had happened between me and Althea during that trip home from Rensselaer, he wasn't ready, in 1988, to let go of those grievances. He'd internalised them, despite my disclaimers, and with a new self-assurance that came in the wake of the publication of *Silent Retreats*, he lashed out:

> Why do I even answer your letters? I must have an enormous self-destructive streak, dwarfed by your willingness and ability to wreak destruction.

> I mistakenly attributed the rumor to your dad, somehow, figuring it was something he and my dad might have discussed in confidence. After I phoned him, I was convinced by the time I hung up that he knew nothing. But I thought it was the last time I'd ever talk to him.

> I drove out to Patterson Springs, to Jim Lemna's house, and asked him. He was my dad's closest friend. Such an indiscretion by my dad could well have been something Lemna carried inside himself and told no one about, in keeping with his great old Catholic code of manhood. Anyway, Lemna said the rumor was 'hawgshit,' and asked what was I doing believing some street

rumor instead of honoring the memory of my father. I believed his denial less than your dad's for some reason. I thought he was sheltering me.

I had never once considered, before that day after Eric's party, that my dad might have done something like that. I took what I heard as truth, and it was a big blow. I was still in mourning. Dad was the absolute center of our family. The death was an enormous shock, and I thought all the shocks were over for a while. But that one rumor, that sole event, changed my idea of him for the next 20 years.

I should have been able to figure it out—this was simply an evil adolescent running off at the mouth. But I couldn't do it, never could, still can't. We were close friends. Why would you do it? I just wonder what the hell I ever did to get all this shit from you?

Anyhow, in adult life (so you know I'm not trying to overstate things), I came to understand why a person would be unfaithful in marriage. The logic of it. And this made me feel less judgmental of him, whether the rumor was true or not, a little more sympathetic. No matter what happened, my position on the matter got to be that I didn't care. Admittedly, that should have been my position all along. It was a long trek. I made it differently than if that party bullshit hadn't ever happened.

The "evil adolescent running off at the mouth" was Herb Budden, not me, but Phil wasn't going to be distracted by facts. He could always "suspend his disbelief like nobody's business."

Then, he took a right turn to the old canard about me and Althea cavorting in a motel room, venting in language that was jarring:

> Luckily, by the time you told me about your opportunity to fuck my mom, I had come through the other thing about my dad, and my feelings for both parents were unconditional. Plus, as an adult, a veteran, and a professional introvert, I knew about treachery by then. By that time, I was just amazed at the hurtful things you'd say to me.

If what you said about my mom was true, that she'd invited you into her room, what were you hoping for by telling me? (Rhetorical question—don't answer any of this.) How did you want this to affect my relationship with her? Were you going after me with this second story, when you already knew you'd got me pretty good with the first one?

I probably seem like a child with arrested development, that I haven't put these things into a more adult perspective, or completely written them off. Did you want to kill me? Because I was born luckier, if dumber? Or because I had that slightly weak look in my eye that let you know you could do or say anything without getting stomped?

Did you want to hurt me real bad so I'd be thankful forever? Did you want to give me something to write about, some good old pain, the kind of pain Hemingway or Salinger say writers should write about, pain and nothing else?

He seemed to have forgotten that neither of the two rumours was true. It didn't matter. False or not, his pain was still real:

I take it all pretty personally. If you just meant it all as irony, grinding about my parents, maybe I was just too dumb to catch it. Is that what you thought? I guess you must read some pretty esoteric guys on the topic of irony. Gore Vidal comes to mind.

I'm the one you permanently damaged. Not Marcella Gasaway or Bobby Green or any of the other little kids in whom you saw some little glimmer of self-doubt that indicated a reasonably easy victim for you to strike as deeply and personally as possible, scarring them for life. It was *me* you hurt for life, and you did it on purpose, and you didn't do it once, or twice, you did it often. And even now, your *Skidmore's Revenge* seethes with the desire to do it again.

Whew. What a letter! And how justified Phil's attacks would have been, if the facts hadn't been in the way. It stunned me then, and it stuns me even now, after he's gone, that he needed to keep owning these lies.

His venom didn't last forever, and there was nothing I could do about it in 1988, nothing I hadn't already tried. It occurred to me that it wasn't surprising that Skidmore was the baddest guy in Deaverland, and always would be. Skidmore and I were assholes.

And just as surprisingly, Phil did a final 180-degree turn in that same long letter, with three further pages of dispassionate and erudite analysis of some of his favourite male writers—Updike, Styron, Hemingway, Joyce, Fitzgerald, Wolfe. In those three pages, it was as if his earlier vitriol, in this same letter, had already become a thing of the past.

I replied meekly, saying that I wasn't "seething" with anything, followed by a bit of small talk about music. My bluegrass band's first album was about to be released on vinyl and cassette. Most of the songs had Illinois themes laced with nostalgia. I sought Phil's advice about a cover photograph.

He was in Birmingham, Alabama, when my letter arrived in Florida, so Cyndie read it to him over the phone. He wrote back to me quickly, giving some tips about a photographer named Larry Kanfer, who'd taken the photo of the Illinois prairie that Phil used for the dust jacket of *Silent Retreats*.

Then, he outlined his future plans. He wanted to complete a novel based on his story "Geneseo" and to write a screenplay about a country doctor. Skidmore was still on his mind, but he had plans to kill him off: "While I expect Skidmore to dip into my stories from time to time, I'm finished with him as a leading character."

That last prediction proved to be short-sighted.

The euphoria of his post-*Silent Retreats* activities had died down. His letter was a mix of dark self-assessments and inflated anxieties. No matter what he achieved, in 1988 or thereafter, he was forever burdened by past disappointments. He drew comparisons between us, always a slippery slope.

> You do have this competitive thing in you real deep, and I have almost no competitor in me at all. I sag under the pressure of competition. It's a mental thing. That must explain how you got me in that leghold all those years ago—a matter of amazement to me even now. If we wrestled again today (let's not) you'd manage it again. As I told you a long time ago, nothing changes.

> I think I had one summer of glory back in Tuscola. At that time, I think, for that brief moment, I was a better baseball player than you. The summer of 1965, after I got home from St Joe. I was on a hitting streak, and was invincible at third base, and my arm never felt better and I could throw harder than anyone I knew. The one thing I struggled with was control—I had a history of making wild throws, but that year was my best year for that too.

> I played the guitar for 15 years, and tennis for 15 years, and never got one bit better at either one. I did take on the manic-ness of racquetball for a while at Murray State, and enjoyed the hell out of that game, but lost regularly, managing to push my level of play lower than that of virtually anyone I'd play against.

> In basketball, I think I had potential, but I was too little in my formative years, and I still play basketball as if I were 5'6". I can't time a rebound, can't shoot from under the basket. One of the great lessons of life for me was watching you play first-string varsity basketball and get cheered our senior year.

The truth was that I'd been a mediocre high school basketball player, at best. But he was on a roll:

> I'd put so many hours into basketball and taken so many biffs from so many coaches whose arrested development as human beings did damage to me. I'm not talking about your dad, who was always a great help to me. And you were out there on the

basketball floor flying high, making that weird reverse layup you used to pull off with regularity to the delight of everybody.

You got to that level by hard work, and (as happened in reverse with me & writing) you definitely benefited from my not being on the basketball team. When we were together, a whole different set of dynamics kicked in. Maybe I held you back in those early high school basketball years. Too much mental telepathy on the bench, too many jokes. I think we contributed to the mental instability of a few coaches.

You were better in sports than I was, even though I think we were equal physically. The difference was mental. My dad was interested in my sports, but in a distant way. He'd been a good football player, but his bad back (football injury) kept him from being the least bit athletic by the time I knew him. Which is why I was always delighted to watch your dad play first base back in good old Ervin Park.

Next, he hit himself where it hurt the most, disregarding all the available evidence:

And you are by far the better writer. Give you ten years, as I had with *Silent Retreats*, and you could blow my writing completely away. You could do it sooner than that. I'm real slow. Your mind is fresher, broader in its reach. Plus you don't give a shit about what people think, which has to be a marvelous attribute for a writer.

I am neither good, honest, nor humble. Half a world away and 20 years down the road, maybe I look that way to you. But I am the walking, breathing embodiment of Hannah Arendt's esteemed phrase, the banality of evil. I'm not mentally tough enough to be mean, or I would be. I grind a lot of anger down into my bones instead of acting it out. I have a paranoid streak a mile wide and I could tell you some stories there.

But my point is, maybe you ought to figure a way to put a little of your anger down on the page where you can see it, if you actually want to get over it and feel better, or whatever. I always sort of figured you really enjoyed being you. I never particularly saw you as crazy or as damaged goods or as someone who had cried so much he couldn't cry anymore. I can readily imagine that a lifetime of incurring people's wrath (at worst), and losing their friendships (at best), could wear one down, especially if a person has a modicum of sensitivity.

He closed with a bit of light relief on the rewards of writing:

Anyhow, writing has a therapeutic effect, if you write the right stuff. It can be satisfying in a big way, apart from acceptance by readers or publishers—in the way writing songs must be for you—'damn, that's pretty good,' you think, and you know it came from you.

It's meditation. It's zen. It's relaxing and energizing all at once. But it is very hard to reach. Very hard to actually sit there day in and day out and do it. The rewards are minimal unless you value the self-satisfaction of having done it.

In July 1989, I toured the USA with my Australian bluegrass band, hawking our first two albums along the way. We played some high profile gigs—in Nashville with the legendary Townes Van Zandt, in Illinois with future Grammy winner Alison Krauss and her Union Station band, in Louisville, Kentucky, as part of the big American Music FanFest, and in Owensboro, Kentucky, on the banks of the Ohio River with Emmy Lou Harris, Bill Monroe, Peter Rowan, and Ralph Stanley.

Phil wasn't able to catch up with me during the tour, but he wrote that he was "listening to the albums often, along with K. T. Oslin and Reba McEntire." What he liked most about the songs, "apart from the familiar voice," was that they were going after "hard issues, aggressively jabbing the complacent, and rattling the cages of the corrupt."

Herb and Bonnie Budden drove over from Indianapolis to see the band play in rural Indiana. We didn't play very well on that occasion, and one of our songs was about the death in custody of an Aboriginal man ("they threw his arse in jail"), which didn't go down well with the right-wing fundamentalist Indiana crowd. One bible-bashing charismatic soul even came on stage with an axe and threatened, in a loving way, to cut off my head. He took special exception our song "Talking in Tongues," which featured barking dogs and screeching cats. I don't think he appreciated the band's Australian sense of humour. But Herb was kind enough to make excuses for us after the show, attributing our rusty performance to mega-jetlag.

Despite his occasional bouts of despair, Phil and I were moving in decidedly opposite directions in the 1990s. Phil was on the rise, even if he had to take two steps forward and one step back.

In Australia, my life was in turmoil—an ugly divorce, a dispute with the government that had me on the front pages of Australian newspapers for a few years, and even a sensational police investigation involving the murder of a model by her millionaire husband, in which, for a while, I was a prime suspect.

I dropped out for rest of the decade, first living alone in my car on the back streets of Melbourne's inner suburb of St Kilda, then hiding in 80 acres of Australian bush with my newly blended family. We lived in the thick of a eucalyptus forest, in a 20-room mudbrick house. We pumped our shower water from the Loddon River, collected drinking water from our corrugated roof, grew our vegetables in an organic garden that was fenced off to keep out the six-foot kangaroos, and cooked on an ancient woodburning stove from Ireland. Our electricity came from ex-Telecom batteries and solar panels. Our hot bathwater came from the Irish stove. Our composting toilet didn't compost, so once a month I hauled the family's dripping collection of shit into the forest, by jeep and wagon, for sacramental burial.

Despite the hard work, it was a good life at the time, a respite from all those city people who were wanting a piece of me. We named our place "Narnia," after C S Lewis's fantasy novels about the magical forest where each pond provided transportation to a better world.

Although Phil's own magic wasn't entirely smooth, it was headed in the right direction. After *Silent Retreats*, he entertained the idea that he might be anointed as one of the Next Big Things in American literature. In 1989, he scored a $20,000 creative writing fellowship from the National Endowment for the Arts to complete a novel. That was serious money in those days, and with it came serious expectations.

New York agents were sending him offers. One of them wrote, "If you are not already represented, and have a full-length novel which you feel is ready for publication, I'd be delighted to have a look." Phil told me about "Hollywood movie inquiries" for his stories "Geneseo" and "Arcola Girls," and said his goal was "to keep at this until I can pay for my house and the kids' college educations, then quit."

He figured he couldn't lose, even if Hollywood didn't bite: "A lot of money is made by writers who option their work to the movies, even though the work ultimately never hits the big screen."

He was giving more and more public readings of his work, including one at Purdue University and another at the annual homecoming ceremony at his alma mater, St Joseph's College. He developed notions of becoming an academic as well as a writer.

"I think Purdue might take me," he said, "if I applied for their open creative writing position." But he hesitated to move from Florida. It would be tough on his kids, especially Michael, who was fully involved with high school soccer.

So he stayed put with Cyndie and the kids in Longwood, Florida, working for the Wilson Learning company for a few more years, pulling in the same crappy salary and writing in back rooms in stolen moments. The NEA fellowship wasn't tax free, and 60% of what was left went to pay off debts and buy a new computer. He couldn't get out of his poverty trap.

In 1990, Phil and Cyndie bought three chairs for their living room. He told me those chairs were the first new items of furniture they'd purchased in 21 years of marriage.

CHAPTER 23

Dumb to Tell the Crooked Rose

I N 1992, ALTHEA SAMPLES DEAVER died at the age of 71. She'd been living near Phil in Florida for a few years after selling the family home in Tuscola to a German professional wrestler. In 1989, she suffered a broken hip and never fully recovered. That accident, together with her lifelong smoking habit, shortened the years of her life.

My dad and mother went to Althea's visitation at the Shrader Funeral Home in Tuscola. They sent me a copy of her remembrance card—a pair of male hands, folded in prayer. These hands had been drawn by her husband, Dr Deaver, in 1963—the year before he died. She had lived without him for nearly 30 years and never considered remarrying.

My dad also attended Althea's funeral, which followed the visitation. It was held at Forty Martyrs Catholic Church, where he'd served as a Sunday usher for many years, showing congregants to their seats. The church was three-quarters empty for Althea's funeral. My dad sat alone in a pew, off to the left, as his old Lac Seul buddy, Father Stephen Deaver from Nebraska, led the service.

In his eulogy, Father Steve pissed Phil off royally by whining about how Althea failed to raise Danny and Maureen as devout Catholics after his brother's death. Phil hated his uncle for saying this to the Forty Martyrs assemblage while standing in his priestly robes next to Althea's casket. As soon as the funeral was over, he ushered Father Steve out of town and they remained estranged for many years. Phil wanted to like Father Steve, who was his last connection to the family's Nebraska past, but regarded him as deeply conditioned by Catholic fundamentalism, a slave to the dogma and expectations of the Roman Catholic Church.

For Phil, my dad's presence at his mother's funeral brought a sense of unity to his past and future:

> The most wondrous of existential spins was the appearance of your dad at my mom's funeral. I appreciated seeing him, talking to him again. Somehow, looking at him, I got a picture of the future and the past all at once, like that thing in Vonnegut's *Sirens of Titan* where time is like a mountain range, all here at once, and you can see it all if you get to the right altitude.

> Your dad was that mountain range, and the funeral took me to a level of detachment where I could see clearly where this mess had always been and where it was going.

Phil's disdain for Tuscola's primitive brigade of coaches had never extended to my dad. He always loved my dad, beginning with that very first encounter in 1957, after I cut my lip in Marguerite McDaniel's sixth-grade classroom. He remembered my dad this way:

> … out there playing first base on the softball diamond, spryly shooting hoops in the gym. I can see him there, in the dim lights, shooting hoops—a big kid, high hopes, bound to be miserably disappointed, but still popping that hook shot and wondering what was going to become of him.

> And I can see him in church, coming in with your baby sister on his arm, with that lip-sync pointy thing he did when ushering, that there was a seat up there for the lady waiting in the back of the church.

I remember helping him put in the insulation and attic ceiling tiles at your house, his silhouette against the bright light of that front set of gable windows. He was always good to me, and always helped me.

At Althea's funeral, none of the speeches were as good or as sad as the words Phil wrote to me afterwards:

"She had been living in St Augustine these past three years," he said, "but missed the wave for having fun. She was cornered by the time she got here, so God had to run a pawn to the baseline to take a queen so he could close the game and avoid a stalemate."

Althea was buried next to Dr Philip Deaver in the Tuscola Cemetery, in a family plot that awaited the remains of their two children.

Two years after Althea's death, Phil's marriage to Cyndie was on the rocks, and they soon separated. Laura was 11, Daniel was 16, and Michael was a freshman on a soccer scholarship at Rollins College.

Cyndie once told Phil, with a deadly aim he recognised as true, "you don't need a wife, you need a mother."

He never wanted the divorce, which became final in 1998. For the rest of his life, he would have gone back to her, if only he could have found a way. But he couldn't find a way. The genie was out of the bottle, and the bottle was broken.

CHAPTER 24

Her Hardest Hue to Hold

I N 1994, PHIL began an affair with Susan Lilley. It was the final straw leading to Phil and Cyndie's separation and divorce. For years, Cyndie had tolerated his bouts of remoteness. She recognised his desperate need to write stories to feel fully alive. She felt his deep remorse for not having done more during the marriage for her and the kids, for failing to live up to his own exacting standards. But she couldn't share him with another woman.

Phil met Susan at a gathering of poets in 1991, when she was teaching at the University of Central Florida in Orlando. She was on her second marriage, to Paul Strasshofer, an Orlando native and classical double bassist, and she was pregnant with their daughter Anna. It wasn't love at first sight for Phil and Susan. Although they moved in the same circles, they didn't get serious about each other until 1994.

Susan had central Florida DNA. Her grandfather, William Anderson, was an early Orlando developer. Her father, Robert Lilley, was an Orlando lawyer and judge. Her mother, Sue Taylor Lilley, was a dedicated volunteer for worthy causes. Susan had grown up in the leafy neighbourhoods of Audubon Park and Winter Park, a stone's throw from Rollins College. As a local teacher and budding poet, she had connections all over central Florida. She even had a foot in the door at Rollins College.

It's not clear who broke up whose marriage. In all probability, Phil and Susan each had a hand in the other's chaos. In any event, Susan made clear to Phil the terms of their future together. They had come together at their respective crossroads, and it went without saying that they would support each other's writing ambitions. Added to Phil's side of the pact was Susan's demand for the total fidelity he hadn't been able to provide to Cyndie. If Susan ever caught him with another woman, there'd be hell to pay.

Four years later, in 1998, with Susan's help in making the right connections, Phil nailed down the job of his life at Rollins College. The English Department asked him what title he wanted, and he suggested "writer-in-residence." That was agreed, in the understanding that he'd also be teaching creative writing.

But in 1994, before Rollins became a reality for Phil, there were still dues to pay at Wilson Learning. Phil held off from formalising the divorce until 1998, because he couldn't afford the legal and support costs on his Wilson Learning income.

Already he was hanging out at the Rollins College library every chance he got. He said it was his "favorite place."

He wrote to me on Mother's Day 1995, his "third without a mother, second without a wife." Cyndie had moved into a place of her own, with Laura, and Phil stayed behind for a while in the Longwood house with Daniel—"the house we lived in for ten years." Michael continued his studies at Rollins.

Although Phil's salary at Wilson Learning had doubled to $78,000 a year, it was "all gone a day after each paycheck" because he was "buried in debt." His work at Wilson Learning was "life-eating"—he worked at least ten hours a day, plus travel that took him away from his writing and his kids. When he couldn't hide away in the Rollins College library, he had to squeeze time for writing on the road.

Phil still had no money. He remembered one time when he gathered his three kids together for a holiday meal but didn't have enough money to buy food. He drove to a gas station that sold fried chicken. He tried to use his gas card to pay for the chicken, but that wasn't allowed. So Phil went back to his kids empty handed.

Although his publishing opportunities had slowed since 1989—after the spike in interest that followed *Silent Retreats*—he did succeed in placing a handful of stories in literary magazines. "Vasco and the Virgin" appeared in *Tamaqua*, "Forty Martyrs" was published by *The New England Review*, and "The Underlife" made it into *Crazyhorse*. Both "Forty Martyrs" and "The Underlife" were nominated for the Pushcart Prize, with "The Underlife" garnering a "special mention." "Forty Martyrs" made the list of the 100 *Best American Short Stories*.

These were significant achievements, but well short of the goals Phil had set for himself after 1988. And none of his longer manuscripts were getting past the gatekeepers. He feared he'd "probably found [his] natural depth in the literary pond":

> The blocker is a novel. I don't have one, and I'm not fond of trying to write them. They take me two years and, when the two years are over, all that time is gone. I only have about five or six of these blind alleys left in me, and I'm not convinced I can crack the code anyway. Still, the agents all insist on a novel, and never a collection of short stories alone unless you're Updike.
>
> With short stories, I can hone things pretty fine over a few months. It takes me five months to complete a story. I'm frequently writing three at a time, and five stories completed in any year is a bumper crop. Last year, with the Great Divide from Cyndie, one story.
>
> Over the past few years, humility has returned, and my rule of persistence has returned. Surely within my lifetime this pragmatic purity of heart will result in another book. It is all I want and all I ask, Lord.

Although his three kids never warmed to Susan, they were handling Phil's split from Cyndie as well as could be expected. Laura was the one most traumatised by her parents' split, but she maintained her straight-A average and was already excelling at soccer. Phil described her as "attached at the hip" to Cyndie. Laura was reluctant to go to Susan's house, even on holidays.

Phil described Daniel, in appearance the most "Deaver-like" of the children, as "not really of this world." Another A student, Daniel was prolonging his adolescence by playing in a rock band, where he put his anger to good use with Generation X vocals. Michael, the oldest, was a dedicated athlete specialising in soccer and running. He'd found some old ankle weights in Phil's closet, and used them for training. Once upon a time, in Tuscola, Illinois, those same ankle weights had belonged to me.

These three kids meant more to Phil than anything, even his writing. He always wanted them to be proud of him, as a writer as well as a father, and they were. But writing wasn't paying the bills. He felt a lot of Catholic guilt over the family breakup. He stayed with the Wilson Learning company for the money and for no other reason, out of a paternal sense of duty.

In desperation after his separation from Cyndie, Phil told his Wilson Learning employers that he'd go anywhere on a moment's notice—"nothing matters, send me," he said. They ran him ragged from Colombia to Europe to Canada to the East and West coasts of the USA, with clients like GM, Pfizer, and MetLife in New York. On the bright side, his salary continued to rise. But following a corporate sell-off to a Japanese conglomerate, new management swept through Wilson Learning, and (as Phil recalled it) there were two categories of layoffs: "people with dicks and people with grey hair." Phil met both criteria.

A new vice president, ten years younger than Phil, came into his office one day, saying, "Well, Philip, what can *you* do?" Not, what *do* you do, which was the right question if the guy wanted to learn something about staff production.

Phil knew the guy was there to pluck a few cattle from the herd, something he could do without an iota of skin in the game. He saw Phil as old and expensive. Phil had no doubt that the stress from his job had contributed to the end of the marriage, or at least to the end of good communication between him and Cyndie, which led to the end of the marriage.

After the separation, Phil dismissed his literary agent and tried to peddle his own stories, with limited success. He predicted he would "struggle financially all the way to [his] pauper's grave." But as usual, he was being overdramatic.

In 1964, when we graduated from high school, George Orwell's *1984* still seemed a lifetime away. The end of the 20th century was unimaginably distant. And now, as we approached the new millennium, neither of us knew what would happen next in our private lives or otherwise.

Phil entertained the prospect of visiting me in the Australian forest. It was a "remote possibility," in connection with his Wilson Learning work for the ANZ Bank. But it never happened.

PART THREE

CHAPTER 25

A Half-Truth, the Darkest of All

"There are others who sit quietly and unattended in the grass watching serene and childlike with serious eyes. Tender voices caress their ears endlessly and they are beyond sorrow."

Cormac McCarthy

IN THE YEAR 2000, known as Y2K to those who believed that computer glitches would cause planes to drop from the sky like grasshoppers, I returned to central Illinois with half of my blended family. The three older kids stayed behind Down Under, de-blended for a while. A prime motivation for the move was to enable the youngest ones to get to know their paternal grandparents, before they died. And frankly, I was weary of Australia after living there for 20 years.

But it was a mistake. I'd spent the previous ten years living in a forest, with nobody telling me what to do and minimal social interactions. I'd had as much to do with koalas and kangaroos and tiger snakes and wallabies as I'd had to do with people. Now I was going to teach at the University of Illinois College of Law and moonlight with a Champaign–Urbana law firm. Any fool could have seen where this was headed.

It struck me, all over again, that America was fubar—"fucked up beyond all recognition." There were more guns than people, white racism was as entrenched as ever, and before long George W Bush had brought his empty brain to the White House, towers were tumbling in New York City, and America was lying its way into a war in Iraq. And it was more than that. While I was dozing among the eucalypts in the Wombat Forest, Americans had taken a collective turn to the right. Even those who passed for "liberal" in the USA were run-of-the-mill conservatives by Australian standards. And everything in America had become polarised. Ordinary conversations had become exercises in trying to figure out which side somebody was on, while a veneer of smarmy politeness kept the lid on a whole lot of loathing that was ready to pounce at the drop of a hat. At least that's how it seemed to me after emerging from my sanctuary in the Australian bush. Clearly I was headed for trouble.

And already my mother was showing early signs of the frontotemporal degeneration (FTD) that would rob her of her ability to communicate and, ultimately, in 2009, take her life. It was the same disease that would kill Phil Deaver a decade later.

FTD is a cruel and pernicious malady. The areas of the brain associated with personality, behaviour, and language begin to shrink. The common signs include the blunting of emotions, increasing deficits in speaking and writing, socially inappropriate behaviour, and (for some) stuffing oneself with food. FTD is as bad a disease as you can imagine. It negates any hope of penetrating the wall that surrounds the person you knew. It has been compared to having amyotrophic lateral sclerosis (ALS, or Lou Gehrig's disease)—the motor neuron disease that causes the muscles to weaken, twitch, and waste away—combined with dementia. The cause is unknown. It's not easy to diagnose, particularly in the early stages. There is no cure.

In my 2014 novella, *More Deaths than One*, I wrote about the effects of FTD and my mother's slow descent unto death:

> She lived her life, from beginning to end, without a trace of irony. She wanted only to say and do something very plain, over and over again, variations on a theme: 'I love you.'
>
> And she had a small request from beginning to end, a simple need to fill if it wasn't too much trouble. Could you please love her too, please? And could you tell her so?
>
> And when my father turned on her, she didn't know what to do or where to go or who to tell, because she knew that one day his ashes and hers would mix together in the hands of their five children in Morrisonville, Illinois, and scatter to the wind, and that was all that really mattered.
>
> And when the doctors told her she had FTD, all she asked was whether she would recognise her children, and call them each by name, and they said no, she could not do those things. Sooner or later she could not do those things.
>
> So in the rest home, night after night in her simple room across from a field of corn, she recited the letters of the alphabet one by one, just the way she had taught them to schoolchildren during all those years in all those towns, and as long as she could say the letters she could say her children's names, until one by one the letters disappeared, and then she could remember none of them at all.
>
> And in her uncomplicated nature, she may have been the wisest of us all. And we knew it then, and we know it now. I love: therefore I am.

As I was trying to settle into Champaign, Illinois, Phil was settling in at Rollins College. He thought it was a "miracle" that he'd scored such a perfect job. Perhaps, but it wouldn't have been a miracle without the strings pulled by Susan Lilley and her literary friends in Orlando. When she hooked up with Phil, she believed he was a rising star.

In shifting from Wilson Learning to Rollins College, he took a 50 percent pay cut, so initially he was even worse off financially—but now he had a rare tenure track job, and it came with tuition remissions for his three kids. Plus, his lower income meant smaller alimony payments to Cyndie.

Lots of people would have killed for that job. Phil would have killed for it, but he didn't have to. His sudden ability to refer to himself as a "writer-in-residence" must have seemed like winning the lottery—and it came with job security as well as prestige. It was a remarkable and unexpected pathway out of the domestic and social life he had perceived, increasingly, as "bland." He would hold the Rollins College job for nearly 20 years, and when the time came to honour him posthumously, he was best remembered and esteemed as the person he became at Rollins.

I'd written to Phil in September 1998 to tell him I envied "that writer-in-residence business," and that I'd be returning from Australia to central Illinois. "My main goal," I said, "is to play catch with you sometime."

> Tossing a baseball back and forth along a country fence line would be best, next to a highway, with no one around except the occasional passing car. Maybe a cow or two. If that can't be, I'd settle for a back yard. Or a front yard. Or out in the street. Most likely it will be in heaven.

In February 1999, he wrote that he was into his second term as a college professor, and that he was "challenged to get some writing done." He said the odds were that he wouldn't get as much done as he used to in his stolen moments, but that he "must get busy and beat the odds, unto death." He continued to struggle mightily, in everything he wrote, to find endings with a satisfactory conclusion or denouement, and he felt that this blind spot in his creativity coloured the entirety of his output.

His daughter Laura had just suffered her second ACL injury, during Florida's state championship soccer game. Michael had graduated from Rollins College, majoring in psychology. And Daniel was in his second semester as a 21-year-old Rollins freshman.

Six months later, in a letter Phil sent from Father Steve's parish in Scottsbluff, Nebraska, where he was trying to make amends with his uncle, he made his first mention to me of his "girlfriend Susan." Her birthday was coming up, and he saw significance in the fact that her birthday was on the same date as mine—a date that had become "sealed in the vault of long-term memory."

Father Steve's brand of Catholicism puzzled Phil:

> ... a real dip into mainstream Catholic reality. Not the Jesuit intellectual thing—out here they're arguing about married priests and instant baptism and whether the choral director needs to be fired for propositioning the organist. This is a big deal, since they're both male.

> And on and on. Steve's deep into it, as he must be, and one way to look at it is it's a deep dip into community life in America—jails, hospitals, marriages, counseling, religious schools, and don't forget the collection box and Prozac.

Phil was revising, yet again, his "Sadorus" story, which had already been published in *Sou'Wester*. He had bigger plans for it and wanted my edits. Skidmore was the story's anti-hero, "living on borrowed time, the way he always lived." Kraft Foods in Champaign, where I'd worked, and Eastern Illinois University in Charleston, where I'd studied, popped up in the story. Skidmore was back in central Illinois, asking the first-person narrator (guess who?) to hook him up with a married ex-girlfriend named Marcia Barrett, a name that was awfully close to Marcia Truitt, one of my high school girlfriends. The narrator (again, guess who?) caves in and facilitates the liaison, with a little help from Marcia's brothers. After the rendezvous, the brothers give the all-clear as the narrator drives Skidmore to the nearest airport: "Head down, no bags, he walked in the double doors to the little aluminum lobby of Champaign's Illini–Willard Airport. Bye."

At the start of Y2K, after I'd been back in central Illinois for a spell, Phil and I spoke frequently on the telephone. I wrote to him in early 2001, confessing to a growing disdain for what currently passed for American poetry and saying, rather dramatically, that there was "something dead" in me. He replied in May, encouraging me to "try to write poetry of some kind."

He sent me a big box of poems, including works by William Matthews, Louise Gluck, Sydney Lea, Russell Kesler, Marianne Boruch, Mark Jarman, and Jorie Graham. Syd Lea was the guy who'd accepted "Arcola Girls" for *The New England Review*, way back in 1986. Jorie Graham was one of the writers he'd met at Murray State University. Phil thought she was fetchingly beautiful and once asked her, "Aren't you embarrassed by the movie star pictures of you?" Her reply, he said, was "No."

Before his death in 1997, William Matthews had become a great favourite of Phil's. They'd befriended each other in the 1970s following Matthews's Murray State poetry reading. Matthews spoke in Deaver-like language, looking back to youthful memories, looking ahead to mortality, with a touch of baseball thrown into the mix. Phil's box of books included Matthews's 1984 volume, *A Happy Childhood*, and a photocopy of his poem *Days beyond Recall*, about the Spanish-American philosopher George Santayana who had described himself as "an ignorant man, almost a poet." Mathews preferred to think of Santayana as "a student of the future, and thus of the past":

> The older our poet grows, the more past he has
> to love and powder and dandle, nostalgia
> being a dotage, and so he can use up
> his dwindling future like a cake of soap,

or he can turn to that future expectantly,
the way a Jesuit might search his mirror for a skull,
and from the mists of waking and shaving

a skull will burn like Birnam Forest.
Or he can seethe along the fuse of his ignorance—
almost a poet, almost a future, almost dead.

These were words that Phil could have written, in Y2K or at any other time, or wished he had.

In 2001, I went to the Tuscola cemetery in search of the graves of Phil's parents, but couldn't find them. Both Phil and Herb emailed me with an explanation: the two headstones lay flat on the ground, which made them easy to mow around but hard to locate. Phil was annoyed that Tack Green, the funeral director who'd arranged the headstones, had his own grave nearby under a towering monolith.

In April 2002, he emailed me his own heartbreaking prose poem about his father's stone, *The End of the Father*, as good as any words he ever wrote. He placed his narrator alone in midwinter:

There's ice again on the winter-gray grass,
and the trees are stone cold
and the high red light from the Dixie Truck Stop
is all I've got.

There's a rabbit among the headstones,
silent and still, and back against the old road
there's a shadow I can't identify.
There's another road under this snow somewhere,
how the hearse gets from here to there.
There's an owl, or something, in the shadows overhead
washed in the black of winter and the red.
What am I doing here anyway, in Illinois
in the winter in the middle of the night?
My father's headstone is here somewhere.
I should know—
but I can't find it in the snow.

After the wreck,
Tack Green, the undertaker, sold us a plot
and a headstone which would lie flat
so it was easy to mow.
It was summertime, thirty years ago.
That day in the sales room of the morgue,
I really did wonder, trying to think of something else,
how long it would be
before Tack Green himself, hefty and red-faced,
would be lugged out here in his own ambulance
black as coal
and dropped waxy and stonefaced like the rest of us
into a hole.
There's a dream I have that comes day or night;
it's a sound dream, the sound of my father's wreck,
a wild skid, the metallic smash and spray of glass.
So fast and then silence, like the silence out here.
I try to listen deep into that dream, peer into it
like I peer into that shadow along the road,
listening terrified for what I've never heard—
the ghost whisper of my father's last word.

Tonight I can't find his headstone;
it's under ice among other stones
in the area of the era of headstones lying flat.
How long did that last? Well,
I do see Tack Green's stone jutting up
a few rows over which, row by row,
in the cadence of how graves in our town go
would mean eight years or so.

That Tuscola cemetery was a village inhabited by ghosts from our past. After receiving *The End of the Father*, I drove out to the graveyard again, this time with my seven-year-old twins whom I'd taken shoe-shopping at Tuscola's outlet mall. There beneath the sod was Harriet Sluss, our Latin teacher with foul breath in death, no doubt, as it was in life. There were Herb's hardworking parents, Jim and Helen, Craig Sanderson's grandmother Dorcas and his Aunt Shirley, who was good-looking but never married. There was Ray McDuffee, the softball pitcher who played with my dad—he was a guy who could hit as well as he pitched, despite shuffling his feet in the batter's box.

I emailed Phil: "It was a strange experience. The wall between the dead and me disappeared for a little while. Now I'm back in the illusion of the living."

In the summer of 2002, he made the first of a few trips to see me in Champaign. He jotted down directions on a scrap of paper I discovered later in his rental car: "Go west on Kirby. Cross Prospect. Turn left at next traffic lights onto Mayfair. Until you reach 1709. On right."

"Bring your baseball glove," I told him on the phone. I was still hoping for that game of catch I'd mentioned years before.

And he did. I waited for him outside my home, across from the St Matthew's Parish he would later write about in *Forty Martyrs*. I stood across Mayfair Road in the vacant space where people walked their dogs and flew their kites. He drove up slowly in his rented car, checking the house numbers. I flagged him down and he pulled over. As he got out of the car, his baseball glove was already on his left hand.

He took a spot in front of the school, about 60 feet away from me, and I lobbed a St Louis Cardinals souvenir baseball to him. He caught it backhanded, slick as a minor league infielder in his prime, then squared himself around to throw the ball back, a bit harder. We stood there for half an hour, two guys in their mid-fifties, playing burnout just the way we'd done when we were twelve. We didn't say a word. We didn't have to.

We hadn't seen each other in 30 years.

It may not have been *Brokeback Mountain*, but tears welled in our eyes. If it had been *Brokeback Mountain*, Phil would have been

Ennis Del Mar, whose name translated, in a corruption of Irish and Spanish, into "Island of the Sea." I would have been Jack Twist, a name that requires no explanation.

Phil stayed at my house for a few days, befriending my family. He was hard not to like, and my whole family loved him. Just seeing him and being with him, after all those years, was a mystery. He was still the same, but he wasn't. We were still the same, but we weren't.

We spent hours together at the Café Kopi in downtown Champaign, sitting across from each other at a table, drinking coffee and writing. I was polishing off my first novel, *Houseboating in the Ozarks*—which still had the working title "Skidmore's Revenge"— and Phil was working on some new stories.

All the while, he was observant. He noticed small details everywhere, things I didn't see.

"Look at that woman outside the window," he said. I turned and looked and saw a university student peering into the Kopi from the sidewalk. So what?

"She's admiring herself in the reflection," he said.

I looked again. He was right. She wasn't doing anything obvious, like brushing back her hair or adjusting her collar, but she was looking at herself, posing, admiring. I hadn't seen it. It was too subtle. But Phil saw it. He saw behind people's gestures, the way he saw behind photographs. He scribbled something into his red notebook.

That notebook was a treasure trove of bits and pieces that eventually found their way into his stories and poems. For more than 40 years, he'd kept reminders of all aspects of his life and work in one journal after another. The current version even held a sketch of his most recent jogging route.

I introduced Phil to a number of Kopi friends of mine, including the Chicago-based poet Paul Freidinger. Paul had grown up in nearby Monticello, Illinois, and we'd known each other since high school. He studied philosophy at Eastern Illinois University while I was there, and together we played endless games of ping pong and racquetball. We also led a series of anti-war protests that got our photographs into the EIU yearbook and nearly got us expelled. Paul and I were perpetual pen pals, and he and his mother had visited me at my outback home in Australia's Wombat Forest.

Immediately, Paul and Phil hit it off, connecting via their central Illinois background, their shared interest in writing, their politics, and their knowledge of baseball. Paul was to make several trips to Florida to hang out with Phil, including traveling to Jupiter, Florida, to watch Cardinals' spring training games. On one memorable occasion, they bumped into the Cardinals legend Albert Pujols at a Cuban restaurant.

Paul came to know many of Phil's Orlando friends and family members and was bemused by the vast scope of Phil's social life. They became fast friends right up to the end of Phil's life—Paul was to be one of the speakers at Phil's memorial service in Orlando. In some ways, Paul seemed to step into my place in Phil's life—with less contentiousness—after I left for New Zealand in 2006.

At the end of his first visit to Champaign, Phil and I decided to take another road trip together, a short one to St Louis, to another Cardinals game, just like when we were kids. He hoped to see Adam Wainwright, the Cardinals' ace pitcher, in action.

"I like Wainwright," he said, more than once, almost like a mantra.

On our way, we stopped in Tuscola. We drove past Phil's childhood home on Scott Street, which looked about the same to me. He pointed out some trees his dad had planted in the yard, and how big they'd grown.

Before getting back on the road to St Louis, Phil and I drove out to the old Chautauqua grounds at Patterson Springs. The area was all built up now, with lots of houses. We couldn't find the Deavers' old property, and even if we had, there would have been a house on it and we'd have been trespassing. We couldn't find the trees we used to hide in during our army games, or the spot where Billy Adkisson jumped us by popping his head out of the water.

On the way to St Louis, a two-hour trip, Phil tried to get us started on a joint screenplay. As I drove the rented car, he tacked together bits and pieces from our various stories, with lots of dialogue and white spaces on the written pages of our would-be script. We gave our first draft a test run in the car, quoting each other back and forth from years gone by, but outside Mulberry Grove we got a flat tyre, fixed it, and never talked about a screenplay again.

When we got to St Louis, we shared a hotel room at Laclede's Landing. The next afternoon, after brunch at Mike Shannon's restaurant, we strolled along the western banks of the Mississippi as a thunderstorm rolled in from the west. But in late afternoon the lightning stopped and the sun burst through the clouds and we wandered over to the stadium.

As we walked outside the ballpark admiring the statues of Cardinal legends, Phil noticed a homemade shrine in a cranny wedged into an outside wall, fenced off with a makeshift metal barrier. We strolled over for a closer look. There were candles and baseball cards and flowers and coins, tiny wooden baseball bats and jerseys and photographs. One of the people in the photographs was Jack Buck, the long-time radio and TV sportscaster for the Cardinals. Phil and I had listened to him on the radio since the 1950s. He'd died six weeks earlier. The other photographs were of Darryl Kile, a Cardinals pitcher who'd died unexpectedly of a heart attack, four days after Jack Buck. At least Jack was sort of old when he died, at 77. Darryl was only 33. His death was a shock to Cardinal Nation. He was the first active major league player to die in more than 20 years.

One of Darryl's baseball cards, with his picture and his lifetime statistics, was within arm's length. I reached through the metal bars to grab it, but Phil said it would be the very worst form of karma to rob the dead. So I flipped Darryl's card back among the other trinkets.

Inside the stadium, we had great seats behind home plate. Adam Wainwright took the mound for the Cardinals and pitched well for six innings, until the manager, Tony LaRussa, decided to pull him out for a pinch hitter in the bottom of the sixth. Once Wainwright was out, the Mets got hot and beat the Cardinals in extra innings.

"Why the fuck did LaRussa take out Wainwright?" I asked as we were leaving the stadium. "He was rolling along."

"Yeah," Phil agreed. "I like Wainwright."

A few months later, Phil sent me a package from Florida containing the latest draft of *Past Tense*, the novel he'd been working on for years, all 118,206 words of it. His cover letter described it as his "life work." He said there were "400,000 or so words in the boneyard that went into finding my way to this draft".

> ... so the journey is as important as the final version or what happens or doesn't happen when it passes through the literary digestive tract that is the New York publishing industry. That being said, nothing is worth even more time than the time I've put into this already, and moving to the next thing is important.
>
> As you can imagine, I have many disclaimers and explanations to provide about this. But I'll let it stand, with all its surprises (I hope) and disappointments (inevitable) and breakthroughs and wild-ass tangents. If you find typos or inanities that are immediately fixable, I'd love to know about them, and, having read the whole thing, if you suddenly divine another possible title, I'd love to hear it. It began with the working title 'The Reconciliations,' long before Jonathan Franzen scored with *The Corrections*, but I ended up liking *Past Tense* better.
>
> Once you've read this, I'll probably want to get my collection of stories to you, so you can see the opus that 'Vasco and the Virgin' is nestled in the middle of. It is called *Dreams of Her and Other Stories*, and it's the post-*Silent Retreats* short story collection, except for six stories that are set aside in a special

set entitled *Forty Martyrs Suite*. You'll see that thing as a whole also, this summer for sure.

Strange. Even the biggest cities only need one martyr, at most, but Tuscola has a church full of 40. As you probably remember from catechism, the original "Forty Martyrs" were Roman soldiers who openly admitted they were Christians, near the ancient city of Sebaste. The story goes that they were condemned by a pagan prefect to stand naked on a frozen lake till they died. One of them didn't like that idea. He renounced his Christianity so he could warm himself in a nearby cauldron. But when he slipped into the hot water, he died of shock. This caused a Roman guard, Aglaius, to hear voices and see angels. He tossed away his soldier outfit and joined the remaining 39, so the number of martyrs stayed at 40. At daybreak, their stiffened bodies were burned and their ashes were thrown in a river. There's probably a moral there somewhere. *Thirty-nine Martyrs* wouldn't have had the same ring to it.

Phil's *Forty Martyrs Suite* didn't make it into print that summer, and neither did *Past Tense*. In fact, *Past Tense* never made it anywhere.

Past Tense was meant to be Phil's farewell to Skidmore, a liberation from his most problematic character: "Skidmore was all over *Silent Retreats*," he wrote, "and continued to carry on and torment everybody in sight in subsequent stories over the years. He was a lot of fun, but with *Past Tense*, he's done."

The draft of *Past Tense* he sent me had a subtitle: "Skidmore on a Mission." In early drafts, the action began in a hotel room in the Galt House in Louisville, Kentucky, overlooking the Ohio River. I'd stayed there in 1988, when my Australian bluegrass band performed at Louisville's American Musicfest, sharing the stage with the likes of Townes Van Zandt, Mary Chapin Carpenter, and the Austin Lounge Lizards, and I'd sent the play-by-play to Phil.

In *Past Tense*, Skidmore engages in soulless sex in the Galt House with his ex-girlfriend, a nun, before a fire alarm breaks it up. I thought this opening scene was gratuitously pornographic and told Phil so. I took particular exception to the words "bone to bone," which he'd used to describe their congress.

"Jesus," I said.

He removed "bone to bone."

Past Tense was driving him nuts, as had the other four novels he'd worked on for years but never completed. I once made the mistake of suggesting that he put his novels aside and concentrate on his short stories, because that format appeared to be his natural medium. He took my comments as criticism and was offended. The publishing establishment's model was that short stories were baby steps toward becoming a grownup novelist. No one, until Alice Munro, had ever won a Nobel Prize for short stories.

He countered with some advice for an essay I was writing, but his words—particularly his reference to the 44-year-old "leghold"—said as much about his own frustrations as they did about me:

> We make up stories about ourselves, and then we make it our mission to make the stories be true. Stop summing up your life and putting it in a frame. Just revise the motherfucking essay.
>
> I'm sorry I said you were whining. I thought it would make you laugh, actually. But while we're talking about it, let me say that the leghold was a spectacular and foreboding metaphor for my life, and I think I even knew it then. I'm not going into it, because to face these things is to announce one's whole life failure, something I just am not in the mood for right now.
>
> The deal on that is that I will find a way to fail. I will find a way to fail. Two roads diverged in a yellow wood, over and over, and I took the fucking failure road. I'm magic in my ability to do this.

In the end, Phil deep-sixed *Past Tense* after sending a copy of the draft to his friend and mentor, Ann Beattie. She was already a literary star. In her feedback to Phil, she ripped *Past Tense* to shreds. It had some funny parts, she said, but it was a mess. She dismissed it out of hand.

But even after Phil consigned *Past Tense* and his other novels to his bottom drawer, Skidmore kept popping up in his head. In 2009, as Phil was close to pounding 31 years of short fiction scraps into his final book, *Forty Martyrs*, he was still tinkering with Skidmore in "The Kopi," a piece of metafiction he'd begun during our café get-togethers in 2002. He came to regard "The Kopi" as a "failed" effort, as he confessed in a 2016 *TNB Self-Interview*. In fact, the story is among his finest works. It failed only in the sense of not fitting, in tone or voice, into his *Forty Martyrs* book. It has an omniscient point of view, with the author jumping in and out of the lives of his characters. It would have wrecked the novel-like plotting of *Forty Martyrs*.

In the *TNB Self-Interview*, Phil described "The Kopi" as "a semi-fictional version of myself confront[ing] all the [*Forty Martyrs*] characters," including Lowell Wagner, Wally Brown, Carol Brown, Vasco Whirly—and Skidmore. He knocks all his characters upside the head, Vonnegut-style.

The story's elderly Skidmore, like me, was a "cross between Donald Sutherland … and an older Nicholas Cage." Phil made Skidmore's external appearance match his interior life—"partially crippled." He entered his own story to declare that Skidmore's "sixth grader was still there, a ghost flickering in the movement of the shoulders, a shade still young and dancing in the movement of the head and neck, youth gone all but the echoes, but there were echoes real and present." Skidmore's current body language had descended from

> … the movements of the 8th grader on the Canadian fishing trip, the 11th grader self-consciously going into his self-conscious batting stance with his self-conscious facial expression, the adult singing the Neil Young song with the very sincere and trademark 'I'm dead inside' look on his face, the real person so

far beneath the layers, poses, and postures that no one could get at him though a lot of people would have liked to.

The "I'm dead inside" line, describing Skidmore, came straight out of my 2001 letter to Phil. The Canadian fishing trip, the Neil Young songs, the layers, the baseball stance, the self-consciousness—all were very close to home.

Predictably, in "The Kopi," Skidmore-in-his-dotage was "an apologizer—he'd learned to be because he was forever owing apologies, and just as his infractions were wilfully and coldly inflicted, so were his regrets and recantations."

The elderly Skidmore was still a "bad boy all right," someone the narrator had long known to be "toxic and lethal." He had a so-called woman problem, but the narrator turns that into a plus, of sorts: "Every woman, Sylvia Plath said, loves a fascist."

Skidmore and his Creator tangle, and Skidmore, true to form, says harsh words that echo the hurtful things he'd said to Martin Wolf 20 years before in "Silent Retreats":

> 'The truth is, you're stupid,' he said to me. "The poems are awful. I should have told you earlier.' He was getting up. 'Pitiable utterances, really, and terribly dumb.' He got his cane.

> 'The truth is we were never friends. We were always on different planets. Anything good that happens with the shit you're writing, it'll just be because you're a nice guy and have a few friends pulling you along. And,' he said, 'as you know, you're not really a nice guy, either.'

His Creator pulls some strings and delivers a character, Barbara Bender, who cracks Skidmore over the head with his own vintage Martin guitar, leaving "cherrywood splinters all over the Kopi floor." But even after that—on the last page of what may be the last short story Phil Deaver ever finished—"Skidmore was out there somewhere, and we weren't done yet."

In 2004, I flew down to Orlando for a return visit. Phil and Susan Lilley were living together now, in her mother's house. Phil called it "the Lilley pad." I stayed with them for a few days and managed to behave myself—although I did wear a stripey-tailed Davy Crockett hat the whole time I was there. In a way, my good behaviour was unfortunate, because it created a comfort zone for Phil's friends and set the stage for my second visit in 2006, which was a total disaster.

In 2004, Phil showed me around the Rollins College campus, introduced me to a few of his students and colleagues, and gave me a guided tour of the Cornell Fine Arts Museum, which bored me shitless.

One of his friends, Hoyt Edge—a philosophy professor and coordinator of Rollins College's Australian Studies programme—swore he remembered me from a sabbatical he'd taken in 1991. It was possible. Not far from Rollins College, in a prison cell in Melbourne, Florida, was an Aboriginal inmate by the name of Russell Moore. At the age of 26, he'd been convicted of a cocaine-fuelled sexual assault and strangulation of an interior designer named Barbara Ann Barber, in an alley behind her showroom.

Hoyt had been trying to help Russell for years, working with authorities in Florida and Australia to get Russell shipped back to Australia to serve a life sentence instead of rotting on death row in America. He'd met with Russell numerous times in the prison.

"He's a really nice guy," he told me, perhaps unmindful of the irony of using such words to describe a convicted murderer. "He never should have been in America in the first place." But Hoyt's efforts to get Russell shipped back to Australia proved to be unsuccessful. Russell was destined to die in his Florida prison in 2021.

At the time of Hoyt's 1991 sabbatical to Australia, I happened to be working with Russell's birth mother, Beverley Moore Whyman, with the shared goal of getting him home from Florida. I got together with Beverley and several of her friends—Aboriginal elders—at the Aboriginal Legal Services office in the inner suburb of Fitzroy, Victoria. I even wrote a protest song about her son—"Koori Man," with the repeated chorus line that "he ain't got no business on death row"—which I performed live at a few Aboriginal gatherings and which later appeared on two of my albums.

Beverley was only 14 when Russell was born, which is why he was taken away from her under Australia's racist child removal policy, which resulted in generations of stolen Aboriginal children. Russell's white adoptive family, the Savages, renamed him "James Savage" and removed him to the American South. They were fundamentalist Christians with missionary zeal. During Russell's murder trial in Florida, his adopted name led to sensationalist media coverage (e.g., "Savage is as Savage does"). But after his conviction, he changed his name back to the birth name Beverley had given him—Russell Moore.

Hoyt Edge had visited that same Aboriginal Legal Services office in Fitzroy, Victoria, and met a white American lawyer who was working on Russell Moore's case. I didn't remember Hoyt, but he remembered me.

During my first trip to Rollins College in 2004, Phil and I attended a book reading by a pallid middle-aged man who'd dyed his hair black to pass himself off as Lakota. He offered secret insights into Wakan Tanka and the Sacred Hoop, in the manner of the late "Native American" writer "Jamake Highwater" (real name: Jack Marks, a journalist of Eastern European Jewish ancestry who misrepresented himself as Cherokee/Blackfoot). The fake Lakota man was accompanied by a silent woman whose dyed hair was as black as his. The Winter Park crowd was lapping it up. Real Indians!

During an interval, I approached these two phonies and asked after several Lakota men and women I knew—Sidney Uses Knife, Madonna Thunder Hawk, Cheeto Mestes, Frank Fools Crow, Gib LeBeau, and Brenda Fast Horse. Any genuine Lakota would have been familiar with one or more of those people, but these two charlatans didn't know any of them. They countered by dropping a few activists' names they'd picked up from newspaper articles—Russell Means, Dennis Banks, and Leonard Peltier. During the second half of their reading, with me eyeballing them from beneath my Davy Crockett hat, they were nervous wrecks.

Phil got a hoot out of my exposé, but some of the other people at the reading were offended. They thought my intimidation was racist. I didn't care. White imposters like these two were legendary on the reservations. There was no end to white exploitation of Indians. Such poseurs were known to Indians as "varionatives," a word coined by Gerald Vizenor (Minnesota Chippewa) in his book *Fugitive Poses*.

Before I flew back to Champaign, Phil and I drove to a Cardinals spring training game at Roger Dean Stadium in Jupiter, Florida. The trip was about two and a half hours long, so in the late afternoon we stopped in Port St Lucie for the night. Phil pointed out a hairdresser's shop across the street from the motel.

"This is Rick Ankiel's hometown," he said. "I want to show you something."

Rick Ankiel was a St Louis Cardinal pitcher who'd had a tremendous rookie year in Y2K, at the age of 20, when he went 11–7 with a 3.50 ERA and was named by *The Sporting News* as the "Rookie Pitcher of the Year." The Cardinals made the postseason that year, and Tony LaRussa chose Ankiel to start Game One of the National League Division Series against future Hall-of-Famer Greg Maddux of the Atlanta Braves. Ankiel didn't allow a run through the first two innings, but his performance suddenly deteriorated in the third. He gave up four runs on two hits, four walks, and five wild pitches before LaRussa took him out. Ankiel joked that he was the first major league pitcher since 1890 to throw five wild pitches in a single inning.

In his next start, he was removed in the first inning after throwing 20 pitches, the first of which sailed over the head of Braves batter

Timo Perez. Four more wild pitches evaded the glove of Cardinals catcher Eli Marrero.

In his third postseason game, Ankiel came on in relief, faced four hitters, walked two, and threw two more wild pitches. In years to come, Ankiel could never regain his control from the pitcher's mound.

Phil believed he knew the secret of Ankiel's collapse. His source was Ankiel's high school sweetheart, a St Lucie hairdresser. Phil pointed her out through the shop's glass window. She'd cut Phil's hair a few months back.

"Drugs," he said. "She told me Ankiel was high on cocaine every time he took the mound."

I don't know whether that was true or not, about the drugs, but it was the kind of fall from grace that Phil chewed like catnip, especially when baseball heroes were involved.

That night in our motel room, I woke at about three o'clock to pee, and Phil was sitting in a chair under a dim light, writing God-knows-what in his little red notebook. Probably more ruminations on the mind and soul of Skidmore, sparked by our road trip to a ball game.

On the way back to Orlando after the game, we talked about those old divisions between us—the 1966 rumour about Phil's dad, and my trip back to Tuscola from Rensselaer with Althea in 1968. Phil said these things were "still a problem" for him, "perhaps the deepest problem between us for over thirty years." So all over again, as we stared ahead down the highway, I explained that I hadn't started any rumour about his dad and that nothing had happened with his mother. As always, his left brain seemed to accept these truths, but his right brain couldn't let go. He said these things were buried in his heart.

Later that year, Phil came back to Champaign for another visit. Once again, he stayed at my home, and this time he established himself as a legend in the eyes of my kids by capturing our Australian bearded dragon, which had escaped outdoors from its homemade cage. We thought we'd seen the last of it. I still don't know how Phil did it. I'd cornered enough lizards in the Australian outback to know that grabbing hold of them wasn't a walk in the park. But when the kids got home from school, the bearded dragon was back in its cage and Phil was their hero. Phil wrote to explain:

> I was coming out to your pool for a swim and I looked over to the side of the deck, and I saw this lizard there, sitting in the sun next to the trampoline. And at first I didn't think anything of it, because we have thousands of lizards in Florida. But then I did a double-take and thought, Jesus, that thing's huge, and they sure don't have lizards like that in Illinois!

> So I got down on my hands and knees, next to the Buddha statue, and snuck across the deck until I was close enough to grab it. But it darted back under the porch. At least, I thought, I could say I'd seen it and it was okay.

> So I went back to get a towel, and when I came back out, there it was again! Just to the left of that Japanese maple. But this time its back was turned. It was almost like it was *asking* to be caught, but didn't want to take responsibility.

> So I got down on all fours again and snuck along the pine, and this time when I reached out it fit right into the palm of my hand. It didn't even struggle.

"Gosh, Dad," my youngest son said. "You sure do have nice friends."

Phil and I drove down to St Louis for another Cardinals game. This time the Cardinals were playing the Cubs—a great Midwestern rivalry—and we were part of Busch Stadium's largest regular season crowd since 1997. The Cardinals were hot—20 games over .500, their fourth best start in franchise history. The Cubs were mediocre at 46–39, and the Cardinals clobbered them 6–1 that afternoon.

But we didn't get to see Wainwright pitch again. Instead, Jason Marquis was on the mound for the Cardinals, and he was in top form, scattering nine hits in eight innings. It didn't hurt his cause that the Cardinals knocked four home runs out of the park. But our favourite moment in the game was when Tony LaRussa got kicked out by the home plate umpire for arguing over a called strike.

The next morning, back in our hotel room, Phil and I ordered room service breakfast and shared a copy of the *St Louis Post-Dispatch*.

"Look at this," said Phil, pointing to the front page of the sport section. The lead article was about the previous night's game, written by a local sportswriter named Dan O'Neill. Phil read it to me word for word. He was so impressed with O'Neill's writing that he cut out the article and stuck it in his wallet.

Three years later, that newspaper item became the opening piece in *Scoring from Second: Writers on Baseball*, the book Phil edited in 2007. It was amazing to think O'Neill may have written this well every day, unheralded, for a sports page in a Midwestern newspaper. To give you an example of his descriptive prowess, here's one of a dozen casual lines from his article, this one describing Albert Pujols's line-drive home run in the bottom of the sixth inning: "Pujols led off with a rope that got out of the park quicker than Mike Tyson ran out of money."

CHAPTER 26

Before the Devil Knows You're Dead

A<small>FTER MY TRIP</small> to Orlando in 2004, I got serious about gathering my scraps of written words into some sort of novel. I hadn't saved any of this stuff on a computer, so I had to work from bits and pieces of paper I'd lugged back with me from Australia. I had in mind a picaresque form with an overriding theme of circularity, inspired by T. S. Eliot's *Little Gidding*, the fourth and final poem of *Four Quartets*:

> We shall not cease from exploration
> And the end of all our exploring
> Will be to arrive where we started
> And to know the place for the first time.

I settled on a clichéd American structure—a road trip by car through the Midwest by "Duane Leonard Skidmore" and his two youngest children, with flashbacks to real-life experiences—family lore, Lakota and Aboriginal spirituality, liberation theology, the St Louis Cardinals, bluegrass music, failures to communicate. The novel would be told in third person limited, with a narrator seeing things from Skidmore's perspective and with the thoughts and feelings of other characters filtered through Skidmore's warped sense of the world. Skidmore would be intentionally incomplete, almost two-dimensional, sort of like the all-knowing billboard eyes of Fitzgerald's Dr Eckleberg in *The Great Gatsby*. The novel would be sandwiched within a frame, a foreword and an afterword told in the first person by a guy named "Finbar Studge"—a/k/a Philip Deaver—who would provide a context for Skidmore's meanderings.

"Finbar" was a twist on Phil's middle name, Fintan, which he found embarrassing as a child. The surname, "Studge," came from *Breakfast of Champions*, in which Kurt Vonnegut linked the name "Philboyd Studge" to cumbersome writing and assigned it to his metafictional self.

As a point of fact, Vonnegut had his alter ego's first name wrong. "Filboid Studge, the Story of a Mouse that Helped" was written by the Edwardian satirist Saki, and the original Filboid Studge was not a writer, or even a human, or a mouse, but an eponymous breakfast food that started flying off the grocery shelves after a counterintuitive advertising campaign.

My Finbar Studge would be the fictional editor of (the late) Duane Leonard Skidmore's posthumously published manuscript. (After completing his novel, my Skidmore disappeared under suspicious circumstances.) Studge would recall his childhood friend "sitting in a gently rocking boat at Patterson Springs, near the old Chautauqua grounds, with his father Leonard":

> In this snapshot from my memory, Duane Skidmore is only twelve years old, and his whole life stretches before him endlessly, for ever and ever. In my remembrance, he smiles as the sun catches the ripples on the water, and the lake seems alive with a thousand twilight fireflies. In his high pre-adolescent voice, and higher spirits, he sings with his father, round and round and round:
>
> Row row row your boat
> Gently down the stream
> Merrily merrily merrily merrily
> Life is but a dream.

Skidmore's Revenge (the working title) drew on an actual trip I'd made with my young twins—a son and a daughter—to the Lake of the Ozarks, where we'd rented a houseboat for a few days. In the middle of the second night, I discovered that hurricane-force winds were pounding the boat. To make matters worse, the boat had become unmoored and was floundering somewhere in the darkness. I couldn't see a thing except when strobes of lightning flashed. The twins stayed asleep through the storm. I managed to climb into the water, stark naked, swim to shore while gripping a long rope, and retie the boat to a tree, but I cracked my head and cut my arm. Gradually, the storm died out and the houseboat began to rock like a cradle. I dropped off to sleep, dreaming about my parents and years gone by.

In my novel, Skidmore would do the same. Then, he and the twins would complete their circular journey home, and upon arrival, Skidmore—with his occasional urge to purge—would stroll across the street to St Matthew's Catholic Church for an evening confession. Kneeling inside the confessional, he would wonder out loud what the hell he's doing there, but the priest would talk him into staying. Skidmore would conjure up a sin worthy of confession, telling the priest about a woman he'd had an affair with back in Australia—a woman whose husband murdered her. Skidmore would tell the priest that he felt responsible for her death. The priest would sigh and forgive but assign an unusual penance. Skidmore would be obliged to find a pew in the darkness of the church and stare at the crucifix above the altar. Nothing more. Just look at Jesus nailed to the cross.

Skidmore would do as he's told, and in a moment of epiphany he would come to understand the symbolism of the cross as the opposite of the metaphorical journey he had just completed. The lines of a cross didn't complete a circle. They didn't come back to where they started. Instead, the lines each pointed away to eternity from the heart of their intersection. In my novel, Skidmore would experience a sudden mystical connection with everyone and everything in his life—past, present, and future. All the people he'd ever known would have a resting place along the extended arms of the crucifix, and Skidmore would be at peace.

But being Skidmore, his sense of harmony would be short-lived. At Sunday mass the following morning, the priest would read a gospel passage about Jesus being led into the desert to be tempted by the devil—Matthew 4:1-11—and interpret it as meaning that, with one exception, Jesus was tempted in every way, like the rest of us. The exception, according to the priest, was that Jesus was never tested by any need to redress sins of his own—because he didn't commit any.

"Some test," Skidmore would snarl as he fumbled with rosary beads in the church's back pew. "Some test." After all, he would remind his readers, what kind of saviour curses a poor fig tree (Mark 11:20-25; Matthew 21:18-22) and makes it wither from its roots, never to yield again? What kind of guy frightens a poor farmer's drove of pigs over a cliff to drown, on the rationale that the pigs were demons (Mark 5:1-20; Matthew 8:28-34)? What kind of criminal vandalises merchants' tables and scatters their precious doves (Mark 11:15-18; Matthew 21:12-13)? What kind of sexist tells a woman who's crawling across the floor begging for food crumbs that she's a dog (Matthew 15:26)? These cruelties may or may not have been sins, exactly, but clearly Jesus could have done with a little anger management from time to time.

Before mailing the novel to prospective publishers or agents, I sent a manuscript to Phil. I'd changed the title from *Skidmore's Revenge* to *Houseboating in the Ozarks*, along the lines of Richard Brautigan's 1967 novella, *Trout Fishing in America*—a change that provided Phil with a sigh of relief. He suggested some word changes and structural shifts and had some nice things to say.

"Incredible, fantastic, superbly written," he wrote. "In many places poetic in just the right way so you can get away with it in the third person limited voice of your main character."

He threw in a few more adjectives: the writing was "exquisite," with "gorgeous lines" and "smart turns."

> The chapters end on just the right notes, carefully, to deliver powerful ironies and smart points and poetic flourishes that are never showy, always embedded in the fictional reality and completely right in tone and voice.

And he wasn't satisfied by heaping such over-the-top praise on my manuscript. In keeping with his lifelong self-deprecation, he also had to put himself down, saying that his own writing was "awful" and that my sentences were "so much better" than he "could ever do." This was absurd, and I told him so.

But together with his positive feedback, he had some concerns, mainly with my failure to "adequately fictionalize" the novel's supporting cast. Except for "Duane Leonard Skidmore," I'd used people's real names in the manuscript (the way Jack Kerouac did in his early drafts of *The Dharma Bums*), and Phil advised that now that the story was complete, I could "change all the names, and it won't hurt the novel at all. You've had enough use from the real names—they helped you focus and do characterization, etc." He wanted "the Deaver name out of it, and Freidinger's, and Budden's, and Sanderson's," and he said that "whoever else's actual names are in there should be out also. Use a phone book." This was good advice, and I followed it.

A bigger concern was that I'd camouflaged a lot of real-life incidents from our actual backgrounds—his and mine—and even with the names changed it wouldn't be hard to figure out who was who. He wanted big revisions to those passages. In asking me to separate my work from his, he used a fishing metaphor drawn from our childhood trip to Canada's Lac Seul. I needed to do a better job of disguising identities "so we, in our separate writing careers, aren't tangled up in each other's lines."

And he didn't stop there:

> Skidmore comes out of this novel looking pretty good, in that exasperating way the audiences always were positively taken by my own Skidmore character. But you've written a novel that is a time bomb in your own family. That's the incubus that lurks within *Houseboating in the Ozarks*. If you publish it as it is, many people in your family will be devastated.
>
> Because you have interestingly and ostensibly (you have your secrets and your limits on self-revelation) wide-open borders to your own privacy, and are (ostensibly, though you have your limits) willing to self-deprecate and try to make Skidmore the bad guy as a shield for your defense of some rough handling of loved ones, you assume people will go along with it. You aren't respecting their privacy because in a way you think that privacy is hypocritical and perhaps even telling a lie.
>
> These things are fixable before you publish, but some of them (the parental things) pose the need for a deep revision that will cause the novel to take two more years to write, from start to finish, which is about how long it takes us mortals. And the book will be better fiction, better psychology, and just plain better. You have to ask yourself why you would resist that.

He wasn't wrong, but his advice put me in a tight spot. I didn't mind changing the names of characters. In the end, I even changed "Duane Leonard Skidmore" to "Christian Leonard Hooker," which was a better name anyway. But I couldn't write Phil's kind of book, and I didn't want to. I couldn't start hacking out pages and paragraphs—it would destroy the flow. To put this another way, I wasn't good enough to write the kind of book he wanted and I sure as hell wasn't going to spend two more years trying to do it.

I wasn't cut out to be a people pleaser. Unlike Phil, I didn't care what past friends or family thought of me or my book. Tuscola, Illinois, may have been his ancestral and spiritual home, his "middle of the middle," but it wasn't mine. The only reader I really wanted to make happy was me, with him running a close second. By the time I'd finished *Houseboating in the Ozarks*, I was untroubled by the likelihood of offending certain people.

"When a writer is born into a family," said the Polish poet Czeslaw Milosz, "the family is finished." I didn't want to go that far, but I didn't want to hold back for fear of hurting people's feelings.

Phil was even more exercised about my plagiarism. I'd shamelessly lifted a paragraph about my Hooker, a/k/a Skidmore, straight from *Silent Retreats*, and put it in the mouth of Finbar Studge, in an indented paragraph in *Houseboating's* foreword:

> Hooker was a razzle-dazzle guy. He could unanswer more questions in a week than most men in a lifetime. It had become a pattern in his life. Give him a relationship and a couple of months on his own resources, and Hooker could bring more ruination than whole defoliation programs, whole societal collapses, whole holy wars.

Not only that, I'd ripped off some lines from one of Paul Freidinger's early poems, *Be Like Water*, and put them in the mouth of Hooker's precocious eight-year-old daughter, Sharon Hooker, who wrote verse in her diary accompanied by drawings of stick-like creatures wailing away with oversized teardrops.

"If that happened to me," Phil said, "it would annoy the fuck out of me, I'll tell you that."

I guess it would annoy the fuck out of most people. But it wouldn't have annoyed the fuck out of me, and Freidinger never said a word about it.

Phil drafted an "attribution paragraph" to fix the plagiarism:

> Certain small pieces of this text, 310 words in all, were taken from the work of Philip F. Deaver and Paul Freidinger. Used by permission.

"It's assholey but also not right to do otherwise," he said. "It's a toxic issue. Act before it's too late."

I resisted. "Plagiarism is so last century," I replied in my smart-aleck way. I reminded Phil of how many written words from my own letters he'd lifted verbatim for *Silent Retreats*. I argued that Shakespeare stole plots and language from published sources—in *Antony and Cleopatra*, for example, the Bard of Avon cribbed from Plutarch's description of the Egyptian queen floating down the Nile on a barge of gilded splendour.

In his mounting anxiety, Phil evoked *The Exorcist*.

> You're like the little girl in that movie when the devil is expelled from her but first her eyes have to turn into red lights, her head does a three-sixty, and green bile gurgles out of her mouth. I don't know how come this is so painful for you. A little attribution paragraph, as I wrote for you, is all that's needed.
>
> You didn't do anything wrong, and I wasn't accusing you of doing anything wrong. You *do* have permission from Freidinger and me, but in this climate, that's not enough.
>
> My attribution paragraph will cover your publisher also. Or if the publisher doesn't think the paragraph is needed, it might at least want short letters from me and Freidinger granting permission, sitting in its files as back-up.
>
> If you do this small thing, it will rank in retrospect with the change of Skidmore's name to Hooker as among the smart things you did to place this book on a solid footing.
>
> Don't be mad at me. I'm a mere earthling, and your pal.

Phil was being perfectly reasonable, but I didn't want to do it. To my way of thinking, I'd already given him credit by gifting one of his Skidmore paragraphs to Finbar Studge, his alter ego. And Freidinger didn't care.

In the end, Phil gave up the fight for attribution, but he still had two big worries. In separate passages in the novel's epilogue, written by "Studge," I mentioned the 1966 party rumour about his dad and the 1968 motel scene with his mother, albeit with names changed. Herb became "Ellinghaus." Phil's dad became "Harry Studge." Althea was "Rosa." I was "Hooker." In the epilogue, poor old Hooker can't imagine why Studge was *still* mad at him after all those years— "especially when it was only [Hooker] and nobody else who came over the night his father died and sat with him in the Rambler station wagon outside his house for a couple of hours."

For Phil, horsing around with the memory of his parents, even when camouflaged, smacked of revenge. He believed I was trying to get even because his short story, "Infield," had fingered my dad and me as the sources of the rumour about Dr Deaver:

> I'd like for you to delete every thinly disguised reference to my mom and dad from your book. This is possibly your long-awaited revenge for my brutal inclusion of aspects of you in my character Skidmore, and you may figure it's okay, under the Layer System, to do it back to me. After all, your working title was 'Skidmore's Revenge.' Bingo.
>
> Years later, I've understood your explanations for what happened at the party and what happened in that motel room, blah blah blah, but at the time those things hit simple little Danny Deaver with the precise force you knew they would, and if you didn't know how they would hit me, then you're fucking autistic or insane or something. Actually, they're the meanest things that ever happened to me.
>
> If you don't jerk all the stuff about my parents, I'll still be a friend and I'll still be a huge and jealous admirer of your talent. I'll also understand how in a smart adult author the Layer System can work to accomplish a very sophisticated and ironic version of revenge—and I'll understand at last that it hurt you that I was mad at you all those years (you couldn't see why), to call

you mean and to 'brutally' base the original Skidmore on you. If I was wrong to do it, your novel contains exponentially more wrongs, or perhaps you're squaring accounts all around and not just with Studge. Something in you WANTS to do it.

He said he was struggling with how much of this same history to include in *Past Tense*, which was still a continuing nightmare for him, even after Ann Beattie's savage criticism led him to scrap it. He kept resurrecting it for the rest of his life.

Maybe it's time for you to say that Skidmore in the version of *Past Tense* you're familiar with was troublesome for you, even though there is less connection between you and him than before, or so I say. Perhaps you, having fallen fully on the Skidmorian sword, would like some greater input on this character in *Past Tense*.

Let me know because I'm in the middle of another revision and can move load-bearing walls if anything in this almost-certainly-not-to-be-published work has privately gnawed at you or pissed you off. Just say. One good turn deserves another.

Frankly, I'd rather not go into these particular things about my parents in my own novel and be guilty of exposing them to renewed rumors, in fact reviving them and spreading them just to make my novel work.

In that spirit, he suggested a tit-for-tat, encouraging me to find "some fictional parallel thing" instead of alluding to the 1966 and 1968 incidents in *Houseboating in the Ozarks*.

The truth was, as he knew, that his characterisation of Skidmore never caused me any pain at all, so there was no tat to exchange for a tit. I wrote back to tell him so.

"You didn't hurt me and never put me in mind for paybacks," I wrote. "You are way off the mark."

There is nothing in *Silent Retreats* or *Past Tense* that causes me any trouble. I want you to work on your novel with absolute and complete artistic freedom, and if you want my father and mother to drop dead or copulate with dogs who eat their flesh afterwards, that's okay with me. Whatever works for you. Grab the golden ring. *Past Tense* is very, very good in my estimation, and I wouldn't tinker with it much if I were you. Stick to your guns. Mull it over and do what you and you alone decide to do with it.

I never said anything negative about your parents. Even the two things in *Houseboating* that got you so upset weren't negative about them. You really shouldn't have reacted to either of those things in the first place, let alone carry them with you for thirty years.

In February 2005, I received a letter from the president of Dufour Editions in Pennsylvania, thanking me for sending him my manuscript of *Houseboating in the Ozarks*. "I'm rather fond of it," he wrote, "and would like to publish it."

Phil said he was happy I'd found a publisher, but fretted that after our 2004 heart-to-heart on the drive back from Jupiter to Orlando, I may simply have "mainlined [his] expressions of concern, in a gleefully mischievous and mean way, straight into the book along with [his] expressions of resistance." He said he planned to celebrate my success, "unless the book sees print in a way clearly designed to piss me off." I wrote back to raise the white flag of surrender.

"Here's what I'll do," I said. "I'll take out anything you want me to take out, or rewrite anything the way you want, regardless of what the publisher says. I do ask that your feedback come quickly, because things are moving fast at this end." I added: "Frankly, I don't even care if the publisher pulls the plug and rejects my book, because friendship is more important than a stupid novel."

I was starting to get agitated. I expanded the email conversation to include Herb Budden and Paul Freidinger, as well as Phil:

Deaver still objects to a stream-of-consciousness passage near the end of the novel, where Hooker is speculating why his old

186

friend Studge has been so annoyed with him over the years.
There is no meanness in it, and Hooker comes clean that there
was nothing to either one of the subject matters. There is no
maligning of anyone dead or alive, unless it's Hooker himself
and his own extended family. Hooker gets the brunt of it in
the whole novel. Deaver himself broadcast at least one of these
matters very clearly and unambiguously in his excellent story
'Infield,' ten times more than my tiny reference at the end of
this thing, which (like everything else in this solipsistic novel)
is Hooker-directed.

It is hard to take this stuff out, because it is a sort of central
meditation by Hooker about his difficulty in making or
maintaining friendships. Hooker's sensitivity is not like other
people's. He can't figure out why these things happen. Basically,
people just don't like him, which he doesn't complain or feel
sorry about, he just ponders it. He knows what the problem is,
his lack of understanding of the most basic shared sensitivities
of a civilized society—but he either can't or won't do anything
about it.

I love Deaver a whole lot, and I loved his parents who were
very very good and great people. By opening my big mouth in
my twenties I pissed him off and hurt his feelings, but neither
of the two subjects should have had that result. I didn't start
the rumor about his dad, and I never believed it to be true, and
even if it was true I couldn't have cared less. And the other
rumor about his mother was nothing at all, absolutely nothing,
except for me being an asshole by mentioning it. Certainly
Deaver's mother was entirely blameless, and was guilty only of
being very sad because her son was going off to college and her
husband and father had just been killed. There were no sexual
undertones or overtones at all except in my juvenile mind.

But to this day, neither Hooker nor I can figure out why it was
such a big deal, and to this day I can't figure out why Deaver
can write all sorts of shit about Skidmore that everybody in
Tuscola and everywhere else knows is about Forrester and the

writing portrays him as a very bad person, mean and nasty and awful, and the real-life me didn't care a whit about this or about being what most people would regard as being "maligned," but Deaver is so damned sensitive about things!

Hooker wouldn't care WHAT Studge said about Hooker or Hooker's parents or Hooker's dog, and that's not to say that I have the moral high ground or that Deaver has it, or anything at all except that Hooker is just weird and can't figure out why people get so excited about this stuff. IN NO WAY IS ANYTHING IN MY NOVEL 'DESIGNED TO PISS OFF' Deaver or anyone else.

I heard nothing more from anybody. I emailed Phil to thank him for all his help in editing the manuscript. I also emailed Herb, thanking him for his suggestions along the way. Herb replied that he was "very fucking pleased and happy" for me. He said he knew how much "heart and soul and sweat" I'd put into the book. He thought it had "something most other modern fiction doesn't have—readability." He asked for a signed copy when it came out.

Contrary to what Phil may have thought, I hadn't "mainlined" anything, from the Jupiter conversation or anything else. And I didn't feel mean. And when the book was published, the stuff about Studge's mom and dad—with names changed and stories camouflaged—stayed in.

CHAPTER 27

Drop by Drop upon the Heart

IN THE SPRING of 2005, Phil's book of poetry, *How Men Pray*, was released. Anyone who needs convincing about Phil's artistry and versatility needs to read this collection, start to finish—and re-read it. With each visit, there will be new rewards. Phil took his time with all his prose and poetry, but what he produced in *How Men Pray* was magical.

His poems are at once heartbreaking and comforting—"snapshots of the legendary America of promise and disappointment," wrote the poet Carol Frost, "a mixture of colloquial address, irony, and tenderness toward our losses and our loneliness." The only thing missing was Phil's own appreciation of how good a poet he'd become. As Richard Goodman was to observe, Phil "was a better poet than maybe he thought he was or wanted people to think he was."

The award-winning poet from Purdue University, Marianne Boruch, who (unbeknownst to Phil and me) had spent her youthful summers in Tuscola as we were growing up, reviewed Phil's work:

> *How Men Pray* is a book of dreams and remembering, of the slow shining way the past swallows us and we survive, almost.

Here, there's a father's watch with blood on it, a sister's small pink dress, a mother's four weeks to live, a grandfather's magnifying glass that enlarges a lost world. Philip Deaver slips through such things, painful and treasured, and calls back to us.

Phil sent me a signed copy of *How Men Pray*. The book was dedicated to the memory of his parents, "Philip and Althea," and my copy came with an inscription hearkening back to the beginnings of our escapades at Patterson Springs: "For Forrester—from your blood brother. PFD."

Phil was delighted with the reception for *How Men Pray*, and another burst of readings followed in Florida, Illinois, and elsewhere. I was able to get along to two of them, in Champaign and Tuscola.

The Tuscola reading was hosted by Flesor's Candy Kitchen. Known simply as "Gus's" in the old days, the Candy Kitchen had been established by Gus Flesor in the 1920s, and it was Tuscola's favourite high school hangout for generations. Gus retired in 1969, and his son Paul closed the business in 1975. Its fixtures were purchased by an antique dealer who stored them in a warehouse.

Twenty years later, against all odds, Gus's granddaughters Devon and Ann reopened the Candy Kitchen, providing life support for Tuscola's dying downtown area. They were able to salvage Gus's original fixtures—the marble soda fountain, wooden booths, etched-glass mirrors, and stained-glass lamps. Every stool, copper kettle, popcorn machine, and glass candy case was safely accounted for.

Marianne Boruch had driven over from Purdue University to join Phil at the Tuscola reading. She recalled that her grandfather, one of the few Democrats in Tuscola while she was growing up, and Gus Flesor—a diehard Republican—had been good friends. She read several works from her latest volume, *Poems: New & Selected*, with precision and control, and without dramatic mannerisms or eccentricities. Every word in every line seemed perfectly chosen and articulated. Then it was Phil's turn.

It was the first time I'd seen him at a podium, and his gift for poetry was equalled by his rapport with the local crowd. He delivered his lines with a slow, steady, melodious voice. I don't know if Tuscola realised how lucky it was to have two poets of this calibre in a small town. It may not have been the San Francisco Renaissance, but Boruch's *I Imagine the Mortician* and Phil's *The Train Along the Toe* were right up there with Ferlinghetti and Ginsberg, Snyder and McClure. After the readings, they sat next to each other on Gus's fountain stools to sign their books.

Phil's next reading, at Champaign's *Pages for All Ages* bookstore, was a solo presentation, and it was equally well-attended. A few of his admirers drove up to Champaign from Tuscola, and Phil read *Fossils* for them, a poem about our old friend Billy Adkisson of Patterson Springs fame, who found a trilobite "among the rocks, / that collected on the bank / when the water was higher – / it was encased in stone, / a perfect specimen."

I was seated on a folding chair next to our former Tuscola High School classmate, Janet Ochs, who'd been the inspiration for Phil's short story "Sadorus." We listened as he carried us from Billy's triolobite to a Florida cemetery:

> The woman buried here last week
> had many friends
> whose flowers wilt on her grave today.
>
> The man next to her
> doesn't share her name—
> she's buried
> forever in the ground, closer to him
> than she might have been willing to stand
> while waiting for stamps at the post office—
> who knows,
> in the clatter and crunch of things now,
> whose dead profile staring up we'll rot beside,
> whose blood will mix with ours

when the tap root of the post oak
pries open our shells
and a chance tilt of the land
allows the water through?

Phil's poetry soon came to the attention of Garrison Keillor, the raconteur who created *A Prairie Home Companion* and, since 1993, hosted *The Writer's Almanac*, a daily radio program of poetry and historical interest pieces. To Phil's enduring astonishment and joy, Keillor selected two of his poems—the sardonic *The Worrier's Guild* and the ethereal *Flying*—to read later in the year on *The Writer's Almanac*. Phil could never figure out how Keillor discovered his poetry. My guess was that Billy Collins, the Orlando-based writer (and poet laureate of the United States from 2001 to 2003), who knew Keillor well, may have played a hand.

Phil discussed *How Men Pray* in an interview with *Frostproof Review*. He described his poetry as initially "preoccupied with death," but gradually he'd "started to address the harder stuff, such as living on." He said his poetry was "more personal than the fiction." His poems looked behind the surface and into the shadows, in much the same way as he studied photographs and paintings for hidden layers of meaning.

"The poetry looks back on my family and my parents," he said, "the big and much-lamented past. It looks back fondly on my kids growing up. And of course it stares into the shadows."

Meanwhile, Phil was still considering how to put Skidmore on the shelf. In the interview with *Frostproof Review* he was asked, "What's up with your fictional rogue character, Skidmore?" His answer:

> I'm just finishing a novel called *Past Tense* that's taken me a long time. It revisits the characters from my short story collection *Silent Retreats*.
>
> The novel is really about men, in exactly NOT the *Deliverance* sort of way, starring Skidmore, scuttling along the bottom and occasionally daring to eat a peach.

The critics hate aimless, haunted pilgrimages and the aimless authors who write them. Many of my characters are still on that road … Skidmore particularly, I guess, with the baby boom horde chasing him and running from him.

For many of my characters, drifting is the thing. They fail to attach. Commitment issues, all that.

He told *Frostproof Review* he'd recently completed another story, "Coal Grove," part of a "set" he was calling *Forty Martyrs Suite*, stories that "can be read like a collection, the stories read in any order, to the same overall effect despite all the interconnectedness."

Phil confessed to being "awfully skeptical about adults changing, in any big way, even when they see how they should":

Changing by the force of their own wills, I mean. I know you can change rather rapidly if a nuke is dropped on the neighboring town or the farm is taken away or you're heavily invested and the stock market does a terminal dump. Or your life might bottom and you turn firmly to Jesus.

But I don't see many people changing their lives by the force of their own will, absent outside forces. Yet I don't know what we'd do if we didn't at least think we could change our lives as needed.

He wanted Nick, his protagonist in "Coal Grove," to be "at least humanity-normal in his level of moral ambiguity." Nick lied a lot and two-timed his lover, and could be regarded as "awful, evil, bad"—but Phil wanted to "let him off the hook," at least for one day, and not sentence him to what conventional society thought he deserved.

If Nick had any Skidmore in him, Phil may have been contemplating a partial pardon for his old pal.

CHAPTER 28

Know Not What We May Be

"There is another world, but it is in this one."
Paul Éluard

A S PHIL'S BOOK of poetry, *How Men Pray*, was being released, Dufour Editions was making its final pre-publication edits to my novel, *Houseboating in the Ozarks*. Phil's previous angst about false rumours and plagiarism had eased in the whirl of activity that came with the publication of *How Men Pray*. He volunteered to promote the novel and sent me a rudimentary marketing strategy.

"In the old days," he said, "it was tours and TV gigs. These days, you gotta push your publisher just to get a book-signing in the likes of Carbondale, Illinois, and you gotta pay your own way."

He said he'd promote the book in the Florida region. Herb could "help in Indy." Phil's sister Maureen would buy one on Amazon and tell her literary-minded friends. He recommended readings at Flesor's Candy Kitchen in Tuscola and at Champaign's *Pages for All Ages* bookstore.

"Do Chicago too," he wrote. "And one more great thing," he added. "I have the Tuscola class of 1964 email list from the reunion.

Last summer I sent out a mass email of crass self-promotion and sold perhaps 20 books. If you spend a day thinking on this you could reach a couple of hundred. We're all in to help."

He also offered to search for a reputable writer who would put a blurb on my back cover, but he couldn't find any takers. Ann Beattie, Robert Stone, and Connie May Fowler all declined. One writer he contacted, William Trogdon, who went by the catchy fake-Indian name of William Least Heat-Moon, replied to Phil that blurbing was the equivalent of slutting, and he'd never do it for anybody. (I refrained from observing that using a snazzy Indian name to sell books was "slutting" at its very worst.) In the end, Phil wrote the *Houseboating* blurb himself, taking a shot at Trogdon and his fellow autobiographical trip-writer Robert Pirsig, the author of *Zen and the Art of Motorcycle Maintenance*:

> This oddly graceful book, with its two storms, a real one and one of the soul, and its author, will turn out to be important.

> Chris Hooker, deeply distracted in midlife, gets ripped out of himself by the innocent but eerily knowing voices of his kids. Twins! A boy and a girl! Perfect! This is the grit and rip you never see in books that purport to depict the real lives of men in these crazy, awful, corrupted times. Heat-Moon, Pirsig, heads up. This is where we went next.

Dufour Editions liked Phil's blurb and went with it. The due date for the release of *Houseboating in the Ozarks* had been pushed back to the end of April 2006. At the same time, I was making plans to leave America once again, which didn't allow much time for a marketing campaign.

It had never been smooth sledding for me and my family in central Illinois. On one occasion, my kids and I were on a street corner, opposing the Iraq war, and we got rewarded with a steady chorus of drive-by fuck-yous and middle fingers, mostly from local white Republicans with American flag decals on their car windows.

My honeymoon period as president of the St Matthew Parish had worn thin. No one had a clue what I meant when I muttered "liberation theology" or "historical Jesus," and no one wanted to know.

I added salt to the wound by taking the local Catholic Church to court to try to stop the parish from obliterating the parkland across the street from our home. The church wanted to erect a six-million-dollar basketball gym for the parish's grade school kids. The rallying cry was "Building on Christ," an oxymoron that struck me as insane. "Erection for Jesus" might have been more to the point. If my recollection of the New Testament was accurate, Jesus never had occasion to talk about the importance of upmarket basketball gymnasiums. The parish priest denounced me, by name, from the pulpit, and a group of women elders joined in a prayer circle across the street from my home after Sunday masses, saying the rosary and asking God to have mercy on old Beelzebub.

I stopped going to church, and the kids were moved to an artsy private school. But the rot had set in, and it kept getting worse. The law firm I worked for threatened to sack me because of my habit of riding a motorcycle to work while wearing a yellow Bob Marley T-shirt. Clients had complained. "That shirt means 'kill whitey,'" my boss said.

And all our neighbours were Bush supporters. The question that started going through my mind was, What the fuck am I doing here?

Australia wasn't an option—been there, done that. But New Zealand sounded good. It was only a three-hour flight across the Tasman Sea from my three oldest kids in Melbourne, and it was environmentally friendly, sparsely populated, and pro-feminist. Except for the hobbits and All Blacks, it sounded pretty good. I flew down to Wellington in March 2006 to check out jobs and houses, and made a commitment to move there in June.

On 31 March 2006—the day after I got back to Champaign from Wellington—I had to dash down to Middle Tennessee State

University in Murfreesboro for a "Baseball in Literature and Culture Conference." It was a seven-hour drive, and I was scheduled to give a reading. I never would have heard of this conference except that Phil had emailed me six months earlier to say he was submitting a proposal, and he hoped that Freidinger and I would do the same.

"We could meet in Murfreesboro," he wrote to us, "and Forrester could tell them how to spell Murphy and borough. Let's goferit."

The whole idea was crazy. Phil wanted me to read from a second novel I'd just fired off in record time, *Begotten, Not Made*, about a cross-country walking trip during the Great Depression by an eccentric fiddle player, Adolph Fanke, and his deaf sidekick Sancho. It was written from beginning to end in free verse, in Brer Rabbit talk. I referred to it as "de nobbel."

Several passages of *Begotten, Not Made* had baseball riffs, including one about the late Darryl Kile, the St Louis Cardinals pitcher, comparing him to Jesus Christ. That's the passage Phil wanted me to read at the conference, as a standalone poem.

Phil and Freidinger were bemused by de nobbel. Phil said it was "funniest when I imagine it being read to me." Freidinger sent me a friendly review, comparing it to *Catch-22*, where you had to be crazy to be sane and sane to be crazy:

> De nobbel is often tender, sometimes lurid, painful. Comprised of built-in vignettes, its beauty is that it's situational, apparently with historical accuracy, and filled with ingenious anecdotes.
>
> The approach is similar to *Houseboating in the Ozarks*. The journey takes us from New Harmony, Indiana, to Al Smith, to WWI protesters and socialism, to Russian immigrants and Rasputin, to Dust Bowl Okies who are con artists, to Native American philosophy/religion coupled with Indian thieves, Hollywood debauchery (I loved the insane asylum section), and Adolph's death before completion of the mission, a mile or so from the end of the road.

The whole thing relies on suspension of disbelief—not necessary with the historical narrative, but essential with the mental state of the narrator, the dialogue, the intrusion of Derrida, and the other historical events that are tied in.

The joy in Adolph's life is in the act of playing music. He loved his kids and family, and tried to do the right thing, but the music ruled. Sancho's fantasy is bitterly destroyed by the sight of a real woman being reduced to a slobbering lunatic, locked up, sex at its ugliest, and this ruined him as much as Adolph's physical journey killed him.

Everything was lined up for our Murfreesboro conference, but at the last second Phil got cold feet and pulled out while I was still in New Zealand. I found out about this on the day I got back to Illinois, but decided to attend anyway because the brochures were already printed with my name as one of the featured speakers, along with Bill "Spaceman" Lee.

The Spaceman had pitched in baseball's major leagues for 14 seasons, and he'd written a humorous autobiography, *The Wrong Stuff*. What could I do? I made the seven-hour trip from Champaign to Tennessee in my banged-up Oldsmobile.

The only thing I got out of the conference was a story I wrote afterwards about my Murfreesboro experience, which was published in 2010 in a West Virginia journal. I called it "A Kilgore Trout Moment," because in Vonnegut's *Breakfast of Champions*, Kilgore Trout was invited to participate in an Arts Festival in the Midwest but he didn't really know why. His bizarre novels could only be found in porn shops, as filler texts for obscene photographs, and he was an all-round grotty guy.

It wasn't hard for me to identify with old Kilgore at the Murfreesboro baseball conference, as I lurked around avoiding human contact. After arriving in the evening and signing up, I spent the night trying to sleep in the Oldsmobile in an empty driveway.

Around midnight, a guy with an iron pipe tapped on my window and threatened to kill me if I didn't leave immediately. So I spent the rest of the night in the parking lot at the Double Tree Hotel. In the morning, Trout-like, I carried a plastic bag of toiletries past the lobby desk to freshen up in the hotel spa.

Later that morning, when my name was called at the conference, I read my baseball poem in Brer Rabbit talk. Then I drove home.

Here's a snippet from the poem I read in Murfreesboro. I'd mastered the Brer Rabbit accent by reading bedtime stories to my kids over a 20-year period. Try to picture a roomful of hard-nosed baseball guys, in central Tennessee, listening to this shit:

> Darryl Kile wonder de same ting in de minor leagues,
> Starin troo de bus winders fer hours,
> Or alone in de cheap hotel.
> Did God murder he own son?
> Did God pick up where *Abraham* leabe off wif dat po boy *Isaac*?
> Was de def er God's son ter make up fer de *banishment* & *def*
> & *sufferin*
> Er all he little chilluns, just cause dey wanter hab de sexes?

> Who be redeem? wonder Darryl Kile,
> Who sin Jesus die fer, ours er he fodder in hebben's?
> Dis fodder try ter make tings right at last?
> Dis fodder *learn* from he own *mistakes*,
> He own *cruelties*,
> He own *pettiness* & *manipulation*?

> & gentermens!
> & dis *agony* in de garden, dis *crucifiction*,
> Dis de price God pay in he own *twiss mine*?
> Dat *cross* be de 2nd def er *innocence*?
> What come next? *Mo* misery & sin? *Mo* drinkin er de blood?

When I got back home to Champaign, I was busy. The latest exodus from America was only two months away. I had a novel that was just released, a house to sell, a family to move, a new life to start in a new country. But I couldn't manage to get out of Dodge without leaving behind one last stretch of scorched earth. And I found the earth to scorch in Orlando, Florida.

In a rush of blood to his head following the news that *Houseboating in the Ozarks* would be published, Phil had arranged a springtime reading at Orlando's fancy Urban Think bookstore, featuring the two of us, followed by a radio interview and another couple of presentations at Rollins College the next day.

He was being generous. Since 1998, he'd grown accustomed to helping writers launch their works, so he wanted to help me too, even though I was a shameless plagiariser, a liar, and a ruthless violator of privacy.

It all made a peculiar kind of sense, and I was grateful, but I should have known better. A perfect storm was brewing. Strangers would be staring at me, up close in confined spaces, and they'd try to engage with me in adult conversation. For sure I'd clam up, either during my readings or afterwards or both. At the post-reading party Phil had arranged at the "Lilley pad," I'd be doing my usual trick of looking for a closet to hide in.

That's what I'd do, because that's what I'd always done and it's what I'll always do. It was all so Asperger, but I didn't have that label at the time. All I knew was that I would be a one-man wrecking crew. Nothing was more certain than that my social deficits would be deeply offensive for the neurotypicals, who would regard Skidmore-in-the-flesh as the narcissist and arsehole they'd come to expect, even to long for.

And besides, I didn't really care if anybody bought my fucking book. I was headed for New Zealand, and America was about to fall off my radar all over again. But I said yes, I'd come to Orlando, and I thanked Phil for his kindness.

Phil picked me up at the Orlando airport. He had two cardboard boxes filled with copies of my book, which the publisher had sent directly to him in anticipation of the readings. I gave Phil a signed copy and he drove me to a seedy motel on the outskirts of town.

It was the weekend of the 2006 Kentucky Derby, so after I freshened up I got a taxi to Susan Lilley's house to watch the horse race on TV with her and Phil. The second favourite horse that year, in a field of 20, was an undefeated thoroughbred named Barbaro. He had Florida roots, having won the Florida Derby five weeks earlier, so the Kentucky Derby had a bit of local flavour. Everybody in town wanted Barbaro to win.

Susan's mother, Sue Taylor Lilley, took a seat next to me on the living room couch to watch the race. Poor Sue was dying of cancer, but as things turned out she outlived Barbaro. He won the Kentucky Derby that day, but shattered his leg in the next big race, the Preakness, and had to euthanised.

Phil and I made side bets on the Derby, and I won five dollars when Barbaro came home six-and-a-half lengths in front of the pack. That was the moment when I made my first mistake. I'm not a drinker, and don't even know the names of drinks or how to drink. On the rare occasions when I have a drink, I can't handle it and get drunker than a skunk in five minutes or less. But I accepted Phil's offer of a giant glass of Florida red wine to celebrate Barbaro's win.

It tasted all right, and the thought occurred to me that if I consumed just the right amount of alcohol before going to the reading at the Urban Think bookstore, I had a chance to pull it off. So I asked Phil to pour me a second glass of red wine, and a third. He didn't give it much thought, because he could hold his drinks with the best of them.

So far, things were going smoothly. Susan Lilley was still finding me mildly amusing on that first day and gave me a copy of her 2006 chapbook of poems, *Night Windows*, with a note that read, "Hope you enjoy these snippets of Florida life. See you in New Zealand!! Susan." All was well. Or so it seemed.

After the Kentucky Derby, Phil drove me over to a local country club for a late afternoon snack on the verandah and, under his guidance, I ordered some mixed drinks with bizarre names. I think a few of them were called "Mai Tai." He could tell I was getting soused, because I started talking the Brer Rabbit talk from de nobbel. I also started using rap-singer hand gestures to emphasise my gibberish.

And still I wasn't done drinking. When we got to Urban Think, the manager, Bruce Harris, offered us some white wine and I skulled three glasses in quick succession. Phil had done good advance work for the reading, and a sizeable crowd of local intellectuals and wannabes was gathering. I thought it was my job, as the visiting big shot, to help welcome the customers, so I stood by the door and shook hands like a greeter at a Walmart store.

"Hi, I'm Skidmore," I said to one booklover after another. Bruce left me alone to welcome the guests as he put the finishing touches on his makeshift stage, adjusting a set of ceiling lights so they'd shine straight into the reader's face.

When everyone was seated and the murmurs died down, I went behind the curtains and waited, chugging another two glasses of white wine. Phil was first up and he read a couple of his poems to an adoring audience. Everybody knew who he was and everybody loved him. At Phil's invitation, our old friend Herb Budden had flown down from Indianapolis for the occasion, and he smiled broadly as Phil finished his set with *Your Mars Looming*, an evocative meditation on the movement of stars and planets. The stage was set for an anti-climax, something I'm really good at.

I opened, for no particular reason, by pounding out chords on a borrowed guitar as I sang Dylan's "Tangled Up in Blue" and Neil Young's "Heart of Gold." My rhythm was, at best, flexible, and I sang off key, but on the bright side I managed to remember most of the lyrics— no small achievement under the circumstances. The audience wasn't quite sure what was going on. A few of them applauded, cautiously.

When I was done singing, Phil came back on stage to pry the guitar from my hands and slip me a copy of my book. He made a few introductory remarks, laying it on thick about me being Skidmore and us being blood brothers and how far back we went, all the way back to the sixth grade in Tuscola, Illinois. Everybody in Urban Think had read *Silent Retreats*, and they knew all about Tuscola and Skidmore the troublemaker. Phil shook my hand, smiled, and waved goodbye to the crowd. For a brief moment, the room was full of warmth again. Then, I was left alone on stage, sitting on the reader's stool with the lights shining on me and a copy of *Houseboating in the Ozarks* in my hand, with a lot of advance billing to live up to.

The ritual of book-reading is pretty weird at the best of times. It involves a lot of formulaic role-playing. The authors are supposed to be funny or wise or both, with a lot of self-deprecation, and they tend to read in measured tones, making eye contact when they've said something sort of profound or poignant. If it's going well, the audience oohs and ahhs a bit, and at the end there is applause in just the right measure, followed by book signings and small talk, and then everybody goes home.

I perceived my designated role for the Urban Think crowd as that of an aging enfant terrible. I mumbled incoherently from *Houseboating in the Ozarks* for around 15 minutes, about the near-fatal thunderstorm on the Lake of the Ozarks, widening my eyes like a B-grade actor and making those rap-singer hand gestures each time the lightning flashed or the thunder boomed. Then, without warning and mid-sentence, I stopped and staggered off the stage. Things were quiet for a few moments, then there was polite applause. I took a seat at a folding table near the exit and sold about 40 books, signing each one "Love, Skidmore." And that was that.

Until the party.

Phil had arranged a huge gathering at Susan Lilley's house, with plates of finger food and bottles of alcohol. There must have been a couple hundred people there, spilling onto Susan's back porch and into her back yard. Some faces were vaguely familiar from Urban Think. A few were holding signed copies of my book. Others were people I'd never seen before, colleagues of Phil's and Susan's from Rollins College, students and writers and academics.

I had a poison headache and could hardly walk, but I kept drinking anything that was put in front of me. I was still alive enough to know that this party was supposed to be a big deal and that I was meant to be the guest of honour. In my stupor, I devised a survival strategy of avoiding meaningful conversation by hitting on anything that moved my way, because I'd heard that the Irish poet, Seamus Heaney, did that sort of thing at his post-reading parties.

I was just horsing around, fantasising about being a best-selling author at a launch party. One of my hittees was Dr Lezlie Laws, the ex of old Trogdon/Least Heat-Moon himself, known affectionately as "Cherokee." She tried to get me to sing something, anything, other than my two Urban Think songs, but I couldn't remember anything else and she soon tired of me. The other was a blonde woman who'd crashed the party. She sat with me in the back yard on the grass, drinking and discussing the meaning of life, till Phil and Herb came out with a blinding flashlight, shining it straight into my eyes and demanding that I mingle with the party folk.

"What are you doing?" said Herb. "You're being rude as shit."

I stumbled into the kitchen and whispered something stupid to poor old Sue Taylor Lilley, something her daughter Susan interpreted as hit #3, on her own dying mother. Susan went apeshit, and I drifted back outside, ready to bid farewell forever to all my new fans. One of Phil's grownup sons, Michael, came up to me and offered his hand in friendship.

"It's an honour to meet you," he said in a kindly voice. "I've heard so much about you."

I shuddered to think what that might have been. No one had ever said such a thing to me before. The situation struck me as ludicrous. Nobody could really have been "honoured" to meet me, Mr Nothing from Nothingsville. Or at least nobody should have been. I stared blankly at his outstretched hand.

"Why would you say such a thing?" I asked. I was bewildered. My question was genuine, not intended as aggressive. "It sounds like a line from some movie script," I said. Which was true.

As I turned toward the street, I saw young Michael's hand close into a fist. It would have been okay if he'd punched me out. I was so drunk I wouldn't have felt much. But he thought better of it.

The blonde girl from the back yard grabbed my arm and guided me to her car. She drove me back to my fleabag motel, let me out, and drove off. I found my room and slept like a dead man.

When I woke the next morning, I didn't feel so good. Phil came to the motel around noon and took me out for coffee. One of his ex-students, Suzannah Gilman, happened by our table. Phil introduced her as a "lawyer-poet." I said that was an oxymoron, trying to be funny, but it was a conversation stopper.

After she left with her takeaway coffee, Phil said she was the fiancée of Billy Collins, America's poet laureate, and a friend of Susan Lilley's. I recalled that Collins's appointment as poet laureate had caused quite a stir in academic circles. One guy had written that "Collins hits the popular jugular with a vengeance because he thrives on one thing: accepted mediocrity." Still, I was impressed that I'd met the girlfriend of America's poet laureate.

Next came the radio interview Phil had arranged. He listened in his car and thought it went well, which was a surprise.

"You killed it," he said, intending a compliment. But Phil always said nice things about other writers, even me, no matter what. If it was true, it was a miracle.

The evening reading at Rollins College was for Phil's creative writing students. I think he promised them some sort of credit, or a day off from class, if they attended. I hadn't eaten all day and I'd started to sober up. This time I didn't fuck around with a guitar and this reading went better than the one at Urban Think. Hoyt Edge, the Rollins philosopher who said he remembered meeting me in the 1990s at the Aboriginal Legal Services office in Fitzroy, was there. He even laughed at all the right times, when I meant for my lines to be funny, which made me feel borderline human.

A question-and-answer session followed the reading, and I slipped in words like "alliteration" and "iambic" and "allusion" and "evocative," which impressed most of the students. After the session, Phil and Herb wanted to take me out for a meal to talk about the good old days in Tuscola, but I'd been offered a ride by a student who said she liked my prose. She and I found a restaurant and ate and drank till I was falling asleep at the table. She dropped me off at the motel where I spent another happy night alone among the dead.

Next morning, Phil and Herb knocked on my door. They'd obviously been talking with each other and they were royally pissed off, especially Herb. I couldn't blame him. Phil was about to take him to the airport for his flight back to Indianapolis, and I'd spent almost no time with him. He called me a narcissist and a sex addict, which is probably how I came across at Phil's party, despite the fact that I was a human sex-free zone for the entire weekend. The only time I'd scored was when I bet on Barbaro to win the Kentucky Derby. When Phil came back in the afternoon to take me to the airport, he said that neither Herb nor Susan would ever speak to me again. Phil was always good at making predictions, and this one stuck.

But looking back, Orlando must not have been quite as bad as it seemed at the time. The reading at Rollins College and the radio interview had been disaster-free, and quite a few people from Orlando stayed in touch for a few years afterwards. Some of them even visited me in New Zealand. Although I couldn't quarrel with Herb or Susan for hating me, I couldn't remember half of what had happened.

Nine years later, from far away in New Zealand on the occasion of the 2015 Kentucky Derby, I sent a belated thanks to Phil.

"Thanks for attempting to set up the readings that weekend," I wrote. "I shouldn't have let you do it. I should have known how I'd act. It's always the same. I'm better off in exile. I guess that's just the way it is."

Phil's reply was pithy and ironic. He was probably in the early stages of FTD.

"What I regret about your trip in 2006," he said, "is that (a) I can't find the *Houseboating* book you signed for me and (b) I poured you a giant glass of red wine and you went crazy."

He was still being relentlessly kind. I had to set the record straight:

> Nah, my going crazy had nothing to do with red wine. I was crazy anyway. You were nice to set that up for me in Florida. I do appreciate what you tried to do. I sort of don't even feel sorry, although I know I should be very sorry. I just do this. I can't explain it. I'm not always a destroyer. But put me in the situation like the thing in Florida, or a dozen variants, and I will destroy.
>
> I just never should have been there, talking in front of people, going to a party that was sort of, I guess especially, set up for me. It was inevitable that I would set out to destroy. I always do, at anything remotely formal or celebratory or official, or where certain rituals of behaviour are anticipated or expected. In those circumstances, I'm wired to go crazy and destroy.
>
> I can actually be semi-appropriate in smaller circumstances, where there are no behavioural expectations. But put me at a dinner party, or a conference, or a team meeting, or a graduation ceremony, or drinks after work with colleagues, or something where somebody is being honoured, and I will be the visitor from hell. I knew that when you were kind enough to set up the Orlando readings for me. I know it now.

In the past nine years here in NZ, the only real problems I've had have been with such occasions, conferences mainly, and I've sabotaged ruthlessly. When I act that way, people think it's 'out of character,' but it's not. They say they thought I'd be the life of a party or a great conference participant because I seem so intelligent and engaging. I explain to my bosses that I have a form of mental illness and offer to provide a doctor's certificate. They say not to bother because I do my job well, and they just won't invite me to any more after-work drinks or conferences or any of that shit, and everybody's happy.

He wrote back: "I get it. Wishing you the best with your writing." That was strange, because I wasn't writing anything at all, and hadn't said I was.

When I got back to Champaign from the Orlando debacle in 2006, there was more packing to do. But before leaving America, there was one last item on the writer's calendar. Phil had arranged another reading for late May, one week before my departure. This one would be at Flesor's Candy Kitchen in Tuscola. There would be three of us on the agenda—Phil, me, and Paul Freidinger—three boys from central Illinois.

CHAPTER 29

Like an Eyelid's Soundless Blink

Phil's sister Maureen travelled over from Indianapolis for the Candy Kitchen event. I hadn't seen her since 1964, and when Phil introduced us she was pretty frosty. She'd probably heard a whole lot of bad stuff about me, much of it true, over the previous half-century. And she probably took it for granted that Skidmore was completely me, and I was completely him.

Herb Budden didn't make the trip from his home in Indianapolis. No surprise after my bombing campaign in Orlando.

Paul Freidinger invited Liza Ford to the readings. A dear friend of his going back to our college days in the 1960s, she drove all the way to Tuscola from downstate Jacksonville for the occasion. I hadn't seen her in 35 years. She'd grown up as Elizabeth "Lish" Joyce in nearby Danville, Illinois, and was married for a while to her high school boyfriend, Harry "Buff" Ford, a close friend of mine and Paul's during our English studies at Eastern Illinois University. There at the Candy Kitchen, I introduced Phil to Liza and they started flirting with each other right away. Paul, alarmed, warned each of them to stay away from the other. Liza was an alcoholic, unreliable, and suffering from terminal cancer; Phil was publicly committed to

Susan Lilley in Florida and had nothing to offer Liza but a transient covert assignation. But neither of them listened to Paul and that night, after the readings, they found a place to enjoy each other's company. (Several years later, after Liza had died and I'd moved to New Zealand, Paul and Phil bumped into Harry Ford at a baseball game in Jupiter, Florida. The three guys had dinner together. I'd have loved to have been a fly on that wall.)

A lot of Tuscola regulars showed up for the readings at the Candy Kitchen, fans of Phil's. My role, and Paul's, was to provide backup. That suited me better anyway. The Tuscola crowd would be focusing on Phil, and regard me as an afterthought and Paul as an exotic out-of-towner.

Phil read his poem *Shoney's* in memory of Althea, and *Death of the Father* in memory of his dad. He also read an excerpt from his story "Arcola Girls." I sang a couple of songs and read a passage from *Houseboating in the Ozarks*. Paul made several of his poems come alive with dramatic flair, punching the air with a raised index finger.

The following Tuesday, *The Tuscola Review* had us on its front page under the banner "Talent of Tuscola returns with books." By talent, they meant Phil:

> He looks ordinary enough, just an average joe. But he's been published in some of the most prestigious literary magazines in the nation. He's received fellowships from the National Endowment for the Arts; he's a professor and writer-in-residence at Rollins College in Florida and the winner of the Flannery O'Connor Award for Short Fiction, one of the most sought-after awards in literature.
>
> Garrison Keillor even recites his stuff on National Public Radio, a pinnacle of that peculiar fame usually reserved for members of the dead poets' society.
>
> Last Wednesday, writer Philip F. Deaver came home to Tuscola to read for some of the people who made him who he is.

Tuscola has never left Deaver's heart. He mentions the city frequently in his writing. His verses remember his father Philip, a beloved physician Tuscola has never forgotten, and his writing also recalls his mother Althea, equally loved for her work as a nurse.

Our old sixth-grade teacher, Mrs Marguerite McDaniel, was there at the Candy Kitchen. She told *The Tuscola Review* that she was the first person to tell Phil he'd be a professional writer someday. The newspaper reported that Phil said, "I love this lady," and he gave her a hug in front of everyone. Mrs McDaniel was asked about me. *The Tuscola Review* reported:

> Mrs. McDaniel did not recall Forrester having the same degree of inspiration way back then. She exclaimed, "He was in trouble all the time!"

> Forrester agreed. "And I still am," he said.

In words that could have been taken from a description of Skidmore in *Silent Retreats*, the newspaper said I was a "novelist who cultivates the persona of an ex-hippie on the lam." True enough, and the article added the flattering note that my songs "made the night relaxing and entertaining, not a stuffy literary soirée":

> Despite his nervousness, Forrester's writing was assured: wry, comic, and occasionally pointed, which seems to fit his off-kilter personality.

> These two hometown favorites were generous in their praise for their pal Paul Freidinger. The audience appeared to be equally touched by his work, which also contains local references.

> The reading was interrupted by a severe thunderstorm, and there was talk of evacuation to the basement. But soon the cold front passed, and inside the old, well-remembered storefront at Gus's, the warmth of a homecoming continued into the night.

If there was any lingering doubt about the place of Tuscola in Phil's heart and in his writing, he removed it in a companion interview in *The Tuscola Review*:

> Tuscola is in me for good. I'm a Tuscola boy. I suppose, secretly, I want Tuscola to be proud of me, despite most of the people knowing exactly how ordinary I am. When I go back to Tuscola in my writing, I go back in my dreams and emotions. It is home, the center, the middle of the middle, my heart and soul, my base of operation.
>
> My mother and father are buried in Tuscola's black dirt, and I will be too.

When the evening at the Candy Kitchen was finished, Phil said goodbye. We shook hands. That was the last time I would ever lay eyes on him.

It was also the last time I saw Liza Ford. Within two years, she was dead.

PART FOUR

CHAPTER 30

At the Edge of the Universe,
Like Everyone Else

"Once one has glimpsed the finitude of one's existence, it snatches one back from the dream of endless possibilities we once thought were ours."

Martin Heidegger

FOR THE NEXT ten years, from 2006 to 2016, my communications with Phil were mostly by email, sometimes by letter. That may not sound like a tie that binds, until you consider there were more than 2,500 email threads—an average of around 250 per year.

Our correspondence spiked during the baseball seasons, from April to October. Phil was a genuine baseball fan. I wasn't. For me, the St Louis Cardinals were a lifelong habit, and if they weren't involved, I wasn't interested. I knew little, and cared nothing, about the Dodgers or the Yankees or the Braves or whatever those other teams called themselves.

Shortly after my arrival in New Zealand, Phil and I roped my younger brother Jim into a three-way baseball conversation that lasted till mid-2016, when Phil's ability to communicate eroded. Most of these exchanges were simple and straightforward, second-guessing managerial decisions—why didn't the Cardinals' manager Tony

LaRussa have Yadier Molina lay down a sacrifice bunt in the bottom of the eighth? Why did he bring in Allen Craig, a right-handed pinch hitter, to bat against a right-handed reliever? Why didn't he yank Adam Wainwright after the seventh inning, when he was clearly out of gas and Jason Isringhausen was in the bullpen, raring to close out the game?

But sometimes we got philosophical about a particular game, or the game generally, and Phil led those discussions. He really knew his stuff.

I arrived in New Zealand a few days before my 60th birthday and set about finding a new home for the family, who were coming a few weeks later. Phil emailed with some urgency about a project he'd begun before I left. It included me.

Back in 2002, his story "Infield" had been reprinted in a baseball collection, *Bottom of the Ninth: Literary Short Fiction about Baseball*, edited by John McNally for *Southern Illinois University Press*. McNally had a sequel in the works, but in 2005 he got busy with other things and passed the project over to Phil for completion. Phil had already lined up some literary rock stars—Andre Dubus, Leslie Epstein, Michael Chabon, Ron Carlson, Rick Bass, Floyd Skoot, Michael Martone, and William Trogdon (old Least Heat-Moon himself, the wannabe poseur) among them. With this all-star team, he'd found a respectable publisher, *University of Nebraska Press*.

At the 2006 reading in Flesor's Candy Kitchen, he'd asked if I'd submit a story for his project, one about the St Louis Cardinals. I didn't have the energy to start something from scratch, and I was too busy moving overseas, so I sent him a 2,500-word excerpt from "de nobbel," *Begotten, Not Made*, in the Brer Rabbit talk, somewhat modified for Phil's book. It was along the lines of the passage I'd read at the ill-fated baseball conference in Murfreesboro, Tennessee.

Phil was not amused. I suggested he just drop my prose poem from the collection. He replied:

I've not given any thought to removing you from the baseball book. When I invited you into the book, I wanted your good pure writing. You've treated the project like a joke on the world (and me), and counted on my good nature to get it in anyway. Your piece is disappointing because of its phoniness and dishonesty.

I realized, however, that rather than seeing inclusion of your Brer Rabbit stuff as an indication of my good nature, you would see it as another in a string of perceived victories in your lifelong strategy of bullying Danny Deaver. Which takes a lot of the fun out of including your piece in the book, for me.

I stuck to my guns but tweaked the draft in my spare time. It evolved into a eulogy for Darryl Kile, building on the Murfreesboro reading and trickled with biblical passages. I expanded on my absurd comparison of Kile to Jesus Christ and got carried away accusing God Almighty of being an arsehole by taking Darryl's life at the age of 33 (the same age as Jesus was when he was crucified).

With these token gestures on my part, Phil started to mellow. He emailed a long critique, saying that my "baseball commentary is knowing and engaging," but worrying that the piece was "50% about baseball, 40% about Jesus, and 10% about you." To his mind, this created an "imbalance" because

Jesus is heavier than baseball. Baseball is made of leather, yarn, dirt, and grass. Jesus is made of Italian marble. Rest Jesus in one tray of the Lady Justice scale, and you and baseball in the other tray, and on the count of three, let go. Zing. You and baseball go into low orbit.

I thought he'd sort of missed the point, which was precisely that the historical Jesus was *not* "made of Italian marble." But he continued:

I love a lot of the stuff here. The similarities to my own memories, the force of my own feelings about the Cardinals and my past that hit me so hard that day in 2002 when you and I stood outside Busch Stadium looking at the shrines for Kile and Jack Buck.

We experienced the death of Darryl Kile separately and differently, but Jack Buck came from our grounded, common past, a past that was really quaking that day, our first time together in around 30 years.

And we have a lot of Catholic stuff in common. After all, we joined together in conspiracy in catechism classes, hoodwinking Sister Mary Walter by performing mental telepathies. But in our adult days we've experienced religion in different ways, with different intensities, and I'm *not* asking you to move closer to how I've experienced it. I'm just saying there is no way your tight braiding of baseball and Jesus will ride.

In further revision, I'm suggesting you plow through this and for 75% of it stay with baseball and Darryl's death, and with yourself and Jack Buck and all the rest, but deprive yourself (except for the occasional allusion) from crossing the Jordan until the last page.

Then you can tie the knot with all the New Testament you want (stopping short of course of presenting Darryl's resurrected head in the lap of Jesus's mistress followed by some Latin about the power of touching).

I had one more crack at revision, but I really didn't have the time or inclination to change my piece in any significant way. In fact, I liked it, just the way it was. *Scoring from Second: Writers on Baseball* was set to come out in the northern spring of 2007, and the stories had to be finalised by late 2006.

In the end, Phil went with it. He said he was "committed to keeping the piece in unless someone draws a line in the sand and says it threatens the entire project." *University of Nebraska Press* turned a blind eye.

Publication proceeded, and Phil wrote a great introduction for the book. It was accompanied by a 1963 black-and-white photo of him and his dad strolling outside the old Sportsman's Park in St Louis. As usual, Phil found hidden meaning behind a two-dimensional image. In this case, he anticipated the passing of a generational torch, a year before his father's death. In the photograph, he and his dad walked in sync, with identical strides and their heads turned at the same angle to look at an undisclosed object. A dark photographic line gave the appearance of a pipe coming out of young Danny's mouth, just like his dad's for-real pipe.

In his introduction, Phil had this to say about my weird submission: "Forrester is here with what may be our oddest contribution: a mournful, primitive tone-poem melding religion with a contemplation on the death of St Louis Cardinal Darryl Kile and a remembrance of the great Jack Buck." Fair enough.

In 2008, Phil gave an interview about *Scoring from Second* in which he was asked, "What do you miss most about living in East Central Illinois?" His unsurprising answer was, "It's home":

> What can you say about home? Sometimes I go back and stare at my house (it isn't my house anymore, but it's still there). I don't know what to say about it. It's in me, that place, the house, the school, the brick street, the ball diamonds, Flesor's candy store, Forty Martyrs Catholic Church, the courthouse, friends still there who go all the way back with me.
>
> I only wish I could have raised my kids in a town that would remember and embrace them like Tuscola has me.
>
> Two years ago, Garrison Keillor, on *The Writers Almanac*, read a poem of mine called 'Flying.' The real pleasure of that for me was calling home and alerting everybody.

Another testy exchange with Phil involved the Florida poet Russell Kesler, a friend of Phil's and Susan's from their Orlando literary circle. I'd decided to write a book of poetry, probably in a subconscious effort to follow Phil's lead with *How Men Pray*. The only problem was that I didn't have a clue how to write a poem. The best stuff I'd ever done was our Layer System garbage in high school, under the pen-name Garrison "Brown Nose" Forrester.

I started hanging out in Wellington's city library, reading the verse of Anne Sexton, Sylvia Plath, Ted Hughes, John Berryman, Allen Ginsberg, Gary Snyder, Lawrence Ferlinghetti, and anybody else they had on the shelves. I also re-read the poems of William Matthews, Mark Jarman, and Jorie Graham that Phil had sent me years before. And I studied *How Men Pray*.

I wanted to know how words could best express both sense and feeling; why a poet ended a line with a particular word or sound; how cliché could be recycled without sounding like doggerel; how a poem should look on a page; whether and when rhyme mattered, either at the ends of lines or internally; how rhythms affected the impact of a poem; the mnemonic effect of verse. So I read and read and read. And I emailed some of my early drafts to Phil.

I asked him why he ended a line from *How Men Pray* with this word or that, why he capitalised the first word of each line in most of his poetry. His response to these and other questions was not very helpful: "I don't know," he said.

Russell Kesler had a fine little book of poems on the market, *A Small Fire*. Russell's work is grounded in the American South, with screech owls and mockingbirds, shrimping and squirrel skinning. He found meaning in small moments, and he shared with Phil an inclination to remembrance of things past.

Phil sent me Russell's book and emailed his poems *Attic* and *Letter to Laundry on the Line*. I got in touch with Russell directly via email at his University of Central Florida office. I asked him dumb questions: Is it okay to impose a writer's will on a poem? Did Russell have a reader or readers in mind as he wrote? Could a good poem be written without being attuned to silence?

He thought I was an idiot. He said I made him "grouchy." He said he didn't think about readers at all; that if he tried to manufacture a poem, it would "suck." He said that when he began a poem that worked, he was "listening to a whisp of something that requires a lot of silence." He could be "silent in several languages."

Being an "intellectual" was Russell's idea of purgatory.

"I avoid it at all costs," he said. "I can wait on poems. I don't need to make them happen. I'm somebody without them. I get lucky sometimes. Other times, I'm in the garden hoeing my onions and happy as a clam."

He threw some pointed questions back my way.

> When you write your poems with your readers in mind, what do you expect them to take from your poems? Do you want them to feel something you've felt? To connect with something you've said? To connect with you?
>
> Do you suffer over a word until it is the right word, the only word that fits? Do you cleanse the final draft of unneeded words?
>
> Are you trying to make your readers look? Or is it softer, *hoping* they will look? Are your poems love-driven, searching for lovers of the word, the experience behind the word, the experience of the word? Does the word come first, then the flesh?

These were great questions, but it occurred to me that Russell and I were on different planets. Phil bought into the email conversation. I don't think he took kindly to my using Russell's nickname "Rusty" for the main guy in my narrative poems. He acknowledged that I'd "studied up on the nomenclature jargon and lingo and then spread it evenly through a poem" to see if I could get away with it. I took that as a classy putdown.

Phil said my poems were "too much like crossword puzzles with not enough heart." But he wished me well: "Surely in due time you'll achieve enough bravery to disarm and simply write the heart in your remaining days."

Sigh. What could I do? I kept writing my poems, with or without a heart. I couldn't argue with him or Russell. I knew they were right. I tried to explain my emotional shortcomings to them:

> Our point of departure is that the words you use tend to be emotive; when I sense that emotion is upon me, I pull back and leave the poem empty for a reader to fill in or despair over.

> My poems are like inkblots where a viewer recognises something familiar and fills in the blanks. Yours are more like French Impressionist paintings where the reader arrives, in a moment of stillness, at an emotion parallel to something they've experienced.

But I persisted with my poems. And just as I'd done with *Houseboating in the Ozarks*, I didn't stop until my volume, *The Beautiful Daughters of Men*, found a publisher.

By amazing coincidence, the lead poem from my book, a meditation on the Lakota warrior Thathą́ka Íyotake (Sitting Bull), was published in the same issue of *South Dakota Review* as Paul Freidinger's poem *Happenstance*. So bizarre—a similar thing had happened in the mid-eighties, before Freidinger and Deaver had ever heard of each other, when Phil's "Wilbur Gray" story and one of Paul's poems appeared in the same issue of *The Florida Review*.

To give you the flavour of my heartless poetry, here's an excerpt from the Sitting Bull poem, which was inspired by the vandalised statue of Sitting Bull that overlooks the Missouri River from the vantage point of Mobridge, South Dakota. If I let Phil and Rusty down by failing to disarm or to write from the heart, it was because I couldn't do that. But Phil liked the poem anyway:

> So now, prefigured in Lakota lore, he sits
> snow-dusted on this pedestal, his final bluff
> above the long and dark Missouri, a stone's
> throw from the home where he was born.
> Downstream among the rip-raps, our setlines

come up empty once again, those channel
cats and flatheads slicing figure eights
between our eight-inch shads.
As clouds press down upon the hills,
I scrape our bucketful of minnows

against the shoreline stones. You kneel to brush
their silver bodies to the stream, and ask about the missing
feather from his headdress, his shattered nose, the bullet-
pocks across his granite face. I know nothing.
Once he straddled these Dakota skies

like a solitary bird in flight. Even then, he yielded
nothing from his face of stone. The whinnies
of his horses undulated through these grasslands
like the laughter of a holy man
who never meant to die or disappear.

CHAPTER 31

Distant Cries of Reapers in the Corn

"If we have not sinned, how can we repent?"

Chris Borthwick

IN FEBRUARY 2008, the *Orlando Sentinel* featured an article about Phil under the lengthy banner, "A perfect pairing: Author Philip Deaver finds Winter Park's Rollins College a hospitable host for his writing career and the Winter with the Writers program he directs." In the article, Phil reflected on his past, on his present at Rollins College, and on his "future stories from a past rich with perspective."

As one ages, he said, "you start to actually consolidate your experience, in a way .... I don't know how everything will turn out, but I know how a lot of it did."

He was as fulfilled as he'd ever been, and he had a lot to look forward to.

Other people know more about Phil's daily life between 2008 and 2016 than I ever will. He kept writing and teaching at Rollins College, and hosting celebrated writers at Rollins's "Winter with the Writers" series for visiting authors—including such luminaries as Richard Ford, Lawrence Ferlinghetti, Ann Beattie, Jennifer

Egan, Rick Bass, Michael Curtis, Mary Karr, Mark Jarman, David Halberstam, Michael Cunningham, and Jamaica Kincaid.

Phil also gave writing workshops in various parts of the country and expanded his teaching to Spalding University's Master of Fine Arts Program. He struggled, without success, to get Rollins College's English department to approve an MFA program in creative writing. They wouldn't buy it.

He travelled to Bali and Shanghai and Argentina and France and Ireland. More grandchildren arrived. He went to his first live Dylan concert. Sue Taylor Lilley died, and after her house was sold in the spring of 2008, Susan and Phil moved into a condominium in Maitland, Florida. Phil wanted to be a coequal owner of their new home, but Susan was having none of that. She was well aware of his struggles with money. So he remained, in effect, a renter, paying agreed amounts to Susan as he had when they lived in Sue Taylor Lilley's house, his meagre net income going up in smoke.

In 2010, Phil and Susan were married near Ernest Hemingway's old home in Key West, Florida, which had been turned into a museum.

But most of all, as he approached his late 60s, Phil busted his balls getting his novel-in-stories, *Forty Martyrs*, ready for publication. That final project was a lot harder than it sounds. Phil had drawers filled with unpublished manuscripts. His stories had been written in different voices, decades apart, almost as if they had come from two or three iterations of Philip Deaver. One of the manuscripts dated all the way back to his *Silent Retreats* days in Murray, Kentucky, when he was in his 40s, long before he'd ever heard of Rollins College.

From these raw materials in the bottoms of drawers, he had to select manuscripts that could somehow be unified and consolidated into a single whole, with novel-like plotting. The stories had Tuscola in common, of course, with the non-existent college he had previously invented, in the southwest corner of town. He culled his manuscripts' main characters down to six, then seven, and linked their intertwining lives via three major events—a dubious religious sighting, a suspicious fire at the fictional college, and a horrific stabbing incident.

His recent experiment in metafiction, "The Kopi," which resuscitated Skidmore for one final round, couldn't make the *Forty Martyrs* cut. It was a sore thumb, a square peg, with the wrong voice, the wrong structure, the wrong literary style, the wrong timeline. But on its own, it was one of Phil's best works.

When *Forty Martyrs* was accepted for publication by *Burrow Press*, it was one of the proudest moments of Phil's life. His sigh of relief could be heard halfway around the globe, in New Zealand.

Forty Martyrs is a fine work. And unbeknownst to Phil or anyone else at the time, he'd brought it all together as his power over words and language was steadily diminishing in the early stages of frontotemporal degeneration (FTD), which was not yet diagnosed. Phil's efforts met the standards of that over-hyped word "heroic" and the publication completed the circle of his creative life, from *Silent Retreats* to *Forty Martyrs*.

During Phil's eight bittersweet years between 2008 and 2016, I was cranking out some stuff of my own at a pretty fast rate. My book of poetry, *The Beautiful Daughters of Men*, was published in 2008; my third novel, *The Connoisseur of Love*, was released by Steele Roberts in New Zealand in 2011; and my fourth novel, *More Deaths than One*, was published in West Virginia in 2014. In 2012, with his characteristic generosity, Phil wrote a long review of *The Connoisseur of Love* for the *Emerging Writers Network*. It said as much about his own values as a writer as it did about my book:

> *The Connoisseur of Love*, just out of New Zealand, is a collection of twelve short stories, some of them linked. The collection's unifying element is the (third person limited) narrator of all but one of the stories, Peter Becker, an attorney in his fifties or sixties (he ages over the time-span of the stories) who is currently employed as a public servant. Becker is an immigrant

from Germany, living life in a second language (English) which, in the design of the book, he may stumble on in dialogue but moves through like a bird in a tree in narration.

In Peter Becker, Forrester creates an odd character trapped by his own internal life, a cross between Walter Mitty and Larry David's character in 'Curb Your Enthusiasm,' with touches here and there of Mersault (*The Stranger*), Bartleby the Scrivener and, perhaps, Billy Pilgrim. Picture the most trapped-in-the-*cul-de sac*-of-self individual you have ever encountered in life or fiction, quietly careening through his latter years in gentle Wellington with the external world mostly on 'mute' or at least muffled like the adults in the 'Peanuts' cartoons on TV.

All through the collection, we find Peter either alone in his own thoughts or, for brief moments, lonely for connection to others, or, the saddest option, lost and self-conscious in some human interaction thrust upon him. He wasn't born with social connective tissue. Marching in step with other members of the human race challenges him. The closest he comes to regular social interaction is in mixed doubles on the grass courts at Thorndon Tennis Club, where the lines are freshly chalked and clear and he can distract himself with his overly-developed urgency to defeat whoever is on the other side of the net.

Thus, the title of the collection is meant ironically. When in these stories Peter Becker isn't sleeping alone in his house in Khandallah (not that love implies sleeping with someone), he's sleeping there with a pile of tulips or a ukulele.

Twice in these stories, Peter attempts to actually have a date. In one, a six-foot-tall Polynesian beauty from Bora Bora named Lavi captures his attention and he engages her in conversation. He has just refurbished a set of deckchairs he's acquired, and he's been sending out invitations in a rare attempt to gin up a party at his home. Lavi would be perfect to take the fifth chair! The guest list would be complete. Astonishingly she says yes, she would come; they could meet later at a place where she works to firm things up. She gives him the name of the place where she works, a place with which he's familiar. Some days later he goes there to meet up and firm up. Nobody there knows her or remembers anyone by her most lovely and memorable description. She hoodwinked him. He cancels the whole party, so put out is he by her cruel trick.

In another story an attractive woman from the travel agency on the lower level of his building gives him attention—it's rare that someone gives him this kind of flirtatious attention—and he invites her to his house to watch a DVD—'Wild Orchid,' to be exact. She accepts his invitation and furthermore promises to present him with a surprise on that occasion. The prospect excites him, especially the surprise. He goes to a floral shop to purchase beautiful tulips, gets in a twist over the price, haggles with the manager, and ends up walking out with two bunches at half price just so they can get his ass off the premises—this is the Larry David-esque Peter Becker. The pretty woman's surprise, it turns out, is her husband, Erhard, who hails from the same area of Germany as Peter. The woman has happily planned to introduce Erhard and Peter so they could perhaps be friends and reminisce about the old country. Again Peter has selectively perceived what was going on, his heart leaping with the prospect of a date. That's the night he slept with the tulips.

In a story aptly titled 'Remote,' Peter narrates this sentence to himself: 'So far, this Sunday had been a disaster. His wife and daughter were gone for good, his TV remote was missing in action, and here it was mid-afternoon and he hadn't had a single latte.'

That in a nutshell is Peter Becker. Forrester is a master of irony, and when you juxtapose this sentence with the title of his collection *The Connoisseur of Love*, it's irony on the first layer, the simplest interpretation. On subsequent layers, third, fifth, and seventh, this book makes a serious bid (on behalf of its author) to be understood and perhaps even forgiven.

The loneliness and isolation Becker feels is sort of a self-fulfilling spiral. In the story 'Like Water, Till I Couldn't Tell You from Me,' he doesn't attend the funeral of his parents because everybody hates him in those situations, but the fact that he didn't attend deeply bothers him. Though in many ways he's interpersonally numb and blindfolded, he can sense a misstep and he does rebuke himself. In this story he's on the beach, alone of course, thinking all of that over, remembering his parents, trying to rig up a rationalization, a way to forgive himself. A young lad nine years old trots by, shows himself, then darts into the surf and disappears. He's drowning! And Peter runs down, tosses his bag aside, jumps in the water and pulls the boy out, then pumps on the lad's chest until he breathes once more. Peter is a hero. He has saved a random life. On the spot redemption. Thank you, Lord!

I advise students against the 'one person story,' the story that has only one primary character. It's not only the danger of entering a solipsistic 'repeat' loop. It's that the tension and dramatic arc, under normal circumstances, require two people minimally so that there's friction, heat, tension, and rising action. In *Houseboating in the Ozarks*, Forrester's first book of fiction, a novel, a man takes his two children, twins, a boy and a girl, to the Ozarks for a vacation; he and his wife are estranged, and his intent is to connect with the kids and, perhaps by doing so, console them and himself. One of the many wonders of that book is that the man's two kids become real people capable of influencing the outcome of the trip. They grab him by the heart and throw him around. They are bright, funny, and embody their own kind of irony that meshes with Dad's. It was a wonderful, smart, sad book.

So is this one, only this time, unlike Chris Hooker in *Houseboating*, Becker has no one, and so the stories depend on Becker's own narration, memoir-like if it weren't so cagily in third person. The stories are smartly written in Forrester's straightforward clear sentences which have always had an echo of Vonnegut to me. The stories follow a pattern (except for the last one, an attempted capstone which is funny but probably doesn't fit in the set): The pattern is, Becker passes through some torment of human interaction which barely makes sense to him, then retreats to the quiet of home, watches a bit of TV, and goes to sleep alone.

One thinks of *Olive Kitteridge*, and this one might have been called *Peter Becker*, except Forrester wrote it, creating a unique point of view that is so broad it is at once a Gordian knot of irony, a psychological landscape, and a state of mind.

CHAPTER 32

The Ancient Pulse of Germ and Birth

"Look deep into my eyes, Tsarevich, and I will stop the bleeding."

Grigori Rasputin

IN 2013, AFTER his generous review of *The Connoisseur of Love*, Phil reached another low point with his own writing and emailed me to pronounce himself a "failure." He described himself as a "one-hit wonder"—the hit being *Silent Retreats*, a quarter of a century earlier. I wrote back:

> Hey man, you're not a failure as a writer at all! It's a tough game, and you've done extremely well. And you're not finished—67 is a great age for a writer. I'm working on a new novel now, including a whole lot of stuff about metamodernism (postmodernism's successor), with David Foster Wallace emerging as a sort of ghostly character in a *Zen & Motorcycle Maintenance* kind of thing, where metamodernist theory and the ghost of DFW share space within a travel narrative back to Illinois.

I explained that according to the emerging cultural paradigm of metamodernism, postmodernism had been on life support for around

20 years, except in the minds of a few die-hard academic obscurantists with their recycled curricula celebrating those French rascals Derrida and Foucault.

The first half of the 20th century had been the heyday of modernism, which focused on a search for meaning and values in the flotsam of the industrial revolution, the migration of rural people into cities and factories, the great depression sandwiched between two world wars, the holocaust. It's no surprise that people were searching for answers, reimagining the meaning of their lives on earth, longing for common bonds. They needed each other. In that context, modernism was primarily epistemological, exploring the nature and origins of knowledge.

But in the relative comfort of the post-war years of the 1950s, modernism was old and quaint. The previous half-century's hard-earned values and structures were about to be fractured by social upheaval, political realignments, and technological advances such as air travel, television, computers, enhanced medical care, and space exploration. The citadels of authority—universities, churches, government agencies—were no longer able to control their messages of central truths. When they tried, they were met with a barrage of sarcasm, irony, detachment, and suspicion. Truths had become relative, depending on your personal situation—your culture, gender, ethnicity, income, identity, class, sexual orientation, family. Unlike modernism's epistemological foundation, postmodernism was grounded in ontology—as in, who am I and what's happening? Sometimes all you could do was shake your head and laugh along with the likes of Dylan and Warhol.

My email name-dropping of David Foster Wallace caught Phil's attention. Not long before DFW's suicide, Phil had spoken to him at length by phone, trying unsuccessfully to get him down from Illinois to Rollins College for a series of readings and lectures: "I couldn't say a dollar amount that would have brought him down, so we talked about central Illinois." Like Phil and me, DFW was a boy from Illinois. He grew up 20 miles north of Tuscola.

When he first started writing, DFW was drawn to the post-modernism of Thomas Pynchon, John Barth, Donald Barthelme. He was enchanted by the artificiality of narrative. With metafiction, he could intrude into his own work anytime, anywhere, celebrating the legerdemain of his words on paper. DFW was particularly drawn to Pynchon's irony, his Warhol-like propensity to patch together creative work from fragments of advertising, television, popular songs, movies, sport. DFW's first novel, *The Broom of the System*, was criticised by *Kirkus Reviews*, alliteratively if not precisely, as "a puerile Pynchon, a discount DeLillo."

But as early as 1988, in his essay "Fictional Futures and the Conspicuously Young," DFW started to recognise that his generation of writers had seen "literary innocence taken from us without anything substantial to replace it." They were in limbo: "an age between." He became distrustful of anyone "who claimed to know where literary fiction will go during this generation's working lifetime." At the end of the 1980s, he'd grown bored with reminding readers that his stories were fabrications, disenchanted with injecting philosophical asides and ironic commentary into the commonplace lives of his characters. His ennui grew from his innate rebellion against authority. He could only go along with the program, any program, for so long. He felt a growing need to assassinate the postmodern sheriff, along with the multi-headed posse of metafiction, minimalism, and irony.

The publisher's blurb for DFW's 1989 book, *Girl with Curious Hair*, got the message: "The stories in his first collection could possibly represent the flowering of post-postmodernism: visions of the world that re-imagine reality as more realistic than we can imagine." A reviewer elaborated: "Wallace is beyond the calculated fiddle of the postmodernist. He comes to us from a new place, the place the minimalists have only been able to point toward. He is unburdened by any nostalgia for the old order."

By 1993, he'd declared all-out war on irony, even as he continued to apply it as one of his literary weapons. In "E Unibus Pluram: Television and US Fiction," he considered the place of rebellion in art. He became a champion of the single entendre. Now it was his former mentors, the "old postmodern insurgents," who needed a shake-up:

> The next real literary 'rebels' might well emerge as some weird bunch of anti-rebels, born oglers who dare somehow to back away from ironic watching, who have the childish gall actually to endorse and instantiate single-entendre principles. Who treat of plain old untrendy human troubles and emotions with reverence and conviction. Who eschew self-consciousness and hip fatigue. ... Real rebels, as far as I can see, risk disapproval. The old postmodern insurgents risked the gasp and squeal: shock, disgust, outrage, censorship, accusations of socialism, anarchism, nihilism. Today's risks are different. The new rebels might be artists willing to risk the yawn, the rolled eyes, the cool smile, the nudged ribs, the parody of gifted ironists, the 'Oh how banal.' To risk accusations of sentimentality, melodrama. Of overcredulity. Of softness.

By the time DFW got to his magnum opus, *Infinite Jest*, his character Hal Incandenza was neither a Jackson Pollock "force of nature" nor an Andy Warhol "machine." He was something new, and something old; Hal spoke for his creator—David Foster Wallace— who would not be minimalised or contained: "I am not a machine. I feel and believe. I have opinions. Some of them are interesting. I could, if you'd let me, talk and talk. Let's talk about anything."

Encouraged by Phil's incipient interest in the demise of post-modernism, I put him in email contact with Alexandra Dumitrescu, the Romanian-born New Zealand woman who was the first theorist to link the word "metamodern" to a paradigm shift. Her use of "meta" had nothing to do with the self-reflective literary style known as "metafiction." Rather, borrowing the prefix "meta" from the Greek μετα, she meant "after" or "later in time"—while striving toward a higher stage of development. For example, during metamorphosis, a tadpole or a caterpillar undergoes progressive change in the course of natural growth.

As a PhD student at New Zealand's University of Otago in 2007, Dumitrescu wrote an article for *Double Dialogues*, an Australian art journal, titled "Interconnections in Blakean and Metamodern Space," in which she identified a "budding cultural paradigm" that partly "emerged from" postmodernism and was "a reaction to it." In her analysis, postmodernism was hapless and passé—especially because of its focus on fragmentation, individualism, and "the preeminence of analysis over synthesis."

Metamodernism, unlike its predecessors, synthesised what had come before, combining the sincerity of the modernist baby with the detachment of the postmodernist bathwater. Or, in Dumitrescu's charming metaphors, it was "a boat being built or repaired as it sails, or a palace under continuous construction." In her conception, metaphysics, epistemology, and ontology all had their stations along the cross of the new paradigm, but the overriding concern was with ethics. Ethical clarity was not lost in diversity. It was okay to search for values and meaning, even while remaining sceptical. It was okay to be funny and sarcastic, so long as it didn't disconnect us from ourselves and others. It wasn't okay to hurt people, with fists or with words, with lies or with truth. Rationality and spirituality and emotionalism were not mutually exclusive. Love was not stupid. There was—after all—importance in being earnest. The past wasn't dead.

In his 2011 *Metamodernist Manifesto*, the Australian theorist Luke Turner wrote that "[w]e must liberate ourselves from the inertia resulting from a century of modernist ideological naivety and the cynical insincerity of its autonymous bastard child [postmodernism]."

According to Dumitrescu, prominent practitioners of meta-modernism—a/k/a the "new sincerity" or "post-postmodernism"—included the Frenchman Michel Tournier, winner of the Grand Prix du roman de l'Académie française, and the Indian writer Arundhati Roy, winner of the 1998 Man Booker Prize for Fiction for *The God of Small Things*. In 2002, in a scathing speech attacking America's abuses of power in Vietnam, Iraq, and Afghanistan, Roy recalled telling a friend in New York that the only dream worth having was that you live while you're alive and die when you're dead. The friend found this annoying, so Roy elaborated, scribbling on a paper serviette:

To love. To be loved. To never forget your own insignificance. To

> never get used to the unspeakable violence and the vulgar disparity of life around you. To seek joy in the saddest places. To pursue beauty to its lair. To never simplify what is complicated or complicate what is simple. To respect strength, never power. Above all, to watch. To try and understand. To never look away. And never, never to forget.

Other writers with a toe in the metamodernist pond included Haruki Murakami (*Norwegian Wood*) and Jonathan Franzen (*The Corrections*). Filmmakers who searched for wisdom and clarity in the innocence of childhood included Michel Gondry (*Eternal Sunshine of the Spotless Mind, Mood Indigo*), Wes Anderson (*The Royal Tenenbaums, Moonrise Kingdom*), and Gus van Sant (*Good Will Hunting, Finding Forrester*). The freak-folk albums of CocoRosie (*The Adventures of Ghosthorse* and *Stillborn*), Devendra Banhart (*What Will We Be*), and Antony and the Johnsons (*I Am a Bird Now*) came to mind. Or better yet, Sufjan Stevens's concept album *Illinois* or Sun Kil Moon's stream-of-consciousness *Among the Leaves*. In 2014, the Kentucky-born singer Sturgill Simpson went so far as to title his second studio album *Metamodern Sounds in Country Music*.

I urged Phil to check out these works, which "never forgot their own insignificance," as well as the landscapes of Peter Doig;

the Balkan designs of Sejla Kameric; the films of Tacita Dean; the neighbourhood photographs of Gregory Crewdson; the architecture of Herzog and de Meuron; the portraits of Catherine Opie; the poems of Andy Mister.

Phil mulled over these meandering comments and got back to me: "I will now allege, after studying the proposed new paradigm for way too long, that my friend Billy Collins is a metamodernist." As an example, he offered a small poem, *My Hero*, from Collins's collection *Horoscopes for the Dead*:

> Just as the hare is zipping across the finish line,
> the tortoise has stopped once again
> by the roadside,
> this time to stick out his neck
> and nibble a bit of sweet grass,
> unlike the previous time
> when he was distracted
> by a bee humming in the heart of a wildflower.

Phil's first email to Alexandra Dumitrescu was copied to me:

> Hello Alexandra, so fine to hear from you. Forrester is a good guy and he's thrilled to be helping you. We've known each other since sixth grade, so we go all the way back to 12 years old, and we knew each other's parents and siblings. That's how it goes in a really small town.

> I don't think of big ideas when I'm writing a story, but I do have a type of story I write, an approach that seems to have been consistent for over 40 years. Most of my stories are a lot like my poem 'Gray' (attached), offering no answers or conclusions except what might come to mind for the reader. A few years ago, I read 'Gray' to a writing group in Champaign, and one old dude pronounced it sentimental (a pejorative, of course), but I've received an enormous number of emails about it. There is a delicate line that separates a legitimate poem from one that's dripping with sentimentality. It has to do with what one makes

of the poem, whether the intent is to make people cry about the cat in 'Gray' or to understand that the poem is really about the wreckage of divorce. Most people understand that the best poems are about two things at once—one that's kind of in your face and another that thunders in the subtext.

By the way, I'm not yet clear on the differences between modernism, postmodernism, and metamodernism. I worry that the differences might not be clear enough or that the theories might not be different enough to establish a new movement. I do see the downside of group-think mentality in MFA programs, caused largely by the brutality of the workshop format, which drives conformity. I am not the product of such a program, but I have taught small workshops (maximum of six students plus me) and I have controlled the Nazis in such groups who get off on blithely judging the value of the work of the others rather than allowing the muse to wander. The good thing about low-residency MFA programs is that the students live and work at home during their studies. Guidance comes from a mentor who, quite likely in this generation, is not the product of a graduate MFA program but is an isolated writer who struggled the same struggle he/she's asking of the students and who continues to work in isolation. Group think—à la the University of Iowa's Writers' Workshop— is thus suppressed.

I believe this has always been the appeal of Alice Munro—that she worked up there in her house in Canada, untouchable by the dominant influences for 40 years, steady and inexorable, and thus she became a dominant influence of the best kind.

Nice to meet you.

Philip

Phil's poem *Gray*—named for a stray kitten that emerged from the garage of the marital home he had shared with his first wife, Cyndie—closed with the following stanzas:

After the family broke,
and when the house was about to sell,
I walked around it for a last look.
Under the eaves, on the ground,
there was a path worn in the dirt,
tight against the foundation—
small padded feet, year after year,
window to window.

When we moved, we left her
to be fed by the people next door.
Months after we were gone,
they found her in the bushes
and buried her by the fence.
So many years after,
I can't get her out of my mind.

I sent a "reply all" email to Phil and Alexandra:

'Gray' is pure metamodern. A whole host of writers and artists,
e.g., DFW in the 1990s, were struggling with the limits of
postmodernist convention. They were indebted to Barthelme,
Pynchon, Barth, but badly wanted to move beyond the tools of
metafiction, irony, detachment. They wanted commitment and
directness and simplicity but knew that they were taking the
risk of being mocked. They were taking a huge risk of being
vulnerable. 'Gray,' like Collins's 'My Hero,' is plain, simple, free
of irony, free of detachment, expressive of values, timeless. Like
everything else that is now being claimed as metamodernist, it
is pure and new. It is unafraid of being mocked. It synthesises,
it doesn't divide. It bonds. It works.

Alexandra followed up with her own "reply all":

Dear Philip,

I am very glad to hear from you! And happy to have met a friend
of Mr Forrester's. He knows you and your writing reasonably
well, I believe, and he seemed confident that your sensibility is

a metamodern one. (He speaks/writes very highly of you, and your name came up in one of the first email messages he sent to me.)

Below are a few thoughts triggered by your message, on a very early Monday morning (it's not seven yet), but I hope they make sense in spite of my inevitable gaucheries as I write in a second language.

The way I see metamodernism is not as something that somebody—a person, a group—creates, but as a sum of indicators that there are a few things stirring in the hearts of wo/men, which point to another type of sensibility, different from those of the modernist and the postmodernist.

My impression (and probably yours as well) is that people feel the need for something new, a new definition and framework for what they wish to do, for the way in which they feel and create, but the definitions they come up with reek (too strong a word, isn't it?) of their upbringing and education—which were probably steeped in postmodern culture and reverent toward modernism and the avant-garde.

However, one of the blessings of what I/we call metamodern sensibility is that we have learned (from the postmodern and from other people) to be tolerant, to accept the other and see virtues in outlooks completely foreign to our own. A metaphor that comes to mind is that of an international potluck dinner where everybody comes to the table dressed however s/he pleases, bringing a plate of their choice, yet everybody enjoys both the food and each other's company.

Different (even divergent) theories/outlooks coexist and a common denominator/middle ground that ensures dialogue is sought. How to find a common denominator between diverging theories is another matter, but not unsolvable when the divergence is only superficial (as may often be the case).

There may be a lot of wishful thinking in my understanding of metamodernism, and countless places on earth were none of this is a reality or even conceivable, but, again, what I think is happening is a movement towards a metamodern sensibility in a few pockets around the world.

All best wishes, Alexandra

Phil wrote to Alexandra one more time. He was polite, as always, but he made it clear that he wasn't cut out for categorization, labelling, frameworks, or paradigms:

As I indicated in my first note to you, there is no allegiance to modernism or postmodernism or metamodernism or to any literary movement when I write my poems and stories. There is only empathy for everyone.

I'm hesitant to be drawn into this metamodernism pigeonhole. I'm not the best writer around and I'm realistic about that, but if my work gets any recognition, I'd like it to be for its quality, interest, and literary merit. At age 67, I've been working at this since the 6th grade. My initial success was ample, but for some time now it's been very marginal. I keep working. I'm different from Forrester, there in New Zealand, and he knows it. The competition in the U.S.A. is off the charts. Everyone is writing and almost no one is reading.

I do hope to stay in touch, but I have no ambition to have my work associated with metamodernism or any movement, and I hope instead that we can remain literary friends without that.

Warm regards from Florida where today, the third day of December in 2013, it was nearly 80 degrees Fahrenheit and our yard was aflutter with butterflies. :-)

Philip

And with that—although his words "empathy for everyone" were as good as any in describing the heart of metamodernism—Phil Deaver's brief flirtation with the world of cultural paradigms was finished.

CHAPTER 33

By Feigned Deaths to Die

"This is the end, beautiful friend … can you picture what will be, so limitless and free?"

Jim Morrison

WAY BACK IN 1998, Phil sent me a *Harper's Magazine* essay, "Beyond Belief: A Skeptic Searches for an American Faith," by Fenton Johnson, the youngest of nine children from a family of Kentucky whiskey makers. Johnson's essay drew a sharp distinction between two words that are often used interchangeably: faith and belief.

Belief, according to Johnson, comes with preconceived thoughts and wishes. New ideas are judged by how comfortably they fit with what the believer already holds to be true. Beliefs are rules-based, principles-based, dogmatic. Contrasting beliefs are what religious people argue about, what countries fight wars about.

Far from being a synonym for belief, faith is its near opposite. Faith comes without preconceptions. Faith is an unreserved opening of the mind to whatever the truth may turn out to be.

Or, as put succinctly by the late Alan Watts, "belief clings, but faith lets go."

While Phil may have "thought about mortality all the time," he stopped talking God-talk long before his final illness set in. He may have been Catholic to the bone, as Richard Goodman recognised, but he opted for blind faith instead of a belief system—faith in his earthly work, his art, his family, his loves, his friendships.

He settled on the view that humankind, with its mass ego, had created its creator, and done so "to rationalise away the sad fact that we're dust." He "didn't think for one minute that there's an afterlife." He said, for example, that his dad was gone and there was nothing he was more sure of—that his dad died in 1964 and there was nothing left and that's all there was to it.

Contrary to the clichéd belief that "everything happens for a reason," Phil held that everything happens by coincidence. "*Nothing* happens for any reason," he said repeatedly, "beyond the reasons we make up and apply to coincidence."

For Phil, art came first, and events had little meaning without art. For him, every person was a natural storyteller. His faith in stories was almost biblical, without the religious overtones of the Book of John: the word was always there at the beginning of consciousness—then, gradually, it became flesh to dwell among us, within us.

His unblinking need to euphemise reality was clear in his 2013 essay, "Why Write Fiction?" Words could make anything true, if you wrote them the right way, just so. He fancied himself as a word magician. With a spin of his fingertips, things that weren't real could become real, and things that were too painful to hold could be put away, or at least endured.

"We need stories," he said, "so we can bear reality."

Although I envied Phil's faith in art, I clung to my beliefs—in an afterlife, forgiveness and mercy, occasionally-answered prayers, the mysteries of life and death, the Lakota way, the Aboriginal way, the saints, the sinners, the historical Jesus, the ultimate triumph of good over evil—and in "God" as "something other" than me.

One advantage of my belief system was that there was always someone to blame when shit hit the fan. Phil Deaver's decline during the last two years of his life was the kind of thing that made me want to tell the God I stubbornly believed in to get fucked. In my experience, every now and then we need to say things along such lines to those around us. Like most rules, taking the Lord's name in vain is a commandment that begs to be broken. If human beings are really made in the image and likeness of God (Genesis 1:26-27), then good old God has a lot to answer for. Especially when it comes to the exercise of his (it's easier to think of him as a guy) alleged interventionist powers—just have a look at the jealous God of the Old Testament. A real creep. Frankly, sometimes he should be ashamed of himself. And nobody should be *that* jealous.

Don't get me wrong—I give credit where credit is due. But when God acts like a dick, I reserve the right (at considerable personal risk) to shake my fist and rail at him to stick it up his arse. And I'm not alone. For example, old Job from the ancient land of Uz— God's faithful servant—was so tormented by his Creator's role in the drive-by killings of all his children (and other atrocities) that he cursed the day he was born. Who wouldn't? And Job's wife urged her husband to go a giant step further: "Curse God and die." But they both got over it, and so did God. In the end, no hard feelings.

Phil's final illness, FTD, was the same evil that took my mother. God often chooses—or turns a blind eye to—*the one thing* that will hurt a poor innocent mortal the most—a divine twist of the knife, a sick joke accompanied by cosmic laughter, ringing through the heavens.

He gave my grandfather, a professional musician with an eighth-grade education, total deafness by the age of 30. All the poor guy wanted to do was make music.

He worked his omnipotent magic, through a Catholic priest at Quincy College—Father Julian Wood—to take from my father the one thing he loved most of all—coaching sports and bringing out the best in the young men, black and white, who played for him.

He looked the other way, to put it kindly, when my mother—who wanted nothing more in her final years than to enjoy her grandchildren and her children—lost her ability to remember their names or even who they were.

And he took from Phil Deaver, who from childhood wanted to communicate his thoughts and feelings in words—fine words, precise words, evocative words, beautiful words, tender words—the capacity to use or understand written or spoken language.

When young Danny and I were preparing for our Lac Seul fishing trip in 1963 by casting our lines across the yard of his Scott Street home, I asked him which of his senses he'd rather lose, if he had to choose—seeing or hearing. I had in mind my grandfather, the deaf musician. But I thought being blind might be even worse than being deaf. Danny's answer surprised me.

"Most of all," he said, "I'd hate to lose the power of speech."

"That's not even one of the senses, dumbass," I said.

He knew that, but the ability to express what was on his mind was what he feared most to lose.

"I'd hate to be unable to communicate," he added.

And in the end, that was the very thing that was snatched from him.

Phil probably started inching downhill sometime in 2014–15, or maybe earlier. I noticed that his emails—even his baseball commentaries—were gradually getting shorter. As time went on, they became increasingly responsive in nature. By 2016, he was rarely initiating a conversation. When I sent him a photo of my youngest daughter, boasting about her creative writing skills, he sent back five words.

"She's a very pretty girl."

When I suggested that Mike Matheny of the St Louis Cardinals deserved to be baseball's Manager of the Year for 2015, even though the Cardinals hadn't won the pennant, he replied with five more words:

"Matheny. Manager of the Year."

I didn't think too much about it at first. I figured he had other things on his mind. Then, I wrote to him asking who he thought were the best white players in NBA history. Even though his reply made perfect sense, and gave some good news, it sounded (for me) the first alarm:

> Larry Bird and Kevin McHale get my vote. I was sorry to see that Meadowlark Lemon of Harlem Globetrotters fame died at the age of 83. Time flies.
>
> Currently I'm on medical leave from Rollins, and I am giving serious thoughts to retiring. I have no use for the English Dept. here, even though they hired me in 1998. I have never liked that crowd, and they have undermined me all along the way. I just don't like most of them, and I am very happy not to be teaching right now.
>
> *Forty Martyrs* is about to be out, and Ann Beattie has given it a rave review. She's a tough hombre and I confess I was worried about it. But she came through in a big way.

He was right about Ann Beattie. She wrote that she could "hardly stop reading" the *Forty Martyrs* stories, "from first to last."

> These piercingly direct stories contain endless subtleties and subtexts, uniting and dividing them in the most convincing and intricate way. And they're so full of recognizable emotion concerning our interactions with the people who comprise our worlds, public and private—the relationships we've forged while climbing the frail scaffolding of human interaction that we can only hope will support us.

And those were just Beattie's formal words for public consumption. In private, she sent Phil a note that really knocked his socks off:

> Well, these stories just blew me away, and I have a resistance to related short stories (probably because that's usually what editors want, not writers—though this is so deftly done, it's obviously your construct). Everything is totally convincing and the characters are wonderful, including what at first seem to be minor characters who then grow like they're in the Macy's parade. (The minister!)
>
> There were more wonderful moments than I could count, but you always managed to suggest, by your tone and by the way you put the stories together, that this was just daily life, that these might be characters any of us know—and if we don't think we know them, more's the pity, because everybody does have a secret life.
>
> Oddly and perfectly named Whirly, out for his daily run, who happens along when Carol's nearly been stabbed to death. That scene of her 'friend' in the crawl space under the house, who then casually lies at the end of the story that she saw nothing there! And of course the shrink had a one night stand with Carol. Of course he did! The idea of someone doing that with a suitcase of love letters, to begin with! Totally convincing, the way you write it. And of course the lying request in the hospital later. All of that. The lack of courage of Nick, whose life is also a lie. What a truly chilling conversation on the phone when he's told.
>
> The extremely small moments that begin to seem like clues in a mystery, because I guess the whole book is a kind of mystery, but even when it gets 'solved' it only grows larger, because you've so convincingly changed the way the reader perceives of things. Real suspense when Wally is looking for stuff amid the boxes, because by then we know she's kept the letters—but no, he finds about them later, acts later. And he's dying!

And she agrees to see him one more time! And he asks her if he can come back and she says NO! Just great.

I'd also love to have overheard the insurance agent, hearing about the shot-up car they're making a claim on .... but throughout, I did feel, in a good way, like a fly on the wall, and some of that feeling was because nobody was going after me (a fly's ultimate dream) because they were so busy with each other. Yet so seemingly casually, always because in their claustrophobic world (who wouldn't want to escape and drive miles for a beer?), I felt bigger than a fly because I remained in my world (vast, I now see; or, more likely, I haven't focused on it as keenly as you would have as a writer).

I think it's a real collection (novel in stories, clearly) about adults, for adults. And how many times does such a book come along, when every other fucking short story collection is about the end of the world, as narrated by the last living newt? Who needs that dull, so-called imaginative stuff when we can have this: the mystery and splendor of human existence in a small place, during a surprisingly short period of time. I loved it that you actually sent him off to rehab, and that the Jesuit isn't a robot, but a human being. And that you followed him right in, when getting him there was amazing enough (and believable, though I didn't see it coming).

Really, this is an astonishing collection, and the cumulative effect for once is larger with connected stories (rather than smaller). Also, though this was hardly a million laughs, there were many times I did laugh or smile. All the dialogue was wonderful. So I take off my hat to you (gold baseball cap; J. Crew) and thank you for all this pitch-perfect writing, and for such a complex book, about the ordinary within the strange, and vice versa. I am most happy to write a blurb, but I wasn't sure if that was wanted. If so, say the word. If not, thanks for a great reading experience.

Forty Martyrs was to be his last professional triumph. In January 2016, I asked him to send me a copy of his new book. He said he would.

"I'm being very brave when I agree to send it to you," he said. "It is titled *Forty Martyrs*, like our hometown parish."

But he never got around to sending it.

I offered a reciprocal gift: "Hey, my new CD is finished. I think you'll like it. How many should I send for you and your kids etc?"

He wrote back: "Yeah, I'd like to have that. Fifteen."

"Okay," I replied. "Fifteen on their way next week. How are you, monosyllabic bro?"

He sent me his address for the CDs—apparently, he was still living in the condominium in Maitland, Florida.

"I am doing fine," he added. "I'm on leave from Rollins because of a slow bleed in the frontal lobe(s). I don't know what caused it."

"Hope it's nothing serious!" I said. Then I googled frontal lobe bleeding, and wrote to Phil's Rollins College friend, Professor Hoyt Edge:

> Deaver emailed me that he's got unexplained frontal lobe bleeding and he's taken a leave of absence from his job. I can't get any more information out of him and he's been sort of incommunicado for the past several months. How serious is it??? Thanks

Hoyt's reply was a killer:

> Yes, poor Phil. I had wondered if you knew and had thought about writing, but things have been a bit hush-hush, and I didn't want to step on Phil's or Susan's toes.
>
> The upshot is that Phil has frontotemporal degeneration. There are three kinds, and I'm not sure which kind he has, but it looks to me like it has been coming on for several years

at least. He is now not in great shape, and I'm not sure he completely understands what is happening to him. The family is doing research now on the best options for his future.

I think he is currently up with his sister in Indiana. Several months ago I drove him to the airport to fly up there so she could take him to your hometown to read from his new book. He seemed in pretty good shape then and able to function, but I think the problems may come and go and there are progressively some not so good times, a glimpse into his future, I'm afraid. For a year or so he was on disability hoping to get back to work, but he had to officially retire this month—he couldn't have done his job anymore, teaching or writing.

So, all in all, not the same Phil we once knew and still love. I hope things are going well for you.

CHAPTER 34

Your Quaint Honour Turn to Dust

"… understand at long last the breath / of history upon my days, / how what I thought and what happened / turned their cheek to truth / and missed the mark."

Paul Freidinger

AFTER RECEIVING THE devastating email from Hoyt Edge, I made some inquiries of other Orlando acquaintances and learned that Phil had been in some difficulty since at least early 2015. He was having trouble sleeping and he was in a lot of physical pain. He'd developed some foot neuropathy and his right knee was an enduring issue. His prostate had been worrisome for years and his cholesterol was an ongoing battle. But he didn't appear to be struggling cognitively at first, and he managed to focus on staying fit and eating right.

Despite his sleep deprivation and pain, Phil was working his tail off in mid-2015. His priorities were teaching his classes and finalising *Forty Martyrs* for publication, in consultation with the editors at *Burrow Press*. His friends and colleagues thought he seemed a little absent-minded from time to time. But their concerns increased as he missed some of his commitments and deadlines, which was way out of character.

He drafted three new stories for *Forty Martyrs* but struggled to integrate them with the rest of the collection. A new character, Howie Packer, hadn't even existed in early 2015. Phil had to figure him out, discern what was possible, what was likely, what made sense in the context of his other characters and other stories.

As he worked on *Forty Martyrs*, only a few people were aware of his gritty determination to get those last stories completed and published. He'd placed the book on hold for so long that the pressure to finish was increasing just as his ability to do so was decreasing.

Although he didn't know it at the time, the early stages of FTD were already taking hold. He had difficulty keeping the timelines of his stories straight and he couldn't maintain the overall space and time required by a novel-in-stories. He became repetitive. Sometimes he used the same word several times in a single sentence or paragraph and had to remind himself to find synonyms.

He kept telling his friends he felt fine. But slowly, he became increasingly belligerent and irresponsible. He failed to show up to teach classes; he wouldn't return his students' assignments; he neglected mandatory staff meetings; he blew off committee duties. At some public events, such as his readings, his behaviour was very strange and inappropriate. In September 2015, students complained that his syllabus was confusing. In late October, in a presentation at Flagler College in St Augustine, Florida, he repeated the same story over and over again in front of a group of bewildered listeners. Reports of the incident reached Susan. Phil couldn't understand the complaints. He had no sense that there'd really been a problem.

Things got worse. A doctor told him he should stop driving. He could no longer care for his beloved dog Angus. Rollins College tried to fire him.

Susan finally succeeded in getting him to undergo tests, including MRIs, which revealed spots or old bleeds on his brain. At first there was no immediate cause for panic. The spots and bleeds may have been connected with recent falls or with some imperceptible strokes that required monitoring and management.

In November 2015, Susan approached Phil's colleagues at Rollins College to discuss his situation. She managed to keep him from being fired but it was decided, with Phil's consent, that he should take medical leave. Although he'd been an established presence at Rollins for nearly two decades, he was privately relieved to be out for a while. It hadn't always been smooth sailing with some of his colleagues. He regarded a handful of them as bullies who criticised his performance as writer-in-residence and blocked his goal of establishing an MFA program in creative writing. He gave some thought to retiring altogether—but he needed more money.

He remained dedicated to wrapping up the work that was important to him—his Rollins commitments, his ongoing support for his vast constellation of former students and acolytes, and most of all the final *Forty Martyrs* edits. And with more time on his hands, he wanted to enhance his grounding with his kids.

All along, he knew he was aging, but he had no sense of dying any time soon. His favoured plan was to recover from his illness and return to work at Rollins College till he was 75. He often daydreamed about what he'd be doing as an octogenarian. As he'd told the *Orlando Sentinel* in 2008, he had reached a stage in his life when he wanted to "consolidate" his experiences.

"You look back," he said, "and go, 'Well, yeah, I guess I can now see the beginning, middle, and end of certain stages of my life.'"

The publication of *Forty Martyrs* meant everything to him. He missed two of his publisher's deadlines but finally made it across the line. As the autumn of 2015 came and went, *Forty Martyrs* took shape and was ready for publication by *Burrow Press*. When it was finally released, a gala event was arranged in the Rollins College auditorium, which could hold several hundred people. A full house of friends, admirers, students, and fans was expected for Phil's book launch. But it turned out to be a disaster. Phil was unable to read from his own book, so other readers took over as he looked on, smiling vacantly. Susan had boycotted the event, already mulling over thoughts of separation and divorce.

Phil's list of troubles was lengthening. The pain in his legs and shoulders increased. He began taking an anti-depressant. His sleeping difficulties continued through the summer and into the autumn. He was waking regularly at around 4am from night terrors that were so real he had difficulty distinguishing them from wakefulness. In his dreams, he thought someone had entered his home to kill everybody. Sometimes the intruder was an unknown terrorist; other times it was a member of the Deaver family. A recurring theme was that his headstrong son Daniel had crept into the condominium to murder Susan Lilley. Phil would awake with a start, climb out of bed, turn on all the lights. He thought he saw the curtains moving. Eventually he'd satisfy himself that it was only a dream and return to bed, nursing his paranoia till morning. It was nerve-wracking. Each morning, he reported the details of his latest nightmare to Susan. She grew increasingly alarmed.

Early in 2016, Phil's FTD diagnosis was confirmed. He soon lost his ability to use a computer. Because Susan needed certain information to help him sort out his commitments, she accessed his computer and discovered ample evidence of several clandestine affairs he'd conducted over many years. Being discreet wasn't one of Phil's strong points. Susan was humiliated, and most of the people in their social circle sided with her, blaming Phil for his infidelities. Susan managed to talk Phil into a quick "no-fault" divorce, without lawyers. He was in no shape to contest it.

Until the end of May, he continued sleeping in the spare bedroom of the condominium he shared with Susan. Then, he travelled to Indianapolis to stay with his sister Maureen for a while. She and his son Michael had arranged for him to read from his new novel-in-stories at Flesor's Candy Kitchen in Tuscola. It turned out to be his final public appearance, and it didn't go well. He had always loved coming back to Tuscola—fancying himself as local-boy-makes-good or the prodigal son, bathing in the spotlight before an assembly of childhood friends. Of course, it had never been quite the triumphant return he imagined. And on this occasion, he was too far gone to read anything from *Forty Martyrs*, or even to exchange small talk with people he had known all his life. He was completely impaired and it was humiliating for him, for Maureen, for the staff at the Candy Kitchen. His Tuscola friends were saddened and perplexed by his performance.

By then, Michael and Maureen knew they had to get Phil into a place that could take care of him. When he got back to Florida, his family helped him take up residence in Windsor House, an assisted-living facility at Lutheran Towers in downtown Orlando.

In July 2016, after receiving the grim email from Hoyt Edge, I phoned Windsor House and was put through to Phil. He seemed to be in better shape than I'd feared, and we had a fairly good conversation about old times, but he didn't initiate much of it. His overall affect had flattened. There was no laughter, no expression of irony, no sense of fun. But he remembered a lot.

I asked him about *Forty Martyrs*, and he was so happy with the book's publication and with Ann Beattie's support.

"She came through," he said. "Big time."

He said he hoped to be out of Windsor House in a few months. He didn't intend to stay there permanently. He referred to his problem as an "affliction," not as dementia or FTD. He thanked me for sending him copies of my new CD.

I said I'd be coming to the USA later in the year, and maybe we could go to a Cardinals game. He said that would be nice, and he wanted to see me.

"Wainwright," he said. "I like Wainwright."

Those were the last words, spoken or written, Philip Deaver ever said to me.

In August, I emailed him: "Hey Bro—could I come down to Orlando to take you out to lunch/dinner/whatever at the end of September? Let me know and I'll book it!" My email bounced back, marked "undeliverable."

A few days later, I received a message from Phil's daughter Laura, telling me to leave her father alone. The family needed privacy. I understood, but my feelings were hurt. In many ways, I knew him better than she did.

Later, I learned that Phil's sister Maureen had directed Windsor House to deny me access to Phil. Even if I'd travelled to Orlando, I never would have made it through the front door of Lutheran Towers. It seemed that the Deaver family, as well as Susan Lilley and her Rollins crowd, associated me with everything bad that had happened to Phil. I understood their need to blame someone, something, for Phil's inexplicable decline. But targeting me was weird. I'd been away from the USA for more than ten years and I had no magical power or desire to subject anyone—let alone Phil—to frontotemporal degeneration. For 60 years, I'd just taken for granted that he would be part of my life, forever.

In any event, I travelled to the USA in September 2016 but stayed away from Florida. When I got back to New Zealand that November, I wrote a long letter to Phil's family by way of Maureen. I hadn't seen her since 2006, when she drove over to Tuscola from Indianapolis for those last joint readings, which included Paul Freidinger, at Flesor's Candy Kitchen. In the letter, I recounted my memories of Danny

Deaver, going back those 60 years. I added that I respected the family's request for me to stay away:

> I was set to fly down to Florida in September to take Phil out to lunch if at all possible, and talk over some old times, but I first made some enquiries about the diplomacy of such a visit under the circumstances, and Phil's daughter suggested that further communications at this time wouldn't be helpful, so I've stopped contacting Phil. Before that we were regular email correspondents about Cardinals baseball—Phil, my brother Jim, and I. It was a great three-way exchange while it lasted.
>
> I noticed that Phil's participation in these exchanges gradually declined, but didn't think much about it at first. My brother and I kept him in the loop, and every now and then he'd write some observation that was insightful, and things just kept going like that. I'd send him some photos from New Zealand, and some of my new musical or written compositions, and he'd send back comments that made a lot of sense and were helpful.
>
> I think he liked my songs, which are simple and unadorned and narrative in nature. At least his feedback indicated that he enjoyed listening. Most recently, I'd put to music the old Rudyard Kipling poem about 'Danny Deever,' taking some liberties with Kipling's original, and I thought Phil would really enjoy it.
>
> He emailed me a while back, out of the blue, that he had 'bleeding in the frontal lobes and they don't know what caused it.' He said he was on leave from his teaching. At first, I didn't know what to make of this news. He didn't make it sound too serious. But I went online and found out that it was not good at all. I managed to track him down at Windsor House in Orlando and phoned him from New Zealand in July. He sounded pretty good and we had a chat about the usual subjects, baseball and writing. It was the last time I communicated with him.

I think the general impression, among people who know us, is that Phil and I have had a contentious relationship over the years—in fact, although there have been ups and downs, and I would be the first to acknowledge that I can be difficult (to put it kindly), our friendship has been very resilient with many mutual rewards.

Every time I wrote anything—poems, stories, novels, songs— I realise now that I wrote with Phil in mind as my imaginary reader. I pictured him listening to one of my songs and being affected by a line or a rhyme or a twist, and I found it reassuring to think that he'd react that way. My words had to pass an imaginary Phil Deaver test (as well as my own) before I was happy with them. My writing 'pushed the envelope,' as the expression goes, but I always wanted words I'd written to be impressive to Phil. And he welcomed my thoughts on his writing too. Some scenes in *Forty Martyrs* went through changes as we went back and forth in our discussions. It was a way of testing things out. I'm sure he had dozens of other people who played a similar role for him, but I was glad to be part of it sometimes. He would just weigh up anything I said, or anybody said, and make up his own mind about what he wanted in the end.

I guess this is just a long way of saying that I am, once again (the way I was 53 years ago on that summer day in July 1964), overwhelmed and find myself without words to say to you and Phil's children how sad I am. The departure of Phil from my life is like a part of me has died, because in fact a part of me *has* died. Danny was a good boy, and Phil has been a good man. He kept trying, all the time, to be better at the things he did, for himself and for others.

I received no reply from Maureen. I didn't fully appreciate the scope of her well-nurtured rancour until much later, a few years after Phil died. At that time, I emailed her from New Zealand to ask if she'd be interested in trying to find someone to publish, posthumously,

Phil's archived novel, *Past Tense*. I attached an early manuscript of this memoir—*One Dog Barked, the Other Howled*. Her response left no doubt that she clung tenaciously to the false belief that it was me, not Herb Budden, who started that 1966 rumour about her dad's alleged romance with a Tuscola nurse—the same fiction Phil attributed to his Skidmore character in his "Infield" story—and that I had somehow besmirched the reputation of her mother as well.

"I'll tell you what," Maureen wrote with unmitigated venom:

> … you and I will never collaborate on publishing *Past Tense* and it is not yours to do anything with either. More to the point, I would like it very much if you wouldn't contact me anymore.
>
> I am aware that you have an odd obsession with Danny and that you two played 12-year-old games well into your 60s. So it goes. But let's be clear, that's not for me.
>
> You have insulted my parents who never were anything but nice to you and all the Forresters and you have gone to great lengths to expose and sully my brother's life and reputation, and you've presented it to me like a black cat with a dead mouse dangling from his filthy mouth.
>
> You have harassed your last Deaver.
>
> Maureen

There wasn't much point in beating that dead horse. For the avoidance of doubt, I wrote back to say I'd never insulted either of her parents and that her brother was my best friend from childhood, and left it at that.

During that September 2016 trip to the USA, I went to a baseball game in St Louis and picked up a copy of the Cardinals' fan magazine with Adam Wainwright on the cover. From New Zealand, I sent it to Phil in an unmarked envelope. I don't know if he ever received it.

I monitored his progress over the next couple of years by staying in touch with a few people I knew from Orlando. His cognitive difficulties increased. In mid-2017, I was told that he was "seriously diminished." He became even less comfortable in public spaces and lost the ability to carry on a conversation, with family or friends. Few visitors came to see him, but when they did, they usually came in pairs so they could carry on a conversation with each other in his presence and, hopefully, enable him to recognise their voices. He watched a lot of TV—at least, he stared at the set in his room.

As 2017 came to a close, Phil's colleague from Spalding University, Diana Raab, visited him at Windsor House, sensing that it would be the last time. She was accompanied by another friend of Phil's, Darlyn Finch Kuhn. As Diana and Darlyn entered his floor from the elevator, Phil was waiting for them in a public seating area, sitting in a chair and holding a cane. He looked at them but seemed uncertain who they were. He stood up, and they followed him to his room. Diana asked if she and Darlyn could sit on his leather sofa, and he said sure. A few books were strewn across his desk, all face down, next to his favourite Smith Corona typewriter. Diana said, "I've a copy of *Forty Martyrs* for you to sign." Again, he said sure. He reached for the book and wrote, "Dear Diana, thank you for buying my book." Then he wrote the same thing two more times.

When Paul Freidinger learned that Phil had been committed to Windsor House, he travelled to Orlando on numerous occasions to sit with him. Each trip lasted several days. The only other regular visitor Paul encountered was Phil's son Michael, who was loyal to his dad and fully committed to his wellbeing. Michael went to see Phil daily and ran interference in dealing with Windsor House's red tape.

No one else in the Deaver family seemed to know how to deal with the Windsor House personnel or how to meet Phil's needs. In many ways, Michael and Paul were Phil's only lifelines. Almost everyone else—his Rollins colleagues, Susan and her friends, his writer buddies, his social circle, his former students, even most of his family—seemed to have written him off; it was just too hard. His daughter Laura and his sister Maureen loved Phil deeply and visited him occasionally, but they couldn't stand to see him in such a compromised condition. His precocious younger son Dan was living in New York. Diagnosed as bipolar, Dan had been through a tough time that included a few breakdowns and hospitalization. As Phil was getting close to death, Dan was unable to meet with anyone in the family; he never saw Phil before he died. Except for Michael and Paul, and occasional visitors—Laura, Maureen, a few old friends—Phil was alone.

On one magical day, not long before Phil's death, Michael got the idea to bring a baseball and a couple of fielder's mitts to Windsor House. During his visits to Phil's room, Michael had noticed that whenever someone flipped a small item to Phil—a pencil, a paperback book, a snack in a packet—Phil's left hand shot up instinctively and he caught whatever it was, gripping it tightly. So, on that day, Michael escorted Phil to the Lutheran Towers courtyard under the watchful eye of the Windsor House staff. Michael and Phil took their positions about 50 feet apart from each other, and Michael tossed the baseball to his dad. Sure enough, the ball smacked into Phil's glove, and he hurled it back to Michael with a bit of heat. A big grin flashed across his face. For a few precious minutes, they played a spirited game of catch, just as they'd done when Michael was a kid. The staff said they'd never seen anything like it. Phil could barely speak at that stage—he was dying—but he could still whip a baseball back and forth with his oldest child.

On one of Paul Freidinger's last visits to Windsor House, Phil was unable to hold his head up. He was deteriorating fast. He was grossly overweight from inactivity and medication, and he was unable to speak. It didn't appear that he knew who his visitor was, or even that anyone was there. Paul decided to wheel him outdoors for some fresh air, but Windsor House required residents—or someone on their behalf—to sign out before leaving the facility, even briefly. Before Paul realised what Phil was doing, he lifted himself up to the front desk and wrote down his name and Paul's. He spelled "Paul Freidinger" perfectly, in his distinctive handwriting. All along, he'd been fully aware of Paul's presence.

Not long after, Paul asked Michael what he thought about his dad's mental state. Michael said he thought Phil was happy, and it may have been true. The night before Phil died, Michael telephoned Paul and put the phone to Phil's ear, so Paul could say a few final words to him. Perhaps Phil understood.

On 29 April 2018, a message from Maureen was forwarded to me.

> My brother passed away at 12:43 this afternoon at Orlando Lutheran Towers where he had been in assisted living since July 2016. He had been diagnosed exactly 2 years ago today with frontotemporal degeneration (FTD). Phil was in steady decline in recent months but had a sudden drop on Friday. His children Mike and Laura, and their spouses, were with him when he died. This is also the 73rd wedding anniversary of our parents who will be very pleased with their gift.
>
> Our plans are to have memorial celebrations in both Orlando and Tuscola where he will be buried next to his parents, but the dates have not been set yet.
>
> I know this list is incomplete and probably sloppy because I think the computer is about to crash. Please if cousins see that other cousins are not on here, classes from '64, '66, '68 or '70, please share the information. There are so many who cared and want to know—how very lucky Danny was.
>
> Bless you, Maureen

Richard Goodwin's eulogy was the first, written the day after Phil died. Obituaries followed in Florida and Illinois, confirming that there would be two memorial services, one at Rollins College's Knowles Memorial Chapel, the second at a funeral home in Tuscola, Illinois. The obituaries made no mention of the Forty Martyrs Catholic Church, which had been so central to Phil's life; in death, he had no further need of it. Nor was there any mention of Susan Lilley. Her break with Phil had been complete and the Deaver family regarded her as a non-person.

For a fleeting moment, the first Orlando obituary included a final paragraph about Cyndie's enduring love for Phil, which (the obit suggested) had never stopped even after the dissolution of their marriage in 1998. But when I looked again a few days later, that paragraph was gone and it never appeared again. No matter. It was probably true. And Phil felt the same way about Cyndie. As he told the *Orlando Sentinel* in 2008, he was writing a memoir of their marriage, a project that continued for the remainder of his working life. His main audience for this perennial work-in-progress wasn't wide—it was their three children.

> We were seven or eight years together before our first child was born, so there's a whole good life there that they have no access to. And then they see that kind of dismal ending, and they don't even know what we know, which was that wonderful world of growing up in the '60s.

In his marriage memoir, he was still trying to explain himself to Cyndie, still longing to go back to the way it was. He thanked her for being so loving and supportive, so kind and steadfast, for telling him everything would be okay even at the worst of times.

A few days after Phil's obituary appeared, the writer Charlene Edge—the wife of Professor Hoyt Edge—spoke for many with her heartfelt words, "In Memory of Philip F. Deaver: Author and Poet, Mentor and Friend":

> This post is in honor of Philip F. Deaver, award-winning author and poet, professor of English at Rollins College, and tireless writing mentor to me and hundreds of other writers. Phil passed away a few days ago.
>
> More than twenty years ago, I took a class on short story writing taught by Phil Deaver in the Rollins Lifelong

Learning program. That was before he joined the Rollins English Department faculty. What impressed me then was Phil's undivided attention showered on each student's work. He was tireless, present, and mindful of a thousand details at once. His good humor made instruction palatable. I was a new Rollins grad (1994) with an English degree trying to keep my creative life going. Whenever I felt defeated with the story I was working on, Phil made a point of encouraging me to keep working. It was an inordinately long story, and eventually became my book-length memoir, *Undertow*. Phil's best piece of advice for it: 'Drop the melodrama. Just write it straight.'

In later years, when Phil conducted First Friday workshops in the Woolson House at Rollins for students, alumni like me, and writers from the community, he poured out his heart every time. It didn't matter how many people showed up, he'd give everyone a fair listen and offer wise counsel. He shared his own work with us, too, welcoming us into his own writing life. He brought in his journal once to show as an example of keeping the pen moving. I remember he had drawn a sketch of his jogging route in it—for years he was a runner. That journal was a goldmine of bits and pieces of details that eventually made it into his stories and poems.

Phil's masterful writing, dedication to his art, and determination to deal with publishers and submit his work over and over to see it get out there in print, was an important example to all of us.

One of the highlights of my writing life came when Dr. Lezlie Laws, Professor of English at Rollins with whom I'd taken undergrad classes on writing about literature and autobiographical writing, invited me to read my poetry at Rollins's alumni weekend. There, in the Galloway Room, Phil smiled proudly from his seat in the front as I read. He had helped me hone those poems. He had offered suggestions to tighten the lines, bring my work to life. He had nurtured my confidence as a writer.

Over time, Phil and I occasionally offered feedback on each other's work. That was an honor. While I worked on drafts of *Undertow*, Phil offered helpful comments when he could. On more than one occasion, he'd joined us for dinner in our home. He generously provided a promotional 'blurb' to help the book move along its path into the world. He always believed I could write. For that, I am deeply grateful.

It's a sad day but one he would want me to use as motivation to keep writing. That's what he'd want those of us he influenced to do. Keep the pen moving. Tell it straight.

At the Knowles Memorial Chapel service in Winter Park on 19 May 2018, Paul Freidinger was asked to say some words, along with Billy Collins, Lezlie Laws, Diana Raab, Michael, Laura, and Maureen. Cyndie turned up, arm-in-arm with her second husband Preston Perrone. She didn't know it at the time, but in four short years she would follow Phil in death. A memorial service would be held for her in the same Knowles Memorial Chapel. Curiously, her obituary would identify her as Cynthia Deaver-Perrone.

Phil's son Michael described his father's final days—how he and Laura had sat on either side of their father's bed, holding his hands, as Phil began his last silent retreat, dressed in his St Louis Cardinals jersey. Michael recalled that a few days earlier he'd sat with his dad in his room at Windsor House and told him he loved him. A long silence followed, which wasn't surprising, as Phil hadn't said a word in months. But to Michael's astonishment, Phil's lips began to move. "I love you too, boy," he said.

Maureen recounted how Phil's disease robbed him of his ability to express himself, and how difficult that was for him—but she said he continued to listen to everything.

Diana Raab recalled that even before he became ill, Phil commented on the speed of life and the mystery of death. In 2013, he said there was "no doubt in my mind that I want 'writer' to be on my headstone." He had noted, also, that the headstones of both his parents were engraved with their handwritten signatures, but his own handwriting was deteriorating. "I wanna do that too," he told Raab, "but I'd better make the facsimile soon."

A few months later, in a tribute published by the magazine of the *Association of Writers & Writing Programs*, Raab added that when Phil spoke, "people listened because his words glowed with respect, admiration, and wisdom. His passion for writing and the writing process was palpable. He was a writer's writer ... with an uncanny way of making writers feel good about their work."

The memorial service at Knowles Memorial Chapel was as notable for the people who were not in attendance as for those who were. Only a few of the Orlando/Rollins College people I'd met in 2004 and 2006 came to Phil's funeral. The other members of Phil's social circle made their most telling statement by their absence, a form of silent protest in support of Susan Lilley, who wasn't welcome at the service. The Deaver family had quietly declared war on Susan after the divorce, blaming her for being disloyal and abandoning Phil when he needed her most.

But in fairness to Susan, she was in her 60s, had little money, and was left trying to put her life back together. Her divorce from Phil was her third and there was no way she could have supported him, financially or otherwise. For Susan, the divorce was liberating. She continued to express herself in verse. Shortly before Phil died, she was named Orlando's first poet laureate. Unsurprisingly, in accepting the honour, she made no mention of her life with Phil Deaver, or of any influence he may have had. He'd been air-brushed from her Orlando group of friends.

With all the tensions surrounding Phil's illness and death, it may have been better not to have had an Orlando service at all. But the people who attended loved Phil and were able to grieve together.

After the service was over, one of his mourners circulated a Kafkaesque theory about Phil's decline that had a ring of truth but defied medical logic. The opening sentence in Franz Kafka's 1915 novella *Metamorphosis*, according to an early English translation, was the following: "As Gregor Samsa awoke one morning from uneasy dreams he found himself transformed in his bed into a gigantic insect." Generally, it's thought that the insect was a cockroach or a dung beetle. The response of Gregor's family was to shut the door and warn each other not to mention this bizarre transformation to anyone in the neighbourhood. Eventually, Gregor realised that he was no longer wanted by anyone and crawled back into his room to die.

Applying this Kafkaesque theory to the late Phil Deaver had a certain logic, even if it was absurd: i.e., the theory went that he had no alternative but to transform into something less than fully human and die, because that was his only way out of the mess his life had become. By 2015, when FTD started scrambling his brain, he sensed doom wherever he looked. His divorce from Susan Lilley was inevitable; he didn't have a home of his own; he loved his three grown children but his relationships with them had become increasingly challenging; he had never overcome the death of his father—more than half a century earlier—and he never would; he would never have enough money for a comfortable retirement; he was fragmented by his series of secret romances and by the sudden departure of his most recent secret paramour; and Rollins College had had enough of him. That's quite a list. Plus, during the previous 25 years, he'd never achieved the writing success he'd anticipated—the success everybody had expected of him—after *Silent Retreats* was published to general acclaim. He hadn't become the nationally recognised figure Rollins College demanded of its tenured creative writing teacher. In the end, even Windsor House—his final dwelling place—would have kicked him out because he couldn't keep up with its fees. He would have had no place to go, no ability to look after himself, and no one to look after him properly.

Windsor House had been quietly poaching around $90,000 a year from his meagre savings. He was out of money, which was nothing new. Phil could never manage money. At one point before their divorce, Susan talked him into seeing a financial counsellor, who told him he would have to work till he was 80 to have a minimal retirement income, which wouldn't support his lifestyle or his needs. He desperately wanted to continue living his large life, to have nice things, to travel, to eat at good restaurants, to have the best seats at baseball games, to host gatherings of friends and fellow writers. But it was never going to happen.

The second and final memorial service, held in Tuscola on 19 May 2018, was followed by a farewell luncheon at Flesor's Candy Kitchen. Then, without further ado, the earthly remains of Philip Fintan Deaver Jr were buried in Tuscola's black dirt, next to his mother and his father, just as Althea had planned in 1964 and exactly as Phil had predicted in his last interview with *The Tuscola Review*.

Beneath Phil's name, at the centre of his tombstone, is the word "WRITER," followed by a sketch of his favourite Smith Corona typewriter. The overriding ambition of his life on earth—to be known to his friends and acquaintances, and to himself and his children, as a writer—is memorialised for eternity above his resting place. In the end, although he accomplished a great deal, his desire to be known as a writer was greater than his ability to find publishers for his words.

A facsimile of Phil's signature, set in granite, is etched into the right side of his stone.

At last, the things he'd set out to achieve were behind him—living the life of a writer, influencing other prospective writers in positive ways, maintaining the love of his children, honouring the memories of his parents, nurturing friendships. There would be no more layers, no more legholds, no more 20-storey buildings to climb, no more piles of rejected manuscripts in bottom drawers.

The life on earth of my childhood friend was complete. Like his parents, like my parents, and like our grandfathers with the shared name of Lester, Philip F Deaver deserved better.

From time to time for the rest of my own life, I would think of something I wanted to share with him, and him alone—a small joke, a recollection, an explanation, a problem, an idea, a baseball story, a critique of someone's art. Something no other person but Danny/Phil could possibly understand. But he was gone.

CHAPTER 35

Body from Spirit Slowly Does Unwind

Consume my heart away; sick with desire / And fastened to a dying animal / It knows not what it is; and gather me / Into the artifice of eternity.

W B Yeats

IN HIS 17TH century comedy, *The Spanish Fryar* or *The Double Discovery*, John Dryden wrote that "dead men tell no tales." It's a catchy phrase, oft-repeated, but it isn't true.

For example, when my dad died in 2008, my cousin up in Michigan, an Anglican priest, told me that my relationship with my dad would continue to evolve. I recalled D H Lawrence's wife Frieda: "[s]ince Lawrence died, all these donkeys years already, he has grown and grown for me."

"But," my cousin added, "you've got to be vigilant." Insights wouldn't come without an open mind.

I found his words to be true. As I grew older, I could understand what my father may have been thinking and doing and feeling a long time ago, when he was much younger than I'd become. I could see these things from the inside out, not just as a kid observing an old man from the outside. I expect these enhanced appreciations to continue in the years ahead.

The ink was barely dry on Phil Deaver's obituaries when, one way or another, it seemed that he—or someone on his behalf—was sending me all sorts of telepathic messages from the great beyond, revealing hidden tales of his earthly escapades.

First, I learned that after his one-night stand in 2006 with Liza Ford, following our final readings at Flesor's Candy Kitchen in Tuscola, Phil experienced an episode of lapsed-Catholic guilt.

He and Liza stayed in touch for a while with flirtatious emails and phone calls, but when she confirmed that her cancer was incurable, his sense of guilt ballooned. He decided to cut off all communications with her, on the self-serving rationale that it would somehow be better for her in her dying days.

I learned this story from Jeanne Pals, a friend of Liza's from their childhood days together in Danville, Illinois. Jeanne's source of information was Liza herself, who confided in Jeanne as she lay dying.

Jeanne, a graduate of Rollins College, had been living in Orlando for many years. After Liza's death, she arranged a lunch with Phil to discuss her own creative writing ambitions. She hoped he might offer her some mentoring. But their lunch was short-circuited. First, Phil propositioned Jeanne, which may have been second nature for him, but it made her uncomfortable. She fobbed him off. Then, she told him what she knew about Liza Ford.

"When it became clear that I was aware of his affair with Liza," she said, "he could not bear to know me."

Orlando's literary pond is small. Word could get around quickly. And, before the lunch was over, a young man who happened to know them both walked into the café and said hello.

"Phil was aghast," Jeanne recalled. "Someone in Orlando knew both of us. He fled the scene."

In the spirit of journalism's two-source rule, I sought verification of the Phil–Liza liaison. And following Phil's death, I got it. From Lora Goodnight.

After Phil died, I forwarded his sister Maureen's email, announcing his death, to people who may have heard of him at the Café Kopi in Champaign or at some of the readings I'd been to with him. One of the people I wrote to was Lora Goodnight, an old friend of mine from the Kopi.

She emailed back in anger and despair.

"Why didn't you tell me about his illness?" she demanded.

My answer was easy. I didn't even realise they knew each other, except possibly as two participants in a large email chatgroup, in 2008, about American politics.

She said she had no idea Phil was dying, or even that he was sick.

After my move to New Zealand in 2006, I'd stayed in touch with a few acquaintances from Illinois. During the 2008 election year, I took part in a leftish email thread that included my oldest son, who was living in San Francisco, my siblings, old law school buddies, the poet Marva Nelson, my Champaign friends the Reillys, the musician Rachel Jensen, Paul Freidinger, Phil—and Lora Goodnight. Jeanne Pals also signed on a bit later. I'd learned about her from Liza Ford during the readings at the Candy Kitchen in 2006.

All of us were backing Obama for president. We were amazed at how the Republican candidate, John McCain, had sold his soul during the campaign by morphing from a reasonable guy with a reputation as a "maverick" into a scripted Republican hack, evidenced by his terrible lack of judgment in picking the ignoramus Sarah Palin as his running mate. So we let fly with our opinionated emails to each other, seeing which of us could articulate the most outrage and optimism with the greatest eloquence. Lora won the contest hands down, and Phil was smitten.

"Who's Lora?" he asked me by email. I told him what I knew. Much later, I learned that he got in touch with her directly.

In the early 2000s, Lora was living in Champaign. I got to know her because her daughter and my middle daughter became best friends in high school. My daughter introduced me to Lora at the Café Kopi.

During random table-sharings over a couple of years, accompanied by cups of the Kopi's finest cappuccinos, I learned that Lora was a social worker in the local public school system, specialising in children's mental illnesses. She was also an artist—a painter—and a yoga teacher. She rode a motorcycle. And she had a knack for turning a phrase. She was casual by nature, with no particular need for recognition of her creative output. She also happened to be a lifelong St Louis Cardinals fan. For Phil, Lora Goodnight, with her made-for-fiction name, ticked a lot of boxes.

Lora wasn't one of the people I had managed to introduce to Phil, in person, as he and I wrote our stories at the Kopi in the early 2000s, because they never happened to be there at the same time. But I told her a lot about him.

In 2008, before they'd met in person, Phil made an email disclosure to Lora, because by that time they both knew they were headed for a tryst and he wanted to start with a clean slate. He was afraid that if he didn't tell Lora about Liza Ford—his most recent squeeze— someone else might tell her first and blow his cover.

"There's a woman I want you to know about," he wrote. "I met her in Illinois in 2006. We kept in touch for a while, until she got too sick with cancer."

Lora wasn't impressed. She emailed back.

"If I get cancer," she said, "are you going to dump me too?"

That reaction was too harsh. The way he saw it, Phil hadn't dumped Liza. He'd just backed off out of concern for her and her illness.

To say I was surprised, after Phil's death, to learn that Lora Goodnight had been the last great romance of Phil Deaver's life might be the biggest understatement I've made. I didn't even know, until after he died, that he was a dedicated tomcat. I was shocked, intrigued, bemused, bewildered, bothered, blown away. Although I'd indirectly introduced Phil and Lora by email, they were from separate corners of my own life. I had no reason to believe they'd ever met, or ever would.

Even before my emails, Lora was familiar with central Florida. Her brother and his family lived in Brevard County, a stone's throw from Orlando, and her mother spent her winters there. Lora went to Florida a couple of times each year to be with her relatives and to spend quality time on the beach.

Any concerns she may have had about Phil's rendezvous with Liza Ford evaporated when she met with Phil in the flesh in June 2008. As per prior arrangement, they got together in Adrian, Michigan, where Phil was teaching a four-day creative writing course at Siena Heights University. Siena was still affiliated with its founders, the Adrian Dominican Sisters. In that conservative religious environment, neither Phil nor Lora got much writing done.

Afterwards, they stayed in touch. Phil's courtship took the form of sending Lora selections from his body of work, one at a time. First came his final Skidmore story, "The Kopi," which was guaranteed to spark her interest. Next came his volume of poetry, *How Men Pray*, followed by a paperback edition of *Silent Retreats*, signed and hand-delivered during a subsequent rendezvous. By the time she got to the last story in *Silent Retreats*, "Wilbur Gray Falls in Love with an Idea," Lora had fallen in love with her idea of Philip F Deaver. She was hooked. And so was he.

She started travelling from Illinois to Florida more frequently, and in August 2009 she moved from Champaign to live closer to the beach, closer to Phil. At first, he hoped she'd find a place to live in Winter Park, but she wasn't fond of the Orlando area and preferred living by the sea. To his disappointment, she turned down a couple of Orlando-area jobs and found work in the Brevard County school system. Initially, she lived in Rockledge on the Indian River Lagoon; then she moved to Cocoa Beach, a shabby surf town with a population of 12,000, where her rented house was a block from the shore.

She didn't know anyone in Cocoa Beach except for a new friend from work and a few local acquaintances. She set up a small painting studio in her home and rode her bike or walked everywhere she needed to go. Her house had windows with fantastic views and a pretty garden. There were a couple of great vegan restaurants nearby, and a coffee shop that gave the Kopi a run for its money—the Café Surfinista.

Lora spent hours in the South Beach part of town, reading, napping, swimming, daydreaming. She and Phil were less than an hour away from each other by car, if he travelled by the back roads. They stayed in constant touch by email or phone and got together whenever they could, at Lora's home or, occasionally, in Orlando or out of town.

Between 2008 and 2016, they shared more than 4,000 email threads, many containing over 100 emails per thread, and there were literally thousands of attachments—photographs, drafts, past work. They talked about anything and everything—about Lora's abusive father and her long-suffering mother, about Phil's dead parents, about work, kids, friends, memories, birds, light, weather, writing, painting, dreams, baseball, Illinois. And about me.

Their conversations about their parents brought them ever closer. At the ages of 16 and 17, they'd each experienced what it felt like to lose a father. Outgoing in public, they were both fragile at the core in a way, they felt, most people could never understand. They vowed to hold on to their intimacy.

"I don't know what will happen," Phil told her, "but I will love you forever."

When one of them travelled separately, they stayed on the telephone for hours, wearing headphones on the road, waiting in airports, resting in hotels. When Phil gave readings, he left his phone on speaker, so Lora could listen in.

He sent her copies of everything he wrote—every poem and story, every letter or email to someone else, every syllabus, power point, talking point. And every rejection letter. He trusted her enough to show her his precious red notebook, where all his ideas took shape. It contained notes for his creative work and all aspects of his life. It held his running log. He'd accordioned single pages so they'd drop out of the notebook to the floor. It was filled with sticky notes to bookmark certain pages. When he wrote about Lora in his notebook, he used tiny letters so that no one else could ever read these private musings.

They talked about Phil's shared experiences with me—the fishing trip to Lac Seul with our dads when we were kids, our army games in Patterson Springs, school sports, offbeat humour, mental telepathy, our fallings-out, Skidmore, the writing parallels, the differences. It was significant for Phil that Lora knew me and my family and that she liked me. He was relieved when she laughed at the idea that she'd ever had an affair with me.

She told him that he and I were joined at the hip, for better or worse. For Phil, her observations transformed me into a slippery target, less easy to compartmentalise. No one else but Lora Goodnight was in a position to have those conversations with him. She knew me before she knew him.

After Phil's death, when I learned from Lora about their affair, I phoned her from New Zealand and asked, among other things: "Did he like me?" She hesitated, as if it were the dumbest question she'd ever heard. Finally, she spoke. "He loved you," she said.

Phil may have loved me in a bromance sort of way, but he told Lora over and over again, in many different ways, that she was the true love of his life.

She was certainly the love of one of his lives, but (as always) he was living more lives than one. Phil's relationship with Lora was very secret, very private. In his public life, he remained tied to Susan Lilley, living with her in her mother's home. In 2010, Phil and Susan were married on the grounds of Ernest Hemingway's old house in Key West, Florida. Phil posted photographs of the wedding on his writer's blog.

Although Phil's marriage to Susan was upsetting for Lora, she continued to see him. She was unconventional when it came to marriage and relationships. She had never married and had little regard for the masquerade of church-based vows or secular decrees. She was fond of noting that of thousands of species of mammals, only three to five percent appeared to be monogamous. She believed that love isn't something that is chosen. She and Phil hadn't decided to fall in love.

Phil rolled out his mantra that nothing happens for a reason: "Except," he said to Lora, "for the reasons we manufacture and apply to coincidence." She wasn't so sure.

"We need stories," he told her, repeating his standard opening line from countless public readings, "so we can bear reality." Words would be their transactional currency, their medium of exchange. He gave Lora his words; she gave back words of her own, her refinements of his words, her paintings and drawings, and her presence in his life.

He knew how raw the reality of their situation was for her. Whenever she became frustrated by the secrets they had to keep and by his marriage to Susan, he could spin words to change their deceptions into a higher form of truth. He made up stories to suspend her disbelief, stories she could live with. But his magical words came at a cost. If love depended on suspensions of disbelief, how could it be authentic?

"Love isn't some words on paper," Lora told him. "Love is a verb."

Phil thought about that for a micro-second. "So is writing," he said.

Lora recognised the two dominant sides of Phil's nature. On the one hand, his institutionalist core led him to live according to normative social constructs, and to live with and among people who shared them. On the other hand, and privately, he longed for an open, natural, and private life.

This split in his identity was essential to his art. The dramatic tension in this tug-of-war showed up again and again in his stories, especially in his male characters. But in real life, the divided selves could only be maintained with stress and concealment, including a strong dose of willing self-deception. Both the beauty that flowed from him in words, and the socially conditioned reserve that burdened and limited him, sprang from the same well of his conflicted nature. And he knew it.

It was as if each one of Tuscola's Forty Martyrs lived inside him, and he set about knowing each of the martyrs on a first-name basis. He joked that the "biggest cities need only one martyr," even as he knew that he needed 40 masks or more. He understood masks and veils and saw the realities behind surfaces; he knew shadows, and he knew how they were formed by blocking out the light. From earliest childhood, he stared intensely into photographs and paintings, looking for layers of meaning. His stories were layered in the same way. He had his own system of layers long before our childhood "Layer System" came to perplex him.

A line from his exquisite poem *Flying*, about his wish "to put my quiet shadow over all of us," captured both his general sense of darkness from childhood and its effect on people around him, and his desire to live authentically, to reveal who he really was if only he could find a way. But the price of going inside and coming out again, without a mask, was too high for him to pay. Even when a door was left ajar, as it was with Lora Goodnight, he couldn't escape the imprisonment of his own devising.

By marrying Susan Lilley in 2010, Phil postponed, yet again, his reckoning. He loved his Rollins College life and his greatest fear was losing it—losing the public face he showed in lecture halls and bookshops, in interviews and conferences and online postings. At the centre of his shared life with Susan was the perpetuation of that life and that public face. He knew from the beginning that Susan had opened doors for him in Orlando, including the position at Rollins College, and she could shut them again—he was especially vulnerable because his published output was too small to provide security.

And so he nurtured his big external life, where his art and his good name could shine. By keeping them in the spotlight, he could shield his underlife, the source of his art and his drive. And central to that underlife was Lora Goodnight.

His lives were lived in silos, and he didn't want people in one container to know about the people in the others. His lives were like matryoshka dolls of decreasing size, the smaller ones inside knowing about the larger ones, but not the other way around. "There is power in secrets," he said.

He depended highly on routine, so his home life, his centre, had to hold because without it he would crumble. He depended on Susan financially and socially. But he also needed to feel energised and inspired. That's where Lora Goodnight came in. She became his emotional core. She held his lives together, and he loved this about her. His life with her ran parallel to his life with Susan in Winter Park. For him, there was no other way.

Lora wasn't part of his Rollins crowd or his Winter Park circle, or any of the larger life he had as a writer and teacher. She wanted him to escape from that life of commitments and expectations to a light-filled room near the shore, to a shelter from the world where he could write the things that remained in him but had yet to come out.

She told him he had another great book in him, not yet begun. If he kept living that larger life, there would never be room for it.

On any day during their years together, he could have left Orlando to be with her, but he wouldn't, or couldn't, let it happen. He wasn't even sure the things she saw in him were real. He wasn't sure he had another big piece of writing within.

She captured his dilemma in a rough sketch, one her many drawings and paintings of him. A bird sat on a perch in a cage, with the door open to a bright room on a sunny day. A woman stood with her back to the cage as a second bird flew around the room. The caged bird could easily have slipped through the door and joined the other bird in flight. But it didn't. It sat there on its perch.

Lora couldn't see it at the time, but Phil had a broken wing. He was doing the best he could.

After he obtained *Burrow Press*'s offer to publish *Forty Martyrs*, it was time to put up or shut up. He and Lora had been apart for a few months and she was giving some thought to leaving Florida permanently. But their silent stretches were nothing new. When Phil married Susan, he and Lora were away from each other for four months, and later they were apart for six months. This time, in March 2015, she came back to find him oddly calm, with drafts of three new stories for *Forty Martyrs* but no real idea what to do next.

"I'm so glad you're back," he said, over and over. "Thank you for coming back."

For the next five months, she pushed him hard to write every day, to organise his thoughts, to make his batch of related stories read like a novel. His new character, Howie Packer, didn't even exist when she returned in March. Phil had to make him believable and link him, somehow, to his characters Lowell, Veronica, Vasco, Wally, Carol, and Nick. Lora read his three new stories 20 times or more, challenging him on rewrite after rewrite. It was all they talked about as the summer of 2015 progressed.

Although Lora didn't know it at the time, the early stages of FTD were already staking their claim to Phil's mind. But publishing *Forty Martyrs* meant everything to him. In the end, as the book progressed, both he and Lora came to love it unconditionally.

In July 2015, Lora spent a month in New York City with her daughter Sophie, who was now an aspiring model. Phil and Susan, their marriage strained, travelled around New England for the month. Phil said they were aiming to stabilise the marriage. In New York, Lora interviewed for a job with the city's department of education.

On the very day after she returned to Florida, and Phil and Susan had done likewise, Lora was offered the New York job. She told him she had something very important to talk about and asked him to drive over from Orlando. He couldn't get away. They spoke on the phone. She asked if the marriage had been saved. He said it was stable. She told him about her job offer and said she wanted to make clear that the only reason she would decline it was if he left Susan for her—for himself. He could come to live with her, quit Rollins College if he wanted, write. But he said he couldn't do it.

With that last rejection, she shut down. The last time she saw him was in late August 2015, a few days after his 69th birthday. They had lunch and took a stroll together in a nearby park. He was oddly quiet and tearful. He asked if she would still love him after she left. Could he come to see her in New York? Would she still help with *Forty Martyrs*? At lunch, she noticed that he ordered a lot of food and ate it quickly. Looking back, it was an early sign of FTD.

Soon, she was busy making a new life in New York City. Within three weeks of arriving, she wandered into the Strand Bookstore in Union Square. The company's slogan was "18 miles of books," and two inches were taken up by a hardcover first edition of *Silent Retreats*, unsigned, at the bargain price of $9.00. She snapped a photo for Phil. He was blown away and got the idea of doing a reading at the Strand Bookstore as soon as *Forty Martyrs* was released. But it never happened.

At first, Lora worked in public education in South Bronx, helping three- and four-year-old immigrant children and their families. Gradually her work took her to Harlem. It was rewarding, but her life was incomplete. She wasn't having fun. She went to work then stayed home, thinking nothing, feeling nothing, not really talking to anyone. She sat and stared at her TV for hours.

The transition from Cocoa Beach to New York City was immense. It was good to be close to her daughter again, but Lora was 58 years old, working in a new school system, learning to navigate her way through the city. Phil and his troubles seemed a world away.

As autumn came and went, *Forty Martyrs* was ready to go to the final editing team at *Burrow Press*. But before Christmas, Phil shared with Lora, by phone, a long list of things that were going wrong. His physical pain. His terrible dreams. He told her about the student complaints regarding his syllabus, and about the incident at Flagler College where he'd repeated the same story over and over again.

He phoned again. Maybe they could move to Chicago. He wanted to go home to Illinois, but he couldn't go alone. But his idea was absurd. She'd just moved to New York. She had a new job. She'd just signed a lease. It was a ridiculous suggestion. Then, he asked her to come back to Florida—they could get a place together.

She was annoyed with his lousy timing. She had waited so long for him to say these things. He succeeded only in pushing her farther away.

When Ann Beattie gave the *Forty Martyrs* manuscript her rave review, he forwarded it to Lora. "This is one of the best things to happen ever, to me," he wrote. "Besides you."

In February 2016, Lora received an email from Susan Lilley. She'd found out about the affair from Phil's computer and accused Lora of breaking up the marriage. A couple of days later, in a calmer frame of mind, Susan wrote again. She acknowledged that she'd done the same thing to Phil and Cyndie's marriage. She apologised. She told Lora she must be a good person if Phil loved her so much. Then, she chose an odd word as she stepped aside and out of Phil's life forever—she said she "bequeathed" Phil to Lora and wished them well.

In May 2016, Phil wrote to Lora, saying he'd left Rollins College and Susan Lilley and was in the process of getting an apartment of his own. He added that his health was okay, and he was working on a new story. He pleaded with her to come back to him. But she couldn't do it. She needed time.

He kept phoning. Some days he called her seven or eight times in a row while she was at work. Finally, she blocked his calls to get some peace. He needed to get himself together before she could even think about starting anew.

His emails slowed down, then stopped. When they did, she told herself he'd either gone back to Susan or found another woman to take over the mothering role. She would wait, bide her time.

Silent gaps had never changed anything between them. But as the end of 2016 neared, she began to miss him and thought about phoning him. She removed the block on his calls and scrolled through her voicemail, hoping to find his voice. It might be enough to deter her from phoning him, because calling would have meant jumping back to where they'd been before, and she wasn't ready.

She found two voicemails in the "blocked messages" folder. In the first, dated 20 October 2016, he paused, then said, "Hello, this is Dexter Pilkins." That was just like Phil, making up silly names, trying to be funny. In the second message, on 25 October 2016 at 4:25pm—the last communication she ever received from him—he dropped the joke.

"Hi Lora," he said. "It's Phil." A long pause followed, then he said, "Well ... so ... give me a call." He gave no indication that he was in a care facility, or that he was dying. He may not even have been fully aware of his circumstances. He just wanted to see her, or at least to hear her voice.

When Lora learned (from me) that Phil had died, she turned on herself, stunned that she hadn't somehow sensed his condition. She couldn't understand what had happened. She'd filled her time with work and television while she was away from him in New York. If only she'd allowed herself to think about him, to feel his presence, she would have known something was wrong. "I know with my whole soul," she wrote,

> that he sat there and waited for me to come back right up to the end. It breaks me now to think of it, how stupid and selfish I was, thinking I needed a new life without him in it, as if there was ever a way to leave him. There wasn't and there isn't and I am such a fool.

She was convinced, somehow and against all logic, that she bore responsibility for his condition, that his ability to communicate had deteriorated at the very time she had stopped reciprocating. No matter what the medical diagnosis was, in her mind these things were linked as cause and effect. They had not happened by coincidence, she told herself.

She'd forgotten Phil's belief that *nothing* happens for any reason "beyond the reasons we make up and apply to coincidence."

There was so much more she had to say, and even more she needed to hear. She knew she would never get over losing those last months with him, no matter how conflicted they may have turned out to be. No one she'd ever known could do what he could do with words.

And she was alone in her grief. No one in her New York life knew about Phil Deaver. After his death, she confided in a couple of friends, but there was no way they could comprehend her loss. It didn't help when they said she'd done nothing wrong. The magnitude of their soothing untruths, their ignorant efforts to relieve her from her grief, astonished her.

She didn't *want* to be relieved of her regrets. She wanted to own them. She wanted her grief to be part of her and never leave. It came in waves. It came whether she wanted it or not. When it came, she was with him again. She had to find a way to live with it for the rest of her life.

She found some solace in the six words Dylan Thomas spoke to his final lover, Elizabeth Reitell, in New York's Chelsea Hotel shortly before he died: "I love you, but I'm alone." Those words could have been Phil's. Or even hers.

Lora called Phil's old telephone number. The phone rang. There was no answer. There was no recorded message.

CHAPTER 36

The Eye Altering, Alters All

"All finished now. / Had enough now. / Done and dusted now. / Nothing stirring now. / No more trouble now, / and all will soon be well / and nothing remain / and all be at an end."

Günter Grass

IT WAS TWO months after Phil Deaver's death that his younger self, Danny, made his first appearance in my dreams. In that first dream, although we were both in our early 20s, Althea had bought us tickets to a St Louis Cardinals baseball game. Danny and I were together in a cheap rooming house in St Louis, about an hour's walk from the old Busch Stadium, Sportsman's Park, the night before the game.

The next morning, we took part in a rummage sale in the rooming house lobby. I had a bunch of old junk spread across a folding table, as did several other guests. Danny had put price stickers on my items, which included a shaving mirror marked at $10. A guy in a Chicago Cubs uniform wanted to buy it, but I wouldn't sell it for less than $20. I told him that Danny had put the wrong price on it. The Cubs fan didn't want to pay that much.

After a while, Danny and I packed my unsold junk into a couple of cardboard boxes and put them into a storage room. One of the things we packed was an old Scrabble board, with my dad's name handwritten in the margin beneath the board's bottom squares. Then it was time to walk to Sportsman's Park.

Danny and I noticed that we were dressed almost the same—long baggy pants, long-sleeve shirts. But our shirts weren't Cardinal red like they should have been for the game—the shirts were orange. As we walked along, I said to Danny that he should have been a minor league baseball player. "You were good enough," I said.

He agreed. "That would have been fun," he said.

Then, I was about to say to him that he would have had a lot of stories to write if he'd played in the minor leagues, but I stopped myself because I remembered that he could no longer write and I didn't want to hurt his feelings.

We walked a bit further toward the stadium, and he said, "You don't have to be with me just to make me feel good, you know."

I said I wasn't doing that. "I'm just here so we can have some fun at the old ballpark," I said.

We arrived at Sportsman's Park and stood outside, next to a big statue of Stan "the Man" Musial. Then we walked inside. The Cardinals were playing the Cubs. Adam Wainwright was on the mound for the Cardinals.

"I like Wainwright," Danny said.

Then I woke up.

CODA

CHAPTER 37

To Know Serenity, the Dove Must Fly

"We are / alive in the death / of this iteration / of earth."

Jorie Graham

I T WILL HAVE been obvious that the source for most of Chapter 35 was Philip Deaver's final lover, Lora Goodnight. In addition to her many emails after she learned of Phil's death, she sent me copies of much of her correspondence with him and recordings of his voice. She was also kind enough to review early versions of this book. In doing so, she became increasingly nervous.

"Part of me wants to forward some more of his email threads," she wrote, "so you can see the emotional core of him, and of him and me, but it's all very personal and I can't figure out what I'm okay with. It's all very hard."

She said that "his worst fear was that you would kill him and his reputation—with words—because in his mind you'd done it before, true or not, and the vibe of this [the early drafts of my book] is too close to his fears." She said, for example, that he didn't want anyone to know about his affair with Liza Ford, "and there's nothing wrong with that—we all have shit we don't want anyone to know about, don't we?"

"Everything I've told you feels like a betrayal of him," she said. "I don't want to hurt him. He didn't hurt me, ever, and you know how vulnerable he was." Even after she moved to New York, she said, "it wasn't over. It was never over. He waited for me and I didn't get back to him in time."

She explained: "The only reason I told you any of it was because I was and continue to be overcome by grief and you are the only person in my whole pathetic life who can possibly know what I'm talking about. I need to make you understand." She said Phil didn't want "this stuff [his life with her] to affect his kids, Cyndie, his security. He knew what he was up against and what it was going to take to survive it—which he didn't."

I wrote back to her: "I never wanted to kill him or his reputation. I want to honor him." I added: "He was so sensitive."

She replied: "Yes, he was. It was as if he went raw at the age of 17 and never scabbed over."

Not long after that, Lora Goodnight and I lost touch with each other. It's just as well.

In his song *With God on Our Side*, from his 1964 album *The Times They Are a-Changin'*, the 23-year-old Bob Dylan wrote this about his name: "it ain't nothin'." He was probably wrong. His birth name, Robert Allen Zimmerman—the name his parents gave him—wouldn't have cut the mustard.

"The country I came from," he continued in song, "is called the Midwest"—the same "country" where Danny and I grew up, at the same time. In his lyrics, Dylan wondered, among other things, whether Judas Iscariot had carried out the work of God when he betrayed Jesus with a kiss. "But I can't think for you," he sang. "You'll have to decide."

Was it right or wrong for me to write this book? I don't know. I wrote it. You read it. I can't think for you. You'll have to decide.

A since-cancelled comic once said that he didn't want to achieve immortality through his work: "I want to achieve immortality through not dying," he said. That's a tough ask.

Like the lives of most of us mortals, Phil Deaver's life was small, despite his ambition to live large. Not as small as mine, but small. If his life on earth is to continue for a while, it will be in the form of his work. His publications—two novels, a book of poetry, short stories—are out there. But there is more. He left behind boxes filled with manuscripts, online commentaries on his blog, and his precious red notebook. And he left behind his correspondence with hundreds of people.

I've mentioned the voluminous emails he sent me over the last decade of his life. Tucked away in those casual exchanges were a few pearls on the craft of writing, the mystery of mortality, the primacy of family, and ephemera such as baseball and politics. It would be a shame to let them die with him.

I've culled my way through Phil's emails from 2008 to 2016 to give him a final turn at the lectern. What follows is not in chronological order, and it's far from comprehensive. But at least Philip Deaver is spontaneous in these exchanges, letting it rip. Although his emails weren't at the top of his list of things he wrote, it's tempting to recall the translated words of the comtesse d'Arpajon in *Remembrance of Things Past*: "Have you noticed how often a writer's letters are superior to the rest of his work?"

The main things missing in the excerpts below are Phil's meticulous editing, his smile, his self-deprecating manner, his melodious speaking voice, and his fetching need for affirmation. Here is a sampling of his own unguarded words, near the end of his life:

On writing a novel-in-stories:

I'm actually not good at critiquing. I'm involved in the art, not the science—a very messy shirt-tail approach. I'm always writing. One day I'll look up and I'll have a novel, better than the pile of them in the box. I hope.

As I go from stories to a novel-in-stories, I try to imagine the final collection as not linear. Before *Forty Martyrs*, my interconnected stories were still a story collection, not yet a novel. Voice and point of view and everything else except names of characters changed from story to story, and they were written over a thirty-year period. So I tried to imagine that the stories could be read in any order, and a larger story arose, not like going down a road and encountering one thing after another (linear) but like hovering above a town with a pair of good binoculars. However, as I assembled *Forty Martyrs*, an order suggested itself, and oddly it was (with a couple of exceptions) the reverse order in which the stories had been written. I seemed to have had the ending all along and had to write to find the beginning. That's not completely true but mostly true. As I wrote I also discovered things about the beginning that I had to retrofit. All of this is a problem stemming from taking so long to write and in the meantime becoming a different person several times over.

Another thing I was doing was redeeming characters. A story might have an antagonist. In the next story I'd adopt the antagonist's point of view, not for the same story but for a different event, and convert that character to a protagonist or at least a non-antagonistic influence in the story. And so on around the tree, my theory being that most people are antagonists in some situations, but few are Black Bart in every situation.

The new rise in frequency of novels-in-stories is precisely because of marketing. Publishers, such as still exist, feel novels sell better than story collections (seemingly unaware that they, publishers, set that expectation in the market). Louise Erdrich, early on, made a living selling stories to magazines, then pasted them together as novels. It was hard to read a novel of hers and not amble upon whole sections you'd already read.

The publisher of *Olive Kitteridge* cleverly didn't call that book anything on the cover. It is not advertised as a novel or story collection or anything else. I think this was kind of enlightened. The publisher didn't ask Elizabeth Strout to contort her story collection into a novel by whittling away at the stories to make chapters of them. And the publisher didn't call it a story collection. It was just *Olive Kitteridge*, and shortly after introduction they could add 'Winner of the Pulitzer Prize,' after which no label was needed.

On fiction and non-fiction:

I've tried very hard to write a few true things about my life, but invariably I end up taking fictionalized shortcuts. I'm always too happy to self-deprecate, an old habit that goes nowhere. It is impossible for me to write a true story, true down to the minutest detail.

I think it is healthy, as you plan a project, to think through whether a true story is about to be told or a fictional one, because it is so easy to drift off into fiction and not get the true stuff said in the true context.

I'm writing a blog about this now, 'Why Write Fiction?' The upshot is we can't really avoid fiction because if one little bitty imaginative completely made-up riff finds its way into nonfiction, it isn't nonfiction anymore; and then to sell it as nonfiction (because the anal-fixated audience requires the illusion of nonfiction if the book is to be purchased by them, and the willing suspension of disbelief upon which fiction hinges is being bred out of the contemporary reader) is a lie.

So—why write fiction? Because it is very hard to write stuff that is literally true. I fall back on the great Mary Karr, one of the first creative nonfiction writers acknowledged as such. I said to her, 'Mary, I just can't figure out how your life growing up was so funny.' She said, 'Well, I never could pass up a good story.' And that bogus crazy shit about James Frye and *A Million*

Little Pieces. He brings in a novel and his editor, Nan Talese, says, 'This would be better if was true.' So he got in trouble for trying to turn a novel into nonfiction. He should have said, 'Look, Nan. It's fiction. Live with it.' Because if it's partially fiction, it's fiction.

I've tried to make this point a few times and nonfiction writers blow me off because they want to do anything they damn well please and call it true as part of a marketing strategy. I of course am skeptical about marketing strategies, and man oh man does it show.

I'm not saying that one little riff of the imagination taints a work of fact and makes it a lie. I'm saying calling a book nonfiction that contains fiction is misrepresenting it. Of course it could come down to how much fiction is in the 'nonfiction' book and some of the fiction could be excused as simply a different interpretation of the facts or a homerun swing at emotional truth.

We could eventually get to the point where it doesn't matter what's true and what isn't, everything will be called nonfiction because everybody is reaching for emotional truths, and besides the public prefers the illusion that the author held himself or herself to what really happened. Emotional truth is what the best fiction has always gone for, and the reason writers leaned toward fiction for emotional truth was because often reality and what really happened didn't serve emotional truth very well.

There's a literary debate about this everywhere, as fiction recedes and nonfiction (with no obligation to actually be nonfiction) ascends. It's probably best to just define it as a gray area and let it go. Do I think that fiction must be entirely fictional and not what really happened? And that if anything in a novel is nonfiction than it should be classified as nonfiction— in other words, should the reverse of my argument hold also? No. Doesn't that nullify my position? Probably.

I loved *Zen and the Art of Motorcycle Maintenance* and was shocked in 1979 when *Time* listed it as one of the top ten best non-fiction books of the decade. I read it as fiction. I liked the University of Chicago flare it had. I exchanged a note or two with Pirsig in the seventies about *ZAMM*. I didn't know at the time that *ZAMM* was partly fact and partly fiction.

On poetry:

A few years ago I read my poem 'Gray' to a writing group, and one old dude pronounced it sentimental (a pejorative of course). But it's the last poem Garrison Keillor read of mine, and after his reading I received an enormous amount of email about it.

There is some delicate line that separates a legitimate poem from one that's dripping with sentimentality. It has to do with what one makes of the poem, whether the intent is to make people cry about the cat or to understand the poem is really about the wreckage of divorce. Most people get it that the best poems are about two things at once, one that's kind of in your face and one that thunders in the subtext.

This reminds me of 'deep image' poetry, championed by James Wright and Robert Bly in the late fifties. William Matthews, my mentor in poetry, allied with that movement and became its poster boy, like Ann Beattie was the minimalist model. I talked to Bill about it before he died. He said James Wright was important to him, but that W. S. Merwin and Robert Lowell were more important, and that Robert Bly was just plain crazy. Still, 'deep image' did get traction, because it was being explained by poets to other poets, all of whom were in there shoulder to shoulder revolting against T. S. Eliot and Ezra Pound, who were happy to write whole sections of their poems in Latin and Greek, so little did they care to be understood, so little did they care for poetry's connection to an audience (which turned out to be mostly other poets).

On being an academic:

> I am a writer and not a theorist. I'm not an academic. It's why my department and I don't get along. I have a notion that they (the literature side) are in some kind of nationwide conspiracy to prepare a population of students to hate reading, to hate poetry and fiction and the writers who write them. They turn Alice Munro and Barbara Kingsolver into 'subjects' for which there will be syllabi, tests, required papers, and most of all the dominance of their (academic) interpretation. Students who succeed must adopt that point of view and even that way of talking and writing, which is in the opposite direction of being a writer.

> I don't have an academic bone in my body, actually. It's a great credit to Rollins that they brought in a non-academic writer to teach writing.

> Although I hate grading art, I grade my students for learning how to write, and mostly my grades are on their grammar and punctuation, because I figure if they learn all that now, at a young age, they'll be armed to write something good once they are old enough to know what good is.

> I am much less influenced by academics than most writers who write the sort stuff I write. I don't construct highly intellectualized articulations of my intent, mainly because I never know what my approach and intent are until the piece is written. One thing I do know is that the piece won't be hinged to some literary theory that runs through my mind as a sort of measuring stick for each sentence I write on the way to finishing a poem or story.

> I don't think of big ideas when writing a story, but I do have a type of story I write, which seems consistent over 40 years. Most of the stories are a lot like the poem 'Gray,' offering no answers or conclusions except what might come to mind for the reader. Richard Ford and Alice Munro are my marks, though it

is clear now I'll never get there. I'm not the best writer around and I'm realistic about that, but if my work gets recognition, I'd like it to be for its quality, interest, literary merit. I've been working at this since 6th grade. My success was ample early on with *Silent Retreats*, but (for some time now) very marginal. I keep working.

The brutality of post-modernist group-think mentality in most MFA programs drives conformity. I am not the product of such a program, because I learned to write in dark rooms alone, but I have taught small workshops (maximum of six students plus me) and I have controlled the Nazis in such groups who get off on blithely judging the value of the work of the others rather than allowing the muse to wander.

'Low residency' MFA programs, like the one at Spalding University, are different. The good thing about them is that the students live and work at home eleven months out of the year for their two-year programs. Guidance comes from the mentor who quite likely, in this generation, also is not the product of a graduate MFA program but is an isolated writer who struggled the same struggle he/she's asking of the student, and continues to work in isolation. Group-think *a la* the University of Iowa workshop is thus suppressed.

I believe, in terms of fiction, this has always been the appeal of Alice Munro, that she worked up there in her house in Canada, untouchable for 40 years by the dominant influences, steady and inexorable, and thus she became a dominant influence, in my opinion, of the best kind.

William Gass and other post-modernists (like John Barth and Donald Barthelme) never really captured me. I read Cheever's *The Wapshot Chronicle* and it was like reading water. Nothing stuck to the bones. But Ann Beattie, Ray Carver, Tobias Wolff, Tim O'Brien, and other story writers (not the novelists like Irving, Updike, or Roth who were still in the modernist thrall) did interest me and still do. Their interest is in storytelling, and the stories are not self-congratulatory thinly shrouded preenings, but stuff that has represented our generation well.

Most writers don't consciously affiliate themselves with a movement or a paradigm or a literary school of writing. They just write. When Ann Beattie was classified as a minimalist in the 70s she didn't even know what a minimalist was, except that Ray Carver was classified that way also, and she thought that's not bad, not knowing that Carver's shit was getting carved up by his editor so that by the time he (the editor) was done with it, it was minimalist. But Ann didn't have an editor like that—she just had Roger Angell at *The New Yorker* who took most of her stuff just as she wrote it.

Ann Beattie knew Carver. When I visited her in York, Maine, a couple of years ago, she showed me a picture of her and Carver. It's an important picture, taken when the two of them were the focus of short fiction in the country. It was a polaroid, but so well preserved, and I asked her about that. She said it had been on the refrigerator with a magnet, and had fallen down out of the sunlight, so the ultraviolet didn't bleach it out. She was unaware how important the picture might be.

I taught classes about Carver, mainly 'Cathedral' and some of his later work. But my favorite of his is 'Errand,' in which (while dying himself) he writes a story of Chekhov's dying, taking the point of view of a bellhop in the hotel where Chekhov died. It's in the same *Prize Stories: The O. Henry Awards* that 'Arcola Girls' was in, 1988, and it was that summer I seem to recall that Carver finally died of lung cancer, age 50.

Ann Beattie also told me that at a Washington, DC meeting of the Academy of American Writers, she sat next to Vonnegut. He was all bandaged up, she said, from that house fire that almost got him. It was widely rumored that that was a suicide attempt, but she said she doubts it. She said he was always very funny, and loved to laugh, all of it dark of course.

In addition to Ford, Munro, and Beattie, my go-to models are
Carver (after he threw off the editor) and maybe a little John
Irving and Updike and Cheever, and I do like some of the
work of Vonnegut and Walker Percy. I am a little suspicious
of Hemingway the modernist, and Fitzgerald was an elegant
writer but cranked himself around to make a living from *The
Saturday Evening Post*. I did know Larry Brown, combat veteran
and fire chief of Oxford, Mississippi, a very country-music-
get-drunk-and-fuck-and-drive-your-truck-into-the-canal
type guy who lived his writer's life on irony (so he supposed,
but I think he lived on innocence).

On offending with the F-bomb:

Fuck is a great word. One of the best words. It's even a fucking
holy word, actually. The problem is using it to impose one's
view on people with different values (central Illinois being the
equivalent of a contemporary learning disability), different
everything and expecting them to adjust. That won't happen.

By 2050, the population on the earth will have added two more
equivalencies of the current population of China, and we stand
a good chance of being killed in a stampede for white bread,
let alone protein? Fuck the Fuck-bomb dude! Listen, I like the
word fuck. But a writer has to gauge his or her audience. The
challenge is empathy.

A reviewer at *The Milwaukee Journal* once wrote, in her review,
that she didn't like how I viewed women. I actually am okay
with how I view women. In fact, my ardent and lingering hope
is that I view women about the way they view men, though I
know that I am delusional because testosterone and estrogen
are the equivalent of beef and octopus, alligator and eggs over
easy, hawk and mouse, and there isn't really a lot of mutual
respect (that made me laugh when I wrote that).

So I wrote to the reviewer and said, excuse me but I am
really trying to be enlightened and I'd like to know what was

objectionable about my view of women in roughly 1969 (art time)? I am interested genuinely in where I went wrong in my book with my view of women.

Her reply: 'Listen, *I* review books here in Milwaukee and *I* object to your representation of women, and *The Milwaukee Journal* has a 2 million population market in this section of Milwaukee and if I have anything to do with the suppression of sales of *Silent Retreats* in this market region, *I* will consider it a point of pride. Don't write to me again.'

Impenetrable, mean, and not receptive to being drawn into a dialogue with the likes of my fucking ass, so it would seem.

Still, I know from Dorothy Parker and others that men are also just plain old men (we're still around) to plain old women (they're gone now, replaced by beauties who hate us), and any match-up is miraculous if only for a few minutes.

All I've got to say is 'Fuck that shit and all the shit and fuck it rode in on.' It means nothing. Art (not competition) is everything. Art. A writer stands alone with his or her body of work, so to speak.

On Hemingway:

I'm reading Paul Hendrickson's book on Hemingway & his boat during the Pilar years. I've always been way more drawn to Hemingway's biography than his work—unlike Edward Hopper, whose bio I'm reading now, whose life was smart but fairly bland especially compared to his paintings, which I invariably love.

Hemingway was a stylist who broke some new ground talking baby-talk (he claimed to have been influenced by newspaper writing) to a bunch of men and drawing them into reading. When he was thirty, he was more famous than Babe Ruth and that is saying something in 1930. It's the same old celebrity crap – and he rode it all the way to the Nobel Prize.

I really do wonder if we'll ever know who he was (it might not matter, truthfully), because he was so deliriously received by a largely unsophisticated audience (who also loved the myth of Davy Crockett and venerated the slaughtering of the Indians and thought it was fun to blast the fuck out of elephants on safari), a bunch of drinking pals (Fitzgerald included), and a number of vapid women who loved climbing under the thumb of macho dicks and becoming part of their myths. Hendrickson's book is helping me understand the Hem biography which I'm realizing has drifted in my mind, as well as in the minds of subsequent biographers with agendas of their own, since the slightly star-struck Carlos Baker. I got all my initial interest in Hemingway from the Carlos Baker biography, which I almost memorized. Baker posited that Ernest had taken too many blows to the head in his life, and that that eventually is what paralyzed him from writing and thus was why he was so driven that last year to kill himself.

One more thing from Hendrickson's book. It was so interesting to see that letter Hemingway wrote to a kid, the son of a country doc in Idaho who was a fishing buddy, who was in the hospital with some illness—a good decent well-stated letter expressing a positive outlook for when they might all get back to Idaho and go fishing again. This was shortly before he killed himself, and the handwriting was consistent with his handwriting from earlier healthier times.

A Farewell to Arms, to me, was primitive when I first read it in college. Even then it was already 30 years old, or two generations of narrative later. Hemingway was the Model T of writers, in a way.

On the other hand, there is a giant difference between being able to do something and actually devoting one's life to it, and in times of (fairly) instant gratification, many good writers in these times don't give themselves over to it. Very few can make a living at it, and that leaves less time for writing and more chance one will be pulled away from it by all the other requirements of living. It is still happy, for me at least, to know that a writer, even one who was drunk, narcissistic, and too good at self-promotion, shaped a generation of writers who came after him. Hemingway did write, really wrote, a lot, for all the other stuff he distracted himself with. He took time out of his crazy life to write; he made publishers millions of dollars in the star system of the 20th century. One magazine, *Esquire*, advanced him the cash for his boat!!

I still love *A Moveable Feast* (even though there are questions about how 'true' it is) (do I care?); it is a work of art, a lot of it written fairly late in his life.

I wrote to Hendrickson after reading his book. For some reason it was in my mind that he had said Hemingway was raised Catholic, or at least that some Catholic-ness got in him. He told me Hem was raised Congregationalist, but that he joined the Catholics after the war, with Hadley, though he didn't practice, then he was drawn into practicing while he was with Pauline Pfeiffer, his second wife, in Key West. Hendrickson said Hemingway really didn't have a religion at all, as became obvious later in his life.

On The Great Gatsby:

It is clear that Daisy loved Gatsby and Tom was pretty awful, but he had her in palatial circumstances, and since she saw herself as a fool, she relied on Tom to hold her life steady. It was worth it to her to tolerate a lot of his fucking around to try to keep things stable. I think Daisy, accustomed to security, when it got right down to it, was a hostage who didn't have the vision or willpower to leave Tom, or the confidence that Gatsby would survive the transfer. She was a victim of the Stockholm Syndrome.

Something else. In Vietnam, many fighter pilots died who needn't have because they were technicians and well trained to fly, using all the tools they had available in the cockpit.

It was a comfort zone. To eject from the plane meant exploding out of the cockpit into the unknown. If a missile was locked in on them and they got that signal, there were precious few moments to push the eject button. One little hesitation to push it, and they would blow up with the plane. Daisy was hesitating to eject.

The rumor that Gatsby had killed somebody in the past seemed planted in order to catch Tom's notice, and hers. Gatsby's situation seemed fragile, tentative, fleeting, because no one understood where exactly he came from or why. If it was all just to lure Daisy back, the money for his whole show was owed and was a house of cards for sure. Daisy was left with a stark choice between the two men and the choice she made was in favour of security and her known world, and she probably figured, maybe even told Gatsby on the fateful trip home from the city, before hitting the pedestrian, she could after all abscond over to Nick's cottage in the trees for the occasional rendezvous because she loved him too. Fitzgerald would have known that was no solution at all, and that Gatsby had to die. In an indirect way, Daisy killed him.

On baseball:

When I was in Little League, age 9 or so, we all rode out of Tuscola one morning on a school bus, to Wrigley Field. Back then it was a three-hour drive up Highway 45. Then we all got a hotdog outside Wrigley and went in. Our seats were a few rows behind home plate, behind the screen. The sun was beating down. When I emerged from the ramp up into the stadium, Roberto Clemente was at the plate for the Pirates. As I stepped into the stadium, very close to home plate, Clemente swung and missed, a fast ball. I heard him grunt as the bat came around, and saw the dust spin up upwards from his feet like a tornado in reverse. His uniform shirt was open two buttons from the top. He was dripping in sweat. He stepped back into the box. I stood at the top of the ramp watching. On the next pitch, he cracked one to right center, a double, and was yelling as he went up the first base line, rounded second, slid aggressively feet first into second.

He wasn't big, no bigger than Sammy Sosa as I recall, but he battled at the plate like it was a war. This is the big leagues, I remember thinking. I didn't know until later how right I was.

Baseball is so peculiar. When you keep in mind that players on teams are mostly successful between 25 and 33 percent of the time, closer to 25 actually on the average, and you watch a team disappoint all year, night after night.

I wonder if we aren't reaching the far limits of the human throwing arm in baseball. Aroldis Chapman is an amazing specimen of human, and watching him hurl the ball at 102 mph is a great experience. He's a closer which means a lot fewer pitches than Adam Wainwright. Perhaps we should rig all pitchers with a bionic arm. The equivalent of putting a speed governor on a Indy race car. The elbow ligaments and maybe the whole arm would just be steel and rubber and plastic, except for the hand of course. Pitchers could all throw 78 or 108, with no harm to the arm. Then the game, from the point of view of the pitcher, would be a matter of control and wiliness, because major league hitters who weren't killed instantly by being hit with a 108 mph fast ball would eventually calibrate up to it and start smacking it around the yard. Or maybe all pitchers become knuckle ball pitchers, the knuckleball being associated with pitcher longevity.

There's no solution actually, for pitchers. The game was invented in a different era. Parts of us have evolved past it, while other parts aren't there yet. Something similar is happening in motor sport.

A few years ago I witnessed one of the bloodiest things ever in sports when I went to the Indianapolis 500. It's hard to call this a sport, but I suppose there's nothing else to call it. They have this 2.5-mile track, and the cars each year, on the average, are going faster and faster. They are rigged with governors so most all of them top out at the same speed, but then advantages are gained via the balls of the drivers to go through the curves faster and faster, and then to be able to accelerate faster than others coming out of the curves. The ability, in Indy cars, to go through curves fast has to do with how the wings on the car are set. The wings use the speed of the air traveling over the car to hold the car on the track and to give it traction on the track.

The year I was there, there was a strange crosswind in the fourth turn and car after car would go into the turn, lose control, and hit the wall at a mind-withering speed. There was no avoiding the fourth turn. Everybody's gotta go through it about a million times in a 500-mile race, but the wings on the cars were not effectively holding them down on the pavement, so it didn't matter if you turned the front wheels to go through the curve, the car was gonna go straight smack into the fucking wall. It kept happening. After a while you couldn't even look. It had nothing to do with the skills of the drivers. Only one variable gave hope. To slow down in the curve, but these dudes weren't wired that way. Slow down? Fuck that. Smack bam.

I think my failure in athletics made me introspective, as has my failure in writing. All those athletic guys from Tuscola, they're all dead now. Early success in something makes high school a hard act to follow.

On politics:

I expect an acknowledgement of my prediction that Illinois would celebrate Lincoln's 200th birthday and Obama's victory, signalling the death of the racist 'GREATEST GENERATION' and the dawn of a better Amerika. A fact that only an autistic could deny the global relevance of.

On his favourite works of literature:

In 2015, Phil was asked what works he would memorize for posterity if he were the character Guy Montag from

Ray Bradbury's 1953 dystopian novel, *Fahrenheit 451* (in which Montag commits his remarkable memorisation skills to the preservation of literary and cultural writings). Phil's list:

Edward Albee's 1962 play, *Who's Afraid of Virginia Woolf*;
Ernest Hemingway's Paris memoir, *A Moveable Feast*;
Arthur Miller's 1949 play, *Death of a Salesman*;
Mark Twain's novel, *Huckleberry Finn*;
Milos Kundera's 1984 novel, *The Unbearable Lightness of Being*;
D H Lawrence's 1928 novel, *Lady Chatterley's Lover*;
John Updike's 1968 novel, *Couples*;
Philip Slater's 1974 book, *Earthwalk*;
Raymond Carver's stories, "Cathedral" (1983) and "Errand" (1987);
Ann Beattie's stories, "Waiting" (1982) and "Find and Replace" (2005);
Alice Munro's 2004 stories, "Silent" and "Passion";
John Updike's 1987 story, "A Constellation of Events";
Robert Stone's 1993 story, "Helping";
Richard Bausch's 1989 story, "Design";
The chapter "Stalking" from Annie Dillard's 1974 nonfiction narrative book, *Pilgrim at Tinker Creek*;
Richard Ellman's biography of James Joyce;
Gail Levin's biography of Edwin Hopper;
Hermione Lee's biography of Virginia Woolf;
William Matthews's 1984 poem, *A Happy Childhood*;
Rainer Maria Rilke's 1922 poem, *Evening*;
Dylan Thomas's 1945 poem, *Fern Hill*;
AND
Forty Martyrs Suite, his own then-unpublished novel-in-stories.

On mortality:

I think of mortality all the time, not in the poor me way, just the folding over of generations. I don't think for one minute that there's an afterlife unless it exists for all species. It is too suspicious that the only animal in all of creation to be invited to live on after death would be the animal with the largest ego, who created creation for his own convenience and to rationalize away the sad fact that we're dust, just like a runover possum or a baby rabbit hit with a lawnmower.

My oldest child is over 40, and I was 29 when he was born. My youngest is over 30, and I was 36, younger than my oldest now, when she was born. Nobody in my life now ever knew my dad, not even close. As I approach 70, perspective hits like a storm almost every day. One of the things I think of is, 'So this is how short life is.' I remember my grandfather in the sixties, in his mid-sixties, trying over and over to tell us stuff to make us realize it, but he seemed so old.

In Western culture we're allowed two weeks for mourning, no matter who croaked, wives, parents, children, and then it's back into harness and often with the fact of the death ceasing to have any reality among those with whom we work. Mourning goes on way longer and will not be denied.

Also, the loss of our parents is one of the gateways to maturing. When they are finally gone, we become truly adult, having no one around who knew us when we were babies—in this way the toddler in us passes away also and we have to step up and be the parents who remember our own youth and help guide our own kids into the world.

In this stage of life I cry too for the past and the tons of loss, but I don't let it drag me down now that I have my art and have a life that accommodates it as much as life can.

Pete Seeger, RIP. Age 94. It was bound to happen sometime, but what a great man. I remember my dad would turn off the radio when 'Ticky Tacky' was played on WLS, because he thought Pete was communist. I think Seeger was a real priest.

Also, Oliver Sacks died. At home in New York. 82. Cancer. Before he died, he said his 'luck had run out' and now he was 'face to face with dying.' He also said, 'It is up to me now to choose how to live out the months that remain to me. I have to live in the richest, deepest, most productive way I can.' Those aren't bad words at any age.

The self-helper Wayne Dyer died too, of leukemia, at the age of 75. As usual, he left no wise words, but anyway he's dead. With his last name, I guess he finally achieved something he was always destined for.

On always becoming as an artist:

To paraphrase the dying words of the great Japanese ukiyo-e artist Hokusai, renowned for his 1831 woodblock print, *The Great Wave off Kanagawa*: "If heaven had granted me five more years, I could have become a real writer."

Philip Fintan Deaver Jr, 1946–2018

Jeshel Forrester ("his name, it ain't nothin'") lives in a cabin on the eastern bank of Lake Rotoiti in New Zealand's North Island. His musical compositions and recordings include six albums of folk/bluegrass music, and he is the author of four novels, a book of poetry, a previous memoir, and numerous short stories. He lived and worked for many years on Indian reservations in the American West and represented numerous Aboriginal clients in Australia. A more comprehensive account of his life and times may be found on Wikipedia.

His music is available at https://jeshelforrester.bandcamp.com and at https://garyforrester.bandcamp.com/album/houseboating-in-the-ozarks.

The curious may contact him by email at jeshel.forrester@gmail.com.